Unravelling Inwards

Unravelling Inwards

A Journey Of Embracing
The Divine Feminine

Camilla Fellas Arnold

TECASSIA
PUBLISHING

Published in 2023 by

TECASSIA
PUBLISHING

Tecassia Publishing
Building 31186,
PO Box 6945,
London,
W1A 6US
www.tecassia.com

ISBN
Hardback 978-1-913916-17-6
Paperback 978-1-913916-16-9
Also available as an e-book 978-1-913916-18-3

For my dearest friend Emily,
thank you for your grace, love and continued friendship.

For Aaron, for always seeing my divinity.

TABLE OF CONTENTS

Reclamation

INTRODUCTION

The day I realised I needed to write this book came in the aftermath of an incident with my best friend Emily. We'd had some major trouble in a shared project we were working on and I'd spent ten days avoiding talking to her — partly in fear of being shouted at and partly in fear of what I might say in the heat of the moment.

I feared losing the relationship to a fight, but my avoidance jeopardised it just as much as an argument. Eventually, in a way only I can, I lost the filter between my mouth and brain and one short, sharp sentence later, I realised I'd seriously messed up. I retreated inwards; convinced I'd broken us beyond repair. I've lost many friendships over the years for much less so it seemed inevitable. My grief was profound and instantaneous.

Continuing my radio silence out of fear, the next day I walked in the rain with my dogs thinking about the concept of this book that had been gifted to me by the universe earlier that week. I lamented that it wouldn't get written, as I believed it was meant for my friend. She had been the one to introduce me to some of the goddess archetypes and divine feminine work. She owned her skills as an intimacy coach. She had the experience and expertise to pull this off; I most certainly didn't.

In fact, up until two and a half years prior, I didn't have many skills or much knowledge in the realms of emotional intelligence, divine feminine and sacred unions. I didn't know any of the spiritual, metaphysical or subconscious mindset reprogramming and healing tools that my friend brought to the table. Emily had shown up at a time in my life when I felt I was truly and permanently broken. She had shown me an alternative life. I was in so much pain and carrying lifetimes of unhealed wounds that meant I walked through this life in a perpetual state of metaphorically bleeding out.

Her offer, a promise that all could be healed, that I could liberate myself and create a whole new life was enticing but I was scared and weighed down. How could I possibly transform myself and the mess I had created?

I felt overwhelmed. Looking at everything that hurt inside didn't feel safe at first. However, Emily was patient and we approached everything at a pace I could manage. She encouraged me to keep showing up every day, reminding me that although it felt like I would be wading through treacle forever it would get easier given time and consistent work.

I'd spent years sitting in my emotional rowing boat, in the middle of the ocean, watching it fill up with water from multiple holes in the hull. Suddenly this woman with a shining, pure heart was sitting in the boat with me and had brought two teaspoons so we could start bailing out.

At first, it felt like we were getting nowhere. No sooner had I emptied a teaspoon of emotional overwhelm, than the boat filled up again. Emily didn't waver. '*Keep going*,' she said, '*you can do this. One day it won't be so bad.*'

I had no reason to trust her, but instinctively I did. No one had ever seen the weight or pain I carried as she did. Her patience, kindness and utter belief that things could change, that *I* could change, *made* me want to trust her.

I had no idea and was simply not prepared for what happened next.

She took me on a journey over the span of two and a half years. Every day she turned up, armed with teaspoons, then tablespoons and eventually buckets, helping to empty my emotional boat. She introduced me to the goddess Lilith. She showed me hope and possibility.

I have always been a spiritual person but have not had much guidance or support in the past. I certainly carried too much of a persecution complex to fully embrace it. With Emily's support, I began to explore my spiritual gifts, peeling back layers of societal conditioning to reveal my true self.

She taught me how to heal emotional trauma. I faced so many demons head on and she stood by my side every day, encouraging me to keep going. Over time I felt emboldened and began to believe it myself; *of course, I could change and heal. Of course, I could manifest and create the life of my dreams. Of course, I could have it all.*

I learnt about energetic matches and sacred unions. This helped me bring into balance and heal my marriage which had been impacted by my depression and stress caused by some serious harassment from our neighbours. At various times it had felt like we were no more than roommates, such was the divide between us. I had no intention of walking away from my husband; the bond between us had always been too strong. However, neither of us had been particularly happy for some time and had no tools or knowledge to fix it. In the process of healing myself, I eventually had more headspace to work on closing the gap in my marriage and bring harmony back to our household.

Over time and through the journey of undoing and unlearning, I became incredibly close to Emily. I'd never been one for having close or long-term friendships, especially with other women. I tended to turn up in people's lives and turn them upside down with my cataclysmic nature. This usually didn't go down too well, meaning people ran for miles and I often ended up alone.

I'd grown used to and accepted it until Emily showed me a new path of support and loving friendship. After that, I didn't want to go back to the way things were before. Realising my 'uncalled for' comment could cost me the friendship that had changed my life, I was devastated. I could feel my ego and inner critic piping up, feeling vindicated. *What a fool you've been Camilla, to think that things could be different. It was never going to work out in the long run.* I was rapidly unravelling and going back to my old ways of thinking. I retreated inwards, feeling miserable.

And then a miracle happened; *she rang* and I dared to answer. After some awkward silence, false starts and stilted conversation, we began to talk about what had happened. How she felt, how I felt. What we had been thinking and how everything had fallen apart in under two weeks. I remember clearly telling her I understood she had every right to never speak to me again. I waited with bated breath for her to agree and walk away.

Society ingrains the sisterhood wound within women as deeply as the witch wound is passed through our lineage like a family heirloom. Pitted against each other, we are encouraged to envy, compete and sabotage our fellow sisters at every turn. In keeping us divided, we are unsupported, unable to fully access and embrace our true power — honestly, it is the greatest power there is.

And yet, this incredible woman transcended all of that to accept my profuse and frequent apologies with the grace of the goddess herself. Our mission, our work together was of far greater importance and was not worth being thrown away over what had transpired.

As she told me she didn't want to walk away from our friendship, everything changed for me. Her grace and forgiveness changed me. Her embodiment of feminine compassion and divinity at that moment went against everything I had been conditioned to believe by society. Although I could barely hear it, much less accept it, it was one of the most profound moments of my life.

Here was a woman, hurt and metaphorically bleeding by my hand and she *forgave* me. She loved me. She wanted us to work it out together. When she uttered what has become a mantra for me, 'you're not perfect and I love you,' I fell apart internally. I felt the weight of her every word and inside every one of them was simply love, kindness, compassion, forgiveness; true divinity in the mortal realm.

It was something I had not experienced. Something I didn't even know was possible to come from a fellow sister I had hurt so deeply. The walls that had been forming around my heart instantly shattered, and my inner critic fell silent. My brain stalled and I didn't quite know what to do. This had never happened before. I'd never been given a second chance at a friendship after a fight or disagreement. *What was I meant to do with this?*

I kept throwing back my wounded inner thoughts about being undeserving. She didn't flinch. She continued to radiate the same love and patience that she always had from the day we met. Eventually, I ran out of steam and stopped trying to push her away. It was clear we both wanted to stay friends even if neither of us knew the how. To do that, I needed to shut up and listen.

I thought about offering her the book concept on the phone there and then. We'd barely spoken for ten days so I hadn't mentioned it but something made me hold it back. No, this wasn't meant for her to write it, she already embodied the divine feminine and evoked the goddess with ease. I'd just seen it in action.

No, this was meant for me, in my unsteady, uninitiated, wounded state. This book was meant to document my own journey with the divine feminine, to embody that same grace my friend had extended to me.

In my processing and healing, in my exploring, unlearning and de-conditioning myself from the sisterhood wound, this book was meant for me to write.

This book was my journey of reclamation, of me and the embodiment of my divine feminine. It was a record of the journey towards ultimate oneness in both me and my sacred union with my husband.

This book wasn't meant to be the expert journey, it was meant to be the wobbly path carved from the rock as I go. It is intended to be a rough guide and a beacon, for those who are full of fear yet know they can't stay where they are.

The difference between this book and many others in the self-help genre is that this is not intended to be the only tool for you to work with. We've been conditioned to believe that independence is something to wear like a badge of honour and that our healing journey is a process that we do alone. This is not the case. Some things can be too painful to look at alone or that are hiding in your blind-spot. If you want to really make the best use of this book, use it like a guide alongside engaging with holistic practitioners, coaches, therapists, counsellors, friends, family and whatever other support you desire. We were never meant to do this journey alone.

In writing this book, I've laid out the landmarks that you'll likely come across in your journey and I share not only tips for how to work with those wounds to heal them but also the truth of what this work is really like.

Shadow work is a buzz word in the new age spiritual world that people use to shame others. There is a lot of spiritual bypassing in the online space that makes it sound like this work of exhumation, healing and reclaiming is prettier and easier than it actually is. Having gone right into the deepest parts and cleaned every aspect of myself that I could find for two and a half years means that my account is not anywhere near as pretty. I feel it's important to show you this truth. Yes, the road can be hard and sometimes you may wonder why you ever even opened this can of worms. However, the result when you come out the other side having truly healed is *completely* worth it.

It's also important for you to know that this healing journey is done on both a conscious and subconscious level. To try and do all of this only through conscious work will set you up to fail. To truly transform your mindset, limiting beliefs and heal those wounds deeply ingrained in your subconscious is where you will need to do some of the work. There are plenty of practitioners with various tools that can help you work on the subconscious level such as meditation, kinesiology, EFT tapping, breathwork, homeopathy, Bowen Technique and hypnosis to name a few (see the glossary at the back for definitions). Try them all and find the fit that works for you.

If you want to do the deep inner work and truly heal, let this book be your guide, your roadmap. Having come out the other side of this journey, I now work with Emily in her programmes to support others on the path. This book hits all the same points we've both already walked in our healing so you know what you can expect. Of course, every story is unique but this is a story of the most common landmarks, demons and shrines you may expect to meet on the way through your transformation.

It is meant for the uninitiated or long-forgotten, to be a reclamation of our divine feminine no matter where you are on the journey; to rebalance the divine feminine and the divine masculine in sacred union.

This is a tale of the road less taken and the extraordinary transformations you can experience on the way. It's not written from a practitioner's point of view, if I wanted that I would have asked Emily herself to write it. Instead, it comes from me, not as a practitioner (although I have since begun to get various qualifications for the tools Emily taught me to use). It is written from the perspective of a person who didn't have the tools or knowledge and had to learn from scratch. From me who had to take baby steps every day. From me as that person who thought I would always remain broken, who thought that it was too difficult to take the journey and come out the other side. This tale comes from my heart to yours to show you that it **can** be done. You can do it no matter where you start from when you commit yourself to the process of healing yourself and consistently show up.

I have spent lifetimes walking in the darkness. I thought I would never find my way from the labyrinth but I did. When fear reared its ugly head up at the last hurrah to try and return me to the box, it was nothing less than a goddess in human form that offered me salvation. We need more of those divine beings. The world needs more Emily's to wake up to their gifts, their divinity and reclaim their power. The world needs more of that ancient wisdom and nurture that only the feminine can provide. The world needs more divine feminine balance to rise and meet the divine masculine. This is how we do it.

The way this book has been written, channelled and co-created with the universe means it's an invitation *and* an activation. You might want to throw it against the wall and never look at it again. You may hate every word you read. If that happens – *good*! Take it as an opportunity to turn inwards and reflect on why it's making you feel that way – where it makes you feel triggered is where the growth and transformation lie.

This book is a love letter to anyone who has ever felt they were stuck too much in their human masculine.

A love letter to those who have bled for their sisters and made others bleed.

A love letter to the ones who are looking for balance, grace and divinity.

A love letter to the ones who see how broken society is and are ready for change.

A love letter to the ones who want to restore the sisterhood pride.

A love letter to the ones who are on journeys with their twin flame towards sacred union.

A love letter to the ones who want to leave a legacy of love and divine feminine wisdom as heirlooms for generations to come.

A love letter to the ones who are ready to have their world and life undone by the goddess.

A love letter to the ones who are ready to be truly awakened.

A love letter to the ones who are ready to experience the most divine love.

A love letter to the Emily's of the world that have gone before us and continue to light the way with their shining hearts.

This is my love letter for you, for me and for us.

Exhumation

SURRENDER

Finally arriving at the temple
there you are.
Bloodied, bruised and beaten,
worn down by life.

Crumpling on the pristine stone steps
feeling lost and alone.
Rivers of the anointed flood towards you
and carry you inside.

A thousand hands lovingly caress you,
washing away the debris from whence you came.
With love, they remove all trace,
stripping out the hurt and the pain.

Sinking into golden water,
you shed and rinse away the old.
The version of you who cannot go any further,
traversing the desert in search of oasis.

There is nothing to do and nothing to know,
the fight is over, the battle is done.
Lay down your weapons
and let golden light consume you whole.

When your bones ache from the depths,
and your weariness flows from lifetimes,
when you know you can go no further like this,
when you cry out for another answer
because this cannot be the way.

You will find yourself
bruised and beaten
on the steps of the temple.
With nothing left to give
and nothing left to lose,

ready to begin again.
This is your surrender.

THE GRAVES IN WHICH WE DIG

Society has created this concept of women who are perfect and pretty at all times. Undoing this was never going to be anywhere near as pretty.

As such, I considered naming this section of the book, *Unearthing*, but it is too light. Too delicate. It conjures an image of an archaeologist with a brush gently dusting old bones to uncover the history of a life and civilization. That is not what it looks like. Reclamation of the goddess and divine feminine begins with *exhumation*. It starts with the dead things.

At my point of surrender, I stood above my own metaphorical grave. I had not felt much of anything for years. Numb and disconnected from my body, I was a husk. There had been no singular moment that had done this to me. It wasn't a switch I turned off one winter's night. It had been a long-winded, systematic dismantling of my emotions and self until I found myself at the cusp of thirty looking out at the rest of my life thinking to myself, *I don't want this.*

It didn't seem like there were many options available either. Stay numb and disconnected. Go through the motions of life. Smile when appropriate; look sweet and pretty. Talk about what society says are the happiest days of my life, without actually feeling any part of those memories. To speak of those memories was a factual reminiscence, an intellectual exercise more than anything else. The alternative to feeling numb was to sink into pain.

Depression had long been my episodic friend throughout my teens and twenties. I had stood on the edge of the abyss and wondered what to do more than once. The thought of years stretching before me, punctuated with that darkness terrified me because each time I arrived at the abyss I'd gotten a little closer to the edge. How many more times would I stand that close before I actually tried to jump? It didn't feel like much of an option, but neither did the emptiness I felt.

I spent a lot of time drifting in my work. I described it as 'exploring' different creative avenues to gain new skills but internally I knew it was a desperate attempt to try and find myself.

In my life, I had become isolated. I had a few friends that I saw sporadically though I certainly wasn't able to share these truths with them. I was fortunate to have found a man who felt like the other half of my soul — I'd felt the call from him somewhere in the universe and found him by the slimmest of chances. We had got married but life had eventually turned us into strangers in our own home. I had begun to question my life choices and felt like I was having a total identity crisis. I had no idea who I was or what I was meant to be doing, but I knew that staying where I was wasn't the answer.

The problem is we spend so much time projecting the idea that we need to find ourselves outwards as if we will suddenly find our true selves in a new job or at the end of a rainbow. In buying new clothes we will find ourselves sown into the label or we'll miraculously walk into ourselves as easily as stepping into a new pair of shoes.

It is a clever trick by society to keep us always searching for more. We're forever starving, snacking on junk food of various forms but none of it is truly nourishing. The truth is that we will never find ourselves at the bottom of an empty crisp packet, but rather, within ourselves.

There is an innate knowing in all of us, that this is the case. That the answers we really seek are within, buried in the dirt, yet adorned with flowers as a beautiful distraction.

No one really wants to dig in because they don't know what they will find, or how far they will have to go to find the answers that will truly satisfy them. Instead, we placate ourselves, convinced that another dress is just what we need to feel better. Or it's only one bottle of wine, how can it hurt? It'll be enough to forget we ever felt hurt, lost or numb, right?

These things make us functional in society. They make it look like we're still *doing*, still moving forward when in reality the lights are on but nobody's home. We're dead behind the eyes. Walking corpses.

So there I was, stumbling through life in my zombified state. Convinced that if I could figure out what I wanted to do with my life, everything else would make sense. I was in the midst of trying to build my own book publishing company on a shoestring and I was so sure I'd found myself this time. Little did I know I'd barely scratched the surface.

It was March 2020 and COVID-19 arrived, changing the world. Dim lights started to flicker on my internal level of intuition. Things would never be the same and deep down, I knew it. I also knew I wanted to be part of the change going forward so I suggested to a group of holistic practitioners that I knew about collaborating together. The world was about to have a major wake-up call and needed new soul-led women to lead the way. I wanted to be part of it.

Although I didn't have any of the holistic, spiritual or soulful tools like the women I was talking to, what I did have was practical design, technical and communication skills that none of them possessed. My creative background gave me a very different but valuable skill set that meant I'd be perfect for facilitating whatever collaborative project we dreamed up.

We hopped on a group zoom call to discuss ideas and that is where I first met Emily. She stood out to me immediately although I didn't know why. A few weeks later she rang unexpectedly, inviting me to an online course she was running. I had no idea who she was, how she had got hold of my number or what the course was about. I was also far too polite to tell her to go do one. Days later I found myself stepping into her world of metaphors, Touch For Health and kinesiology... whatever any of *that* meant.

From that moment, for reasons unknown to me at the time, she stuck to me like glue. The group of holistic practitioners had decided to organise an online summit. I remember working with her to figure out her speaking topic which is when she first introduced me to Lilith as a concept, goddess and archetype. She explained what Lilith represented as an archetype, how she worked with her and how Lilith transformed your life. I didn't know what I was looking at, but I felt something stir deep inside. It was a yearning, a longing, gnawing at me. I knew that what I was being offered was irresistible.

I was being shown a way out. A third option from the hell I was stuck in. I was being offered a promise of the opportunity to shed all that didn't serve me and create myself and my life anew. I was being given the opportunity to truly heal and

I knew it, even though I was sceptical that it was at all possible. But between that, being comfortably numb and the abyss, it became an unquestionable choice for me. I wouldn't survive otherwise.

Lilith, The Woman, invites you to become extraordinary. She invites you into the greatest, most powerful version of yourself to create the life of your dreams.

Who wouldn't want that?!

LILITH

In the silence between the beats of your heart
she calls for you.
Siren of the abyss.

With velvet words
and the seduction of despair,
go deeply into the night
to the end of temptation.

She will meet you
on a knife edge,
awakening a fire
of burning mania.
The cathartic release from your eternal prison.

A masterpiece
unfolding along the fine line
of insanity and the night.

Ever lacking perfection
without a piece of your soul
embedded in the canvas.

A blood sacrifice serves only
to pale your face.
Nothing else will do

but to surrender entirely.
Give yourself over to her darkness,
let her will flow through you,

On the knife edge of the abyss.

UNSPOKEN TRUTHS
WE WISH WE KNEW

What no one tells you about working with Lilith is the descent. You will go far, deep into the dark. You will hit rock bottom and then find there's further to fall.

You will dig in the dirt; find the bones of your own skeleton and then the bones of everyone who has gone before you. The ancestors and soul tribe who colour your life, all the past iterations of yourself from across time and space — you'll meet them all as you walk with Lilith.

This exhumation is an important part of the healing and transformation, but don't be mistaken in thinking that it is where you stay. To wallow and live in the wounds is to stay a victim of the past. No, the only way to free yourself is to face the past and the pain head-on and move through it.

Lilith asks you – no, *insists* you – to go beyond the very realms of your known existence. After so long in silence, she demands a seat at the table.

Not many people know the full story of Lilith as she has been conveniently written out of history and vilified. Instead, we've grown to fear her and never access her wisdom and power. What you need to know is that before Adam and Eve in the Genesis story, there was Adam and Lilith.

Lilith was Adam's first wife in the Garden of Eden. They were born as equals, raised from the same clay. When Adam wanted to take the dominant position in their lovemaking, Lilith refused, as to do so would be to concede and become subservient to him. She wanted to retain her power and her personal and sexual equality in their relationship. She didn't accept being dominated by a man who refused to be her equal. A power struggle between them ensued.

Eventually, Lilith invoked the name of God and left the Garden of Eden to write her own story. This is where the original story is erased within society in favour of the narrative of the first humans created by god; Adam and Eve. Unlike Lilith who had been born from the same soil as Adam, Eve was instead born from Adam's rib. Eve being born from Adam's own body created a narrative of subservient, 'less than' women that has been perpetuated in society ever since.

For me, Lilith and Adam represent the original template for a relationship of the divine feminine and divine masculine in balance, also known as twin flame or sacred unions. With this template lost in our ancestry, man has spent millennia trying to control women out of fear and insecurity.

Lilith and everything she represents has been demonised and erased throughout history. She has been deliberately hidden, vilified and forgotten. Instead, we are fed a vision of the ideal woman who is vacuous, beautiful, subservient and therefore, easily controlled. She is agreeable and makes Adam feel like a man. *Welcome to the patriarchy*.

For a man to be in an equal partnership with the divine feminine is to be at his most vulnerable. To be held by her is to be safe, to fall apart, to feel it all and to not be in control. To be seen by her is to become transparent to his very core. To have his heart bleed in her hands and trust her not to break it, but to return it to his chest so that he may feel it all and be free.

The fully embodied divine feminine is wild and emotional. She leads from her heart, loving fiercely and deeply. She is intuitive, sensual, powerful and wise. But for any man who is not embodying their divine masculine, who cannot accept that which he cannot control, he will want to destroy her. And through time, man *has* destroyed her.

However, a new wave has been rising and it is growing ever louder and wilder. Lilith will remain silent no longer. She rises now as the voice of the voiceless. Uncompromising and unyielding, she is steadfast in her beliefs and moves forward with full conviction. She shines a light on the taboo, transmuting darkness to stand fully in her own power.

I thought I had already gone to the darkest parts of my psyche, to the edge of the abyss and back again plenty of times. Nothing prepared me for what was to come with Lilith. It was raw, dark, painful, alluring, sexy and exhilarating all at once. To go deep into your own darkness with her is like walking a tightrope over a black hole.

No stone will be left unturned in your life. Everything will be under scrutiny from her gaze as she encourages you to not settle but to accept only the very best.

Many people think they have done this work with Lilith, but I feel most have barely scratched the surface. The images I see depicted of encounters with Lilith are often not deep or dark enough. While she brings a sexiness that many other goddesses don't, it's more than simply sexy or edgy. It's primal, raw and ugly as hell. She meets you deep in the void where others fear to tread.

As a creative, I've long been aware of the mental health issues that are romanticised in the industry. To be a true artistic genius is to be unleashed amongst the insane and lose yourself entirely to your work. So many are afraid to let go creatively because they fear this darkness and insanity, but it is in this place where Lilith meets us in all aspects of our lives.

In walking with Lilith, I found that her unyielding nature meant I needed to be prepared to walk away from everything. The life, love, friendships, family, and all that I had built; to set fire to it all and leave nothing but ash. As you come up against these things and find yourself questioning whether you can let it all go, there's initially a refusal. It feels impossible to walk away. You may argue with me saying it really isn't *that bad*, that you don't *have* to give up everything; that you have no choice in the matter and you'll find a way regardless.

The truth is, we do have a choice. We may not *like* any of the options presented, however, the choice is always there. Lilith invites you to go deep into it no matter how much you dislike the options. She asks that you be willing to make the choice that brings you personal liberation regardless of anything else. This is often where people start to falter because the magnitude of this freedom, and the power of the ability to choose from this space is too great. It's something we haven't been offered before. We've been taught to stick to our obligations, duties, promises and responsibilities regardless of the personal cost to ourselves. We've been told that we are meant to martyr ourselves on behalf of everyone else and our happiness. This is what keeps us neatly in boxes, small and unsatisfied and consequently, not causing any trouble by reclaiming our own power.

Being prepared to walk away from it all doesn't mean that you *will* lose everything in your life. What it means is that in accepting that walking this path MAY cost you many things, you will find freedom in detachment. There is a boldness that comes with being unafraid to lose it all, which means you can truly dig deep and reach the very heart of things so that you may heal and transform yourself forever. Nothing has a hold over you — except yourself.

Lilith walked away from the Garden of Eden before the apple had been eaten. She knew no sin. She walked away entirely naked, carrying nothing but her belief and integrity. When she arrives in your life, she asks if you are prepared to do the same.

In return for total trust in her guidance, she offers the one thing we crave the most on this journey but have been taught by society is not an option; support.

We've been led to believe that we must go it all alone — no wonder no one wants to face their demons. We are totally unprepared, unarmed and unsupported in the process which is why the journey feels so overwhelming. Emily offered me the complete opposite of this, she offered to walk with me daily and I honestly believe that is what made the difference.

In creative writing, the hero's journey is a well-known narrative structure. You've seen it many times over whether you knew that was what it was called or not. The hero leaves the world they know on an adventure or mission. There are trials and tribulations but ultimately they succeed.

What always strikes me about the narrative though is that the hero is often sent off on this journey alone. They may pick up new friends along the way or have a sidekick for comic relief, but generally, it's a solo journey. The strength that the hero gains in the moment of climax when all hope seems lost is generated internally.

The only other time the hero's journey isn't a solitary affair is at the end of the first act where the hero meets with a goddess, guide or mentor. This guide gifts them something to help them on the journey, then bids farewell and waves the hero off to once again face the demons alone. No wonder we are afraid to journey within ourselves alone, not knowing what we might find and having no backup to help us.

There is this mentality that society has created for us that separates, isolates and divides us. We have forgotten that we don't have to do everything alone. Humans are social creatures and our ancestors knew the power of the tribe. However, in modern society, we have been encouraged to be distrustful of our peers. Rely on no one. If you want something done properly, do it yourself. It's a mentality that gives us the illusion of control and power but ultimately there is no true power for the individual. The power comes at our expense because once divided, we are weak and afraid. This is how the world continues to turn as it does with our suffering.

We've been taught to reject the goddesses who would support and connect us. Lilith has been erased from history in favour of a narrative that puts the subservient Eve as the pillar of womanhood. Mary Magdalene was brandished as nothing more than a prostitute, so we steer clear lest we be associated with someone so 'sinful'. Kali represents destruction and wrath. Hecate, an unsavoury crone of witchcraft — the list goes on. The true nature of goddesses and the divine feminine are lost to peddle a narrative that demonises, vilifies and outcasts women. This is how we lost power.

Instead, the current narrative of society is maintained by keeping us focused on gossip, celebrities, hair, makeup and our body image. If we are too wrapped up in these superficial things, we're too busy to dig any deeper, unable to heal our wounds and regain what we have lost. We are unable to and also unwilling to come home to ourselves because it's not seen as glamorous or easy. Why bother when we have everything we need in this society of instant gratification?

And yet so many of us are deeply unhappy. That inner knowing that there's so much more than this, that *we* are meant for more gnaws away at us. But without that support and guidance, the road seems impassable so it's best not to try, right?

This is where Lilith steps in to guide us. She is the companion on the road that can hold you in those darkest moments as you resurrect those dead things and breathe through the fire so that you may heal yourself. She is the one who can sit without judgement as you crumble. And as you fall apart entirely, in that moment of silence when everything is broken, you will hear her whisper, *'something better awaits you. Keep going. I'm here with you.'*

BREAKING GROUND

Before you can start reconnecting with yourself and start your healing journey, it needs to feel safe. It needs to feel do-able. Without feeling safe, you will never get started. Make it safe to look at the feelings, emotions and memories that are holding you back, however, that may look for you. Without really doing the work to set the stage and make it safe, you'll find yourself forever dabbling in the shallow end and never experiencing the true power and healing of this transformational journey.

Look inside and really ask yourself, what do you need to feel safe? What truly scares you about going on this journey to yourself? Whatever the answers are, this is your starting point. There's no right or wrong, only what makes it feel safe for you.

Know that it is possible to make it feel safe to look at your wounds. It may take time and there may be setbacks or days when it feels pointless or that you've made no progress. For many, this is where they check out because the road seems too long or too hard. Truthfully, it is a long, hard road and I cannot pretend it isn't because it's scary when your bucket gets shaken up. It takes time to get off the window ledge, it isn't something you decide to do overnight and that you will never wobble again. At this point, you're like Bambi on brand new legs trying to stand up on ice. You'll fall a lot and it will hurt. What matters is to get up again instead of falling at the first hurdle and staying down. Get up, dust yourself down and have another run at it.

This initial stage of my rehabilitation took months, however, there is no set time frame for this. Being a loner my entire life had left me highly distrustful of anyone who proposed to have my best intentions at heart. What was their real agenda? In my mind, there was always an ulterior motive. No one would really want to help *me* for no reason and I was sure I had nothing to offer in return. But this damn woman Emily was like a dog with a bone and wouldn't give up on me and for that, I am eternally thankful.

It is my wish and hope for you that you find 'your Emily' to walk by your side in this process; heaven knows you'll need it. Don't try to be a hero. Don't try to be clever and think you have all the answers. The wise women who went before us knew that this journey, life in general, wasn't meant to be undertaken alone.

Don't become a martyr for the cause; seek help and lean on your community, practitioners, therapists, counsellors and all of the above. There is no glory in coming out the other side entirely alone. And there is no shame in asking for support along the way. Make it easier for yourself by giving yourself permission to receive support and have the courage to ask for it.

I was convinced I was broken beyond repair. No one had ever stayed in my life long enough or had any tools to offer that could help me deal with my stuff. The lack of prior long-term support accounted for how long it took me to feel safe — I needed to know she was in it for the long haul, that she wouldn't abandon me and that I wouldn't abandon myself either.

It's important to prepare yourself for this transformation too. It's not enough to accept that you may lose everything and rewrite yourself in the process. No warrior goes unarmed into battle and neither should you. This is not a casual Sunday afternoon stroll in the countryside, where you wish you'd brought your jacket because the air is crisp but you left it hanging up at home so you'll make do.

If you're serious about the deep dive then you need to suit up. Ready yourself for war because this is the biggest battle you'll ever face and the main front is a fight against yourself.

Go in knowing this is a fight to the death. Only one version of you will come out of this alive and she will arrive victorious yet humbled. This battle results in the death of your ego; come prepared.

Bring backup — friends, family, therapists, holistic practitioners, counsellors, coaches, sisterhood, guides and mentors. To go it alone is to sanction the hero's journey narrative society has taught us. Break the mould and lean on your tribe, it will make you feel less insane in the process of dismantling yourself.

Gather your tools — if you already have knowledge of how to cope with overwhelm, emotional turmoil and subconscious mindset reprogramming then great; you will need all of it.

If you don't have any tools, this is where people like Emily and I; holistic practitioners, coaches and other professionals come in. There is no pride in having suffered on the journey. The goal is to release and move through the pain as quickly as possible, not to live in it or wear it like a badge of honour. We're not meant to be martyrs.

There are so many tools available that you can employ on this journey, try as many as you can to find your fit. Everything from Emotional Freedom Technique (aka, EFT or tapping), Neuro-Linguistic Programming (NLP) and hypnosis, breathwork, homeopathy and kinesiology to meditation, journaling and many more besides. All of these have their place to help you move through whatever comes up.

Accept that you don't have all the answers. Allow yourself to receive the wisdom and wise counsel of others, especially those who have already undertaken this journey for themselves. They make the healing process that much quicker and easier to move through rather than trying to do all of it consciously and alone. To embrace their wisdom is to embrace our ancestors and rekindle the spark of ancient knowing and soul remembering that will change the world.

As you go on this journey of breaking down, healing and rebuilding, gift yourself grace. Our inner critic is harsh but this is the voice with which you spend 100% of your time. Changing the narrative and letting your internal monologue be that of kindness, love and grace will help you on this journey.

Imagine you were supporting your best friend with a breakdown, would you be as harsh towards her as you are to yourself? Would you tell her to pull herself together within minutes of her world falling apart? *Of course not.* We hold ourselves to a much tougher standard but here is the truth; healing has no time limit. It takes as long as it fucking takes.

Do yourself the greatest favour and get out of your own way. Let yourself take the time to pick up the pieces and become whole again. We've been taught that bitchiness is an inherent part of female nature, when in fact it is a cost to us to be so unkind to ourselves.

One of the most profound changes I ever made in my internal monologue was to explore my own love languages and then make them reflexive towards myself. There are five love languages; words of affirmation, physical touch, gift giving, acts of service and quality time, which were outlined by Gary Chapman in his book, '*The Five Love Languages: How To Express Heartfelt Commitment To Your Mate*'.

Think about what makes you feel loved and how you express your love to others. What is it that you truly crave from your romantic partner? When you understand what your primary and even secondary love languages are, this is when you can turn them on their head and give that love to yourself.

My primary love language is words of affirmation, so changing my internal dialogue to something more kind, loving and encouraging was the quickest route to helping fulfil this need for myself. I spoke to myself as if I were my best friend, 'keep going, you are doing great. I am proud of you!' It doesn't seem like a lot but sometimes this is exactly what your soul and inner child really need to hear.

If gift-giving is your love language, buy yourself something that will make you feel special and reward yourself for showing up to work. For quality time, organise a meet-up or a date with someone that will make you feel joyful, whether it's a date night or a get-together with a friend you haven't seen for a while, it will lift your spirits.

Some people can find acts of service tricky to figure out, so here's a tip. Order a takeout so you don't have to cook or book a cleaning service so you can relax with one less chore to do. For physical touch, receiving a hug or holding hands with a loved one is what you need so go seek it, don't wait for it to fall from the sky. If you don't have anyone physically near that can fulfil this for you, think about how you can help yourself feel held; hug yourself, your pet or invest in a weighted pillow.

With all of these love languages, think outside of the box for how you can make it reflexive and give yourself what you need. In those moments when it feels like you are all alone, no one could possibly understand or you can't face trying to explain the whole story all over again, remember that the one constant who has been there through all of it, 24/7, 365 days of the year is *you*! Be kind to yourself and it will make the journey easier.

As you start to break ground and let things you'd long forgotten (or perhaps not even known were there) surface, one key thing to remember that goes back to how you talk to and treat yourself in this process is to practise non-judgement. If I had judged myself every time in my sessions with Emily when I realised what secondary gain I had on keeping a certain limiting belief or mindset, I wouldn't have gotten off the starting block.

Remember that everything about the human condition is transitory. We are always in motion, forever changing, growing and evolving. There is no pause button for a single cell in these human bodies.

And yet, humans live in absolutes. We have a singular mindset and always want to define and make things make sense. Know that as you go on this journey, there'll be days, weeks, maybe months or years where you won't be able to define who or what you are anymore because it's changing by the minute. That's okay.

Alice captures this sentiment perfectly in Lewis Carroll's '*Alice's Adventures In Wonderland*' - 'I knew who I was this morning, but I've changed a few times since then.' I can honestly say it's happened to me so many times during this journey, so I very quickly stopped trying to label and define myself in favour of letting it occur instead. It made the process so much easier and took a whole bunch of pressure off that I had no place in adding to my pile in the first place.

I remember one day feeling my head drifting. It had been a long 48 hours of revelations and I felt myself needing a nap to process everything I'd be healing. I woke up a good two hours later and I *knew* I was a different person. I didn't quite know how but I knew it. On an internal, instinctual level, I knew I'd fundamentally rewritten myself from the inside out.

The first outward manifestation of that fundamental shift came about the next day when at lunchtime I went to make my husband a cup of tea, I found myself reaching for two cups on autopilot.

Anyone who knew me before that day would know that there were only two hot drinks I ever consumed: hot chocolate and hot Ribena. It didn't matter where I went, if neither was on offer, I'd have juice or water instead. But that day I reached for a second cup as if I'd always done so. I made myself a cup of tea that I savoured like it was the last cup of tea on earth, (any British tea drinker will know what I mean when I say that!) The next day, again at lunchtime, I felt myself hankering for a cup of tea so I followed my feelings and made one.

Yes for a moment my eyes popped out of my head in confusion, I'll admit. However, I took a breath and let it go. It didn't mean anything about me after all. Intellectually I knew that taste buds change every seven years, so it could be possible it was as simple as my taste buds changing. On a personal level, seeing as I haven't had much sense of smell for decades due to long-term sinus issues and knowing how that has affected my sense of taste, I highly doubted changing taste buds was the reason I'd suddenly become obsessed with tea.

Did it matter to me either way? No. Did I judge myself for it? No, it is what it is. Today I like tea, tomorrow I might like coffee. *Ick!* Okay, probably not on that count, but the point I'm trying to make is that I didn't think of myself any differently for it. I know it's a small example but the principle is the same with whatever changes for you.

We're in love with labels because they make us and everyone around us feel safe. They create a sense of belonging and stability. They also trap us and keep us from becoming who we're truly meant to be.

I've worked with so many people who tell me they want to write a book and they come armed with excuses: *I don't have time, I can't spell, I'm not good enough.* If they keep those labels in their head, they'll never get their book into the world and then no one will know what an amazing storyteller they were. No one can be helped or changed by their words. They'll reach the end of their life feeling unsatisfied because they didn't get around to writing the book.

It is often said that you'll regret the things you didn't do more than the things you did. And honestly, it's the only way you're going to do any of this. Let go of every label and judgement you're holding onto about how you think you should act and who you think you should be. You're about to dismantle it all anyway. Let it go and don't judge yourself. You'll thank yourself later.

OPENING THE FLOOD GATES

As you dig in all sorts of things will surface. Some you knew were coming and needed to transform. Others you knew were coming and hoped that they wouldn't. Others you had no idea were laying in wait. Your emotional baggage, limiting beliefs and memories will pop up in any and every possible order imaginable. There is no way to plan the route or know what to truly expect and when it will arrive. This is why it's important to be prepared.

In the last chapter, I mentioned the importance of not doing this journey alone. To walk it with supportive friends and family and to engage with practitioners and professionals who can hold you and guide you along. While all of this is a crucial part of the preparation, it's important to know what it's going to feel like emotionally to help you feel less insane when your emotional bucket is shaken up. Emily's level of practitioner support meant she checked in with me daily, other practitioners may be weekly or monthly.

In the in-between moments when you're not in a session with a practitioner or can't get hold of your friend on the phone, let me share with you how it can sometimes feel. Know that it's cyclical and comes and goes in waves. Know that while you may feel alone in those moments of sorrow and despair, every heart that has been on this journey before you has stood where you stand and felt entirely alone too. While our emotions and journeys may all be individual, take solace in the notion that we've all struggled and felt alone on this path and still kept going because the result is worth it all.

While you may arm yourself with everything available, including the kitchen sink, you will be caught off guard more than once. Whether it's the cumulative effect of every time you ever felt ashamed turning up all at once, or a memory surfacing of a time someone crossed a line that you'd long since buried and forgotten. Whether it's trying to hold all the balls and simultaneously letting them go, and moving through it while still maintaining basic hygiene, getting dressed and taking the kids to school in the morning. Perhaps it's a combination of all of the above and more besides. Whatever the case, there are going to be plenty of days when you feel overwhelmed.

There were endless days when I didn't want to get out of bed. If I didn't have two dogs pestering me for their breakfast, I probably would have stayed under the covers. There were days upon days when I wanted to scream, shout, say 'fuck it all!' and throw in the towel. There were days when if you'd so much as looked in my general direction or breathed in my vicinity, I might well have ripped your head off.

Then there were the days when the grief rose like a serpent. A cold chill up my spine, coiling around my body, squeezing my chest tighter and gripping my throat until I couldn't breathe. And then my dogs would start hounding me because, *mummy, it's walkie time*, and I'd have to somehow pull myself together. I'd heave on my shoes and coat and walk through my village with a furrowed brow, and lowered gaze, biting my lip to give myself something else to think about rather than crying in a heap on the floor. I'd finally get out of the village onto the fields and I'd sob so loudly I was sure the whole village heard me.

And then I'd see someone coming in the distance and I'd have to decide whether I could pull myself together enough to look normal and say a quiet hello, or whether I needed to change our route so we didn't cross paths. Many a time we walked odd, winding routes to avoid people because pulling myself together at that moment was nowhere near possible.

Sometimes it felt like I'd fallen so far down the rabbit hole I'd never get out. It felt like there would never be an end to the tears, grief, sorrow and regret. That my heart would never stop aching, that my throat would never stop burning with rage and unspoken words. When you're deep in the labyrinth, it feels endless.

If you can detach yourself from the emotions for just a moment, that's when you notice that the grief isn't always the same. It may be profound but it's not the exact same grief as yesterday. When you know that the despair and pain aren't endless, that you will get through this, *of course you will*, and you can appreciate the nuances of the emotions themselves.

It is all experienced in layers. Just when you think you've let go of that thing fully, it pops back up again for one last hurrah as if to whisper, *hey, there's a piece of me you didn't fully see, now it's time to let me go too*. This endless cycle could send you insane if you let it, so don't.

Accept that this is an ongoing process which will undo itself in layers over time. That each time that memory pops up with all its raw emotions for what feels like the millionth time and you wonder why we're looking at that old chestnut all over again. However, now you'll be able to appreciate the new awareness, the new layer and the other angle to it that you are now able to see. Full awareness and understanding never happen all at once, they are gained over time in hindsight.

So many people approach healing work with the mindset that they will go and heal all the things once and in one go. This is rarely ever the case. There are so many threads that intertwine in our lives and we couldn't possibly perceive them and their trajectories at once.

Instead, we need to settle ourselves to the idea that we have no idea what will be unlocked with each thing that we heal. As we do so, things we thought we'd already dealt with will gain a new layer, a new angle and you'll see it again entirely anew and be able to let it go in another way.

When you look at your journey this way, it makes it much easier to deal with the overwhelm because you understand why it happens as it does. Unfortunately, I can't promise you it will make any of it less overwhelming, but it does eliminate the frustration of why you are dealing with the same issue again in more or less the same outfit. As I said earlier, practice non-judgement and be kind to yourself on this journey and you're halfway there.

Know it's impossible to map out exactly what order things will show up in because each thing hinges on other coordinates. The order I may have travelled through these stages may look entirely different from yours. However, in the chapters that follow, you'll find some of the common landmarks that you'll pass on your route. Use it as your guide to know you're well on your way.

WHAT WE SANCTION, PERSISTS

From fear, comes hate and rage. The red mist descends and you're furious, indignant. *Fucking outraged.*

As soon as you start opening yourself up to healing and transforming, all the places and spaces where anyone has ever crossed a line or hurt you are going to start showing up. It will drive you mad because once you see it, you can't *unsee* it. The biggest problem, however, is that we haven't been taught how to or even historically been allowed to *feel* our anger, let alone deal with it.

Men and women have been taught to approach rage so differently. For men, it's the only acceptable emotion for them to feel. Everything else is too exposing, too vulnerable and too feminine. Rage is manly. Rage is what man feels like. All their other emotions are numbed, and emotional intelligence is stunted because it's not manly to feel.

They have been taught that to feel is to lose power, to lose control. That it's only acceptable for men to be stoic, big, brave and angry because the alternative would be to be branded as emotionally unstable and therefore incapable of being in charge or leading the world.

Women, on the other hand, have been taught rage is not acceptable. Rage is not a feminine emotion. Rage is not pretty enough. Rage tells us something is wrong, rage hurts everyone. Rage calls you out when something is wrong. Rage creates instability; it makes us unhinged and therefore makes us 'liabilities'.

Instead, we're taught to repress it and ignore it. Our rage is dismissed as over the top. Unpalatable. Dangerous. Chaotic. We're heretics, hysterical, unhinged. We're mad women. Don't listen to us.

Never getting a chance to express our rage does more harm than good. What isn't expressed stores itself in the body and manifests itself physically in other ways. This emotional dam can create a backlog that builds up across lifetimes passed down through genetic memory, compounding itself until it's buried so deep you can convince yourself it doesn't even exist.

This is where we develop our tendencies to people please, be overly giving, unassertive, and disconnected from ourselves and our needs. We don't know when a boundary has been crossed because we don't know where our boundaries lie. So many people take advantage of this for their own gain — at the cost of you.

Society has conditioned us to believe there are levels of trauma and bad behaviour. That my life experiences and your life experiences are not equal. That if I didn't experience life in a certain way then the trauma, pain, anger, grief and hurt I've felt aren't as valid. This is what truly drives us crazy, trying to measure up our lives against everyone else.

It's almost become a sport that permeates everywhere. Can you become a real guru if you haven't been left homeless with five pence in the bank before making your millions? Why are you experiencing sexual dysfunction if you haven't lived through major abuse and trauma? Why are you depressed when nothing really bad has ever happened to you?

But trauma is relative to lives lived. The worst of my life is the worst of *my* life, not yours. I cannot begin to fathom how much you've suffered and I will not judge it as more or less than mine. My suffering does not diminish your suffering and your suffering does not diminish mine. It is *all* valid.

Of course, certain things are widely accepted as completely abhorrent. But to invalidate someone else's pain because it didn't hit a certain marker is what puts us back in our boxes accepting things 'the way they are' and as a result, nothing changes.

Because if I simply brushed off and said nothing about the time a man exposed himself to me while I was walking my dog — oh it's *just* a stupid man, then he gets away with it. And he'll do it again. Only next time, maybe it won't be from a distance to someone in their twenties. Next time it could be up close to a teen which is even scarier to consider and much worse than what I experienced.

However, it doesn't detract from what happened to me. It doesn't invalidate me and my experience. I still have every right to have felt uncomfortable, unsafe and angry about the first instance. In fact, it's an outrage that he did it to anyone at all.

If the only measure of sexual trauma is the severity of the act itself, and if we can diminish it and brush it off because it wasn't 'that bad' or that someone else had it 'worse'; or if we can pretend that there are acceptable levels of violation and therefore sanction the behaviour, then the cycle of repressed women continues.

You have every right to be angry about the shit that has happened to you. You are entitled to be angry about what has happened to you!

In being angry, you know a line has been crossed and you can express it. This is how we change the world, one line drawn in the sand at a time. One boundary is placed on what you will or won't accept at a time.

Consent is the most powerful currency you own.

TRANSFORMATIONAL RAGE

In my experience, I have found that the goddesses and arche-types often work and arrive in pairs or sets. One goddess may be the most prominent one to work with, often due to layering wisdom from the other goddesses in the set and evolving the work, taking it further than her predecessors.

So it comes as no surprise when at this stage of the journey the goddess Kali steps in to join us alongside Lilith. She is, after all, so widely recognised as being affiliated with destruction, death, rage and transformation.

Kali is the Hindu goddess of time, ultimate power, transformation and destruction. On reading about Kali's origins, what struck me was how she has been so deeply misunderstood. To me, her wrathful behaviour was a result of how she was treated, the effect not the cause.

Imagine, being a balanced and embodied divine goddess and your first appearance in the human world is to be summoned to a battlefield. Would you not be horrified at the atrocities you were witnessing? Would you not be uncomfortable with being summoned to such chaos and pain? Would you not feel like a boundary has been crossed because you've been brought into war without your permission?

In another story, it is said that two demons attacked the goddess Durga and in her anger, Kali was born from her fore-head. Now I don't know about you but if I was going about my business and two demons attacked me, I'd be raging pretty hard too and quite rightly so.

Yet this rage, destruction and even vengeance are what Kali has become solely associated with. She has been called 'the black one', 'the dark one' and 'the dark mother'. These are all derogatory and insulting terms designed to depict her as 'less than'. A goddess to be feared instead of revered. Her visual representation is often depicted holding severed bodies or a garland of human heads. She is shown with her tongue out and with three eyes yet she is entirely naked. They've reduced her beauty and divinity to paint a frightening, uninviting, almost hag-like picture which means when Kali appears most have come to fear her.

For me, this couldn't be further from the truth. Yes, she was born in anger and horror. She embodies and holds a darkness that many fear to tread. However, she models embracing and transforming sacred rage for women and acts as a doula for us here on this stage of the journey.

Kali is not afraid to unleash her anger. When she has been wronged, when she is angry or upset, she expresses it fully. You know when you have crossed her. She will make it more than clear to you in those final moments before she takes your head clean from your shoulders. The last thing you will know in the world is that you have enraged the goddess Kali and will not be permitted to do so again.

And while we have been taught to fear her, to renounce her rage, she demonstrates an ability to express an emotion we have long been forbidden from accessing. Kali brings the duality and ultimate balance to the divine feminine in the expression of rage. She shows us where wisdom and personal truths lie within, once we are unafraid to go into our anger.

It's a powerful moment when you can sit with your rage, without directing it outwards towards anyone, without trying to change or stop the flow of it. To express it, observe it and release it is transformational. Rage is sacred.

KALI

You will find her on the battlefield
and in darkness,
where angels fear to tread.

Her presence; an omen
of thunder coming
cracking open your core.

Doula of sacred rage,
she knows no fear or bounds;
only wrath's wisdom.

Her screams permeate
the very fabric of existence
and the truth it hinges upon.

To walk with her
is to unleash your
divine vortex.

While she holds you in duality
of chaos amongst
the silence of the stars.

OUT FOR BLOOD

Sitting with your rage is where you find out who you really are and what you stand for. To sit with your rage is to face the ugliest part of yourself and to love it anyway without trying to change or deny it. To sit with your rage and accept it is to become whole once again, otherwise, you'll avoid or suppress rage entirely. The ultimate goal is to allow ourselves to feel the full spectrum of human emotions, express them healthily and transform them into something more useful and loving rather than letting them fester, turning us bitter, twisted and scornful.

Rage was where my journey truly began to unravel. I had spent lots of time learning to feel safe to look at the things that scared me. I had started to turn my hope that I might one day be healed into believing it was actually possible. I'd been bailing out teaspoons of my emotional bucket one spoon at a time for months, which provided instant relief for whatever was showing up for me on any given day. However, I didn't feel like I was making much headway against the bigger, deep-rooted issues but I felt that I could maybe have them in the same room as me now.

So when I watched as my friend got railroaded and forced into a corner by a mutual acquaintance, initially I wasn't expecting it to affect me much. It was her problem, not mine, right? I listened to her tell me what had happened, how upset and hurt she felt and then I felt that familiar feeling rising in me. That feeling of 'you've hurt my friend and I don't like you'.

Usually, I would have simply avoided this mutual acquaintance from that moment on but not this time. Oh no. I could not let this one go. I began to feel infuriated on behalf of my friend. How dare this person treat her like that!

What happened next, unravelled me to my very core.

I went into meditation that week and suddenly, out of nowhere, I started to see what looked like a movie playing out in my head. All week I kept seeing these movies in my mind and in them, this mutual acquaintance was hell-bent on hurting me and the people I loved.

What struck me most was that there was so much detail. It was all so vivid I felt like I was standing right there, experiencing it. I had no idea what I was looking at and was convinced it was my imagination playing out the narrative of my anger and frustration.

When I shared them with Emily in a session, she had a very different take. She asked me if I had considered they could be past lives. Had I *what*?

Now I need to backtrack a bit to say, I have always been into all things spiritual. Past lives as a concept wasn't news to me. Odd things have happened to me my entire life that I simply cannot explain. I've unlocked psychic and healing gifts and then promptly locked them up again more times than I can count.

While I'm not aligned with a religion, the personal understanding I have developed of universal consciousness means that past lives and reincarnation were certainly concepts I believed were possible. I just had not had any real experience with them.

The way I see it, we're all made up of matter. Everything in the entire universe is made up of those atoms and you cannot destroy matter — this is a fact. It's called The Law Of Conservation Of Mass. While matter can't be destroyed, it can be transformed into something else. So when we die and our body disintegrates over time, that matter, all the atoms that made the body we inhabited get converted into something else. The circle of life and all that.

Now while that matter could go anywhere in the universe and become anything, for me it makes sense to believe that it perhaps stays in the vicinity rather than heading to the outer reaches of space. The fact that we're even alive is pretty miraculous and a long shot after all so… why not?

My thinking is that if this matter, that energy, hangs around, it's not out of the realms of possibility that a little piece of it from one of our previous incarnations, comes back to form a new body for our consciousness when we decide we're having another run at the whole being human thing. If that energy carries a memory of everything it's ever been, we can tap into it. We can *feel* those remnants of remembering. We get those glimpses of what we once were.

If you look at the soul as a facet of an enormous universal consciousness with all of the power that comes with it, then of course we would ensure that the matter that makes our human vehicles contains pieces of our previous dances with humanity. We would orchestrate it on purpose so that it may help inform our future choices and be part of our soul mission, almost like plot points in a story arc.

With that being my personal understanding, the moment it was mooted that perhaps what I was seeing in my meditations were glimpses of past lives, something clicked for me. It made sense to me on so many levels.

There's a recognition, a knowing that happens when you hear a truth that resonates with your soul. It may not be a loud, full-body YES but when you feel it, there's a peace and acceptance that washes over you. When it fits, it feels right and you know it, even if you can't explain how or why you know it or where the awareness came from.

Looking at the stories that had played out in my mind's eye, I learned more of the back-story and saw why this had become a personal vendetta against me. When viewed through the lens of past lives… Oh. *Of course, that's what they were.* I knew and felt it, deep within.

What I'd seen was the same set of people that I knew in various ways in my current life, targeting me throughout all of time and space. The stories kept playing out. Every day, another piece of the puzzle landed and I was on a roll. With each new piece, I understood more.

One small action from way back when had resulted in anger in them that raged for millennia. They'd chosen to seek me out and exact revenge any which way they could. The same stories and the same vicious cycles continued to play out. We were stuck in this loop of meeting and destroying each other.

The experiences got darker and darker. I could feel myself becoming unhinged in my rage at what they'd done to me time and again. Fortunately, I couldn't lash out — most of them were no longer present in my life. The only one who was present was the mutual acquaintance who had activated the remembering of the bigger pattern. However, lashing out at her didn't feel like a powerful or loving choice for me and my healing. That meant there was nowhere else to explore the root of my rage other than within.

When your insides scream at you that *this is wrong* and you ignore it, the body stores it because it has no place to go. Unlike an animal escaping a predator, there's no way to shake off that adrenaline and happily go about your day. In modern society, it's even worse for we face fears and stresses far beyond what our bodies were ever originally designed to deal with.

A fight with a bear is something our Neanderthal ancestors knew how to cope with, but calling your teacher, *mum* in front of the whole class? No one knows how to ever live that one down. It'll come back to haunt you in five years in the middle of the night when you can't sleep because it never got properly expelled from the body. It's still living in your mind rent-free. It's not anywhere near like fighting a bear as an experience although our bodies don't quite know that.

Then in fifteen years when you accidentally send an email to your entire company calling your boss 'dad' on the first line, you are suddenly transported back to that time at school when you called your teacher 'mum' and feel like an idiot all over again. Your body and mind don't know how to let it go unless you allow yourself to feel the emotions and express them at the time.

Imagine this is then compounded by lifetimes of unexpressed emotions and repressed rage. What happened with me is because I'd been gently opening up and emptying my emotional bucket, it had started to shift some of this repressed rage to the surface. One day I felt angry at someone for upsetting my friend and BOOM. All the memories throughout time and space when I'd ever been hurt or angry arrived at my doorstep.

At first, I was angry – too angry to see anything else. There was no nuance, no layers to what I felt, only rage; lots and lots of rage.

This is when people often lash out but it does more harm than good. To start with, you are lashing out on a very surface level. Your anger is immediate and tied to that moment which is fine but won't clear the backlog of rage within you. It will continue to fester and present itself as resentment, unhappiness and long-term burnout as the fight turns inwards against you. It could even manifest in the form of things like autoimmune diseases and aches and pains that won't go away.

That's not to say you won't ever feel angry again. We're human after all. It's normal and perfectly healthy to feel the full spectrum of human emotions. Any guru who sells this idea that we should look to transcend all these negative emotions and live in a perpetual state of love, light and happiness is, in my opinion, entirely missing the point of what it means to be human.

Life is meant to be lived and experienced, the good, the bad, the ugly; all of it. To don a human body and be imperfect in your ability to handle life, to not be able to float around as some divine being who is above it all, for it to be messy, real, primal and raw, is human. Experiencing our limitations and accepting them without trying to be above them is to touch divinity in the human body.

In short, you may feel like your life is a mess and you're barely holding it together but I fully believe that somewhere out in the universe, a consciousness much bigger than us is astounded by your ability to pick yourself up every day and is cheering you on. Somewhere out there your mess is a rich human experience that an angel cannot fully comprehend yet is in awe at your story.

You're doing great however you've handled it all up to now. And in reading this you'll know more and can do it even better. Don't berate yourself for feeling rage but don't live there either. Otherwise, this is as far as you go.

To transmute sacred rage you need to go deeper within and look at what lies underneath being angry at this one incident.

There are many ways you could do this, try everything and find what works for you. The most important thing to remember is not to direct your rage towards anyone. Don't take it out on anyone, it will just create more problems to deal with and no one will be speaking to you.

Instead meditate on the rage, yes really. Sit with that hot anger and let all those thoughts rattle around in your mind. Have the argument you want to have in your head and get everything off your chest — conduct it entirely in your imagination.

Journal. Write furiously about what happened and how you feel and when you think you're finished, keep writing. Don't judge what comes up but continue to write freely on what spawns out of thinking about anger. Allow yourself to feel those emotions. Then take it one step further.

Lots of coaches will offer a multitude of journal prompts for you to take your pick. Having done training in Journal Therapy myself, I know this isn't where it ends. The catharsis is in the expression of the rage on paper. The healing comes in reflection and rereading what you've written.

Consider how you feel about it, what can you learn from it? How can you transform it into something useful? When rage festers it is just that, rage. When we look at our rage and try to learn from it, we can set better boundaries and gain clarity on what to change in our lives. We set ourselves free from toxicity and honour ourselves.

Sometimes the rage is too deep-rooted and white-hot to verbalise or write down. However, without knowing more about it you can't release anything other than that one incident.

This is where I've found things like EFT tapping, breathwork or a modality that works with the physical body like Bowen Technique is helpful. Work with a practitioner if you don't know how and use that feeling of anger as a prompt. Write down every thought that comes up as you focus on the feeling. These are your breadcrumbs to meditate on and journal on later.

For me, as I looked at my anger to release it, I found it came from many places. Of course, there was how I'd been treated over lifetimes but beneath that was deep wounding around abandonment, rejection and betrayal. Beneath that were things like feeling persecuted and unsafe to be my authentic self.

Ah! The witch wound. We all carry this whether you believe you were once drowned or burned at the stake or not. We all carry this wound because it lives in our DNA, blood and bones. How does the witch wound manifest in modern times though? While this is not an exhaustive list, here are a few examples so you can see how pervasive it can be.

Feeling afraid of being seen and fears of public speaking stem from the witch wound. Rejecting anything supernatural, magical or metaphysical, being interested in say, astrology while keeping it 'secret' is a manifestation of the witch wound in the modern day. A lot of people talk about that moment they come out of the 'spiritual closet' – it is this fear and persecution of being different that means we hide it away and comes from fear of being killed for being a witch. Feeling afraid and being hypervigilant are also other ways the persecution of the witch manifests in our daily lives.

The witch wound and associated magic are tied to our intuition. Therefore, whenever we meet someone in life and don't like them or feel like their energy is 'off' in some way, it is more often than not us tapping into our intuition and feeling into their energetic field and not liking what we find there.

This is particularly common with other women whom we judge immediately upon meeting or sometimes later when an action or response activates the wound within us. Part of what escalated the hysteria, fear and destruction of the witches during the witch trials was that women were pitted against and encouraged to turn on each other, ratting them out to the authorities.

For this reason in the modern day, the sisterhood and witch wound are closely linked and often manifest in very similar ways. It could look like feeling left out or rejected from groups of women throughout life or being bullied at school for anything that marked you out as 'different' from the pack. This is the persecution complex, leaving you feeling unsafe to be your authentic self because it may get you cast out from the group (which in ancient times meant certain death).

When females are in the womb, four months in, they grow all the eggs they will ever carry in their entire life. This means that we spent five months, inception style, in the womb of our grandmother.

When I found this out, the reason why the witch wound holds on so strongly in us suddenly made sense; we receive 'the remembering' from our grandmother. In a hop, skip and a jump, it takes us straight back to the time of the witch trials much more quickly than had we received 'the remembering' passed down only from our mothers.

The witch wound is possibly the most pervasive reason for stopping women in their tracks from shining their light because once upon a time, we died most horrifically for sharing these truths.

Anything that makes us feel vulnerable and seen will reactivate this inner knowing, this remembering. Suddenly our bodies and our souls are transported back to a time when it wasn't safe to be the weird woman who talked to trees or saw visions of the future. To be her was to face certain death. This can manifest as actual pain in your body in the present time. *Of course,* we want to run and hide when that kicks up.

However, instead of running and hiding in the hope it will go away, it's important to remember this time, you came prepared. You have tools to release the fear; you have support in the form of practitioners. Run towards the help and you'll be able to transmute this fear and release yourself. Otherwise, it will come back around again at a later date when you feel seen or try to shine your light.

Most recently when the fear reared its ugly head at me, I was able to face it with the help of Emily as my practitioner. However, years prior, I ran. When the witch wound kicked up for me back in 2012, I ran physically out of my house. No joke. I had no idea why but I knew I had to run.

In 2012, I'd broken up with someone I'd been long-distance dating for two years. At the time I didn't realise we had past life energy in the dynamic but I was about to find out. We broke up at the very end of January. I don't know if I was thinking at the time but I had not realised that a certain day of love was coming up. Valentine's Day rolled around and I was getting ready to go to university lectures, not at all thinking I might see my ex considering he lived in another country.

Boy was that a miscalculation on my part.

I was in my room making my bed and heard the front door open. My mum and I lived next door to my grandparents so this wasn't unusual for them to come and go. I assumed it was my grandad coming to check when I'd be ready to have a lift to university.

Suddenly, there he was. My ex looming in my bedroom doorway. Shit. I didn't see that one coming.

After the initial, 'what the hell are you doing here?' I bolted. I couldn't quite work out what was happening in my body but I knew it was huge. I rang my mum at work to tell her, I ran next door to tell my grandparents. I majorly freaked out.

Then I did the only thing I could do at the time; I told him I had to go to a lecture at university and no, he wasn't allowed to come. I hightailed it out of there without so much as offering him a drink. I was gone for *hours*. I have no idea if my nan checked on him (although she probably did) or what he did (aside from still being there when I got back). Definitely not my finest moment and I always felt it was quite out of character for me.

Until more recently that is, when my past lives started unravelling before my eyes and I saw myself as a witch. Arrested, forcibly taken from my home and subsequently hanged. There are no prizes for guessing who I recognised as the witch hunter. Ding, ding. *The ex who showed up on my doorstep on Valentine's Day.* No wonder I lost the plot when he showed up in 2012 as it activated a remembering deep in my soul.

Here's the thing though. Without going underneath the white-hot rage, I would never have gained that piece of understanding. It would have simply been that; rage and my totally out of character, over the top response to someone coming to try and reconcile our relationship. I wouldn't ever have understood why it affected me as it did. I wouldn't know why in the intervening years I've always felt panic whenever the doorbell rang. In understanding it, I could treat my fear and memories with more compassion and do something about it.

When we can go beyond it, beneath it and find out what is there, we learn so much more and can do something useful with the knowledge. We can release and heal the wound.

Another thing that also came out of seeing that life as a witch was the sisterhood wound. The person who had ratted me out to the witch hunters was a female friend. It's well documented during the witch trials that women were encouraged to betray their fellow sisters and it became impossible to know who to trust.

Being suspicious of one another and subsequent isolation of women has been built upon by society through the years. Instead of supporting one another and finding power, comfort and wisdom in the collective, we've become judgemental and mistrustful of other women. Instead of lifting each other up, we spend time gossiping and tearing one another down.

Women have become envious, jealous and competitive against each other. They have become elitist and cliquey to those who don't fit the status quo. Sabotaging one another and perpetuating fear and isolation if you happen to not be part of the group. *You will conform or you will be left out in the cold.*

This activates a tribal, survival instinct within us. Life has long been about survival of the fittest so any sign of weakness; any sign of not being part of the pack could mean abandonment and certain death in ancient times.

Like I said earlier though, our bodies simply cannot tell the difference between now and then. Your girlfriends uninviting you to a night out activates the same neural pathways and fears of our Neanderthal ancestors who were under a very real threat of death if the pack rejected them. Humans are social creatures by nature; this is why the sisterhood wound hurts so much. It separates us from those who would love us, comfort us and raise us up.

Women disconnected and judging each other works perfectly fine for a patriarchal society which is why it has prevailed for so long. If we're too busy gossiping about Sally looking like a slut then we're kept away from claiming our real power of the divine feminine.

The sisterhood wound first activated for me when I was nine. I remember it so clearly. It was the first time I felt I had to go back into my box. It was the first time I felt it wasn't okay to show my whole self to the world. That's a lot to deal with at only nine years old.

My grandad has always encouraged me to embrace the spiritual and supernatural. We were already two peas in a pod but after my parent's divorce, my mum and I moved next door to my grandparents. He quickly became a grandad and dad to me. We did everything together.

He casually asked me one day if I knew how to heal. He showed me the concept of 'laying of hands' and I was apparently a natural. I found this new found skill exciting. It never occurred to me that it might be unusual because my grandad had discussed it so openly and casually with me. Yes, he is a very special man and I'm so lucky to have had him in my life for as long as I have.

Fast forward a few months to school. It was lunchtime and I was playing with friends. I say friends but honestly, I don't think I'd been truly accepted into the group at that stage.

We were at middle school where several primary schools joined up for four years before high school. They were an already established group of friends from a different school to me. They seemed so cool and I desperately wanted to be part of the group. I traded on my Halloween birthday and apparent witchiness to even be noticed by them. We spent breaks running around chasing 'ghosts' that only I could see. It was fun and I felt like part of the group.

The girls would say my eyes glowed red when I was angry. However, I was so desperate to be included that I ignored the sting every time they said it.

It was during one of these lunchtime ghost chases that one of the girls tripped. She twisted her ankle and instantly started crying while we hobbled her over to a bench.

Just as they were discussing fetching help, I piped up that I had an idea. It was the first time I'd tried healing outside the comfort of home but I knew what I was doing. I *believed* in what I was doing. I held my hands over her ankle for a few minutes visualising white light flowing through them. The whole group were silent, it felt like the world had stopped turning and was holding its breath.

'All done. Try to stand up,' I said with total confidence. Her eyes grew wide as she gingerly took a step, then two, then three.

'I feel fine!' She exclaimed. The whole group cheered jubilantly for about five seconds. I then saw them all give knowing looks to each other and they rounded on me.

'Witch. You're creepy and weird. You can't play with us anymore.' And just like that, I was out of the group. The look of disgust and fear on their faces was haunting. From then on I was an outsider, always on the fringes of groups. Always had rumours spread about me; always looked at like I was gum on their shoes.

It originated from this set of friends but eventually, the bullying was escalated by other girls. I was the perfect cannon fodder. Witch. Having Cypriot heritage from my dad's side, I was dark and hairy. I was an incredibly ill child taking a lot of time off school — mostly due to the stress caused by being bullied. I had a deathly pallor to my face that only served to reinforce me being some weird ghost who occasionally turned up at school.

What I didn't realise is the healing incident had activated both the witch wound and the sisterhood wound. I had no idea what was going on but I never felt safe. I felt like I was walking around having signed my death warrant. In a way, I had. This incident occurred when I was about nine. It's common to find a link between the first activations of our wounds at this age which then set the tone for the rest of our lives until we do the work to heal ourselves. Think back to when you were eight or nine, what was occurring for you then? What happened that may have made you feel violated, persecuted or put back in your box? Unlocking and healing these memories is key to helping you release all the fears that have stemmed from them since.

Very rapidly I became the quietest person in the room. I'd gone from confident and outgoing to almost invisible, full of fear, hate and ready for death. At a parent's evening, my mum was even asked if she had a daughter or a mouse by a teacher because I was so quiet and unengaged in class.

My healing gift was put back in its box. I stopped my epic fancy dress Halloween birthday parties — I had no one to invite at that point anyway. I began to resent the day I was born. I resented anyone finding out and joking that I was a witch.

We fight those wounds and traumas on so many fronts. Invisible enemies can be impossible to win against when you don't know what you're truly dealing with. This is why it's so important, no matter how scary or painful, to dig underneath the rage. It's not pretty, particularly when those emotions and sometimes even pain becomes live again and you feel it physically inside your body. However, it is an opportunity to heal it and free your soul now and forevermore. Otherwise, you'll continue to carry it all, much like karmic debts and it will weigh you down and manifest itself in all sorts of ways.

However, it's not all about past lives. Going back to what I mentioned earlier of this idea that the witch wound has been passed down to us through our grandmothers throughout the centuries, there's another pervasive source of wounding; ancestry.

It's not just your eye colour that gets passed down through your DNA – that's genetics. Your genes carry information that affects your physical and functional attributes and these get passed down to you from your parents.

While your physical characteristics are set from birth, epigenetics, on the other hand, focuses on healing intergenerational trauma. The events of our ancestors' lives and the decisions they made, however big or small, still influence our behaviours, limitations and expectations of our lives when activated. We can transform how we respond when an ancestral fear rears its ugly head within us. That old saying of 'it runs in the family' may prove true but in doing this work you can add this addendum, 'it may run in the family, but it runs out with me.'

This one can be so tricky to navigate, not only because you've got several DNA lines all with their own stories and issues to contend with. It is also the fact that any family you have around you that you currently interact with, will feel the ripple of the work you do to heal the family line and they won't always like it.

Any time over the last couple of years that I have done anything to heal my ancestral lines, my family have reacted to the work I do. As they felt the ripple of the healing and clearing I was doing, it would activate the fear and wound within them and rile up their emotions. The wound escalated during the healing process which meant I experienced arguments galore, showing me all the places where the wound still lived in our family. They have at times stopped speaking to me for days, weeks, months, even years depending on how the ripple kicked back at them.

Because healing that wound, changes who we 'BE' in the world. When done on an ancestral line, it doesn't just affect me – it can go both forwards and backwards along the line. Your family may not consciously know what you're doing but energetically they feel it. They feel that it changes who you are, who they are, how you interact with each other, how they interact with the world, and how the world interacts with them. It changes things on a fundamental level that they can't verbalise but deep inside, they know it.

We're all human. We fear what we don't understand. We fear stepping outside of our comfort zone or outside of the familiar even if it's toxic. It's the ego's way of keeping us safe to keep us within homeostasis. When they feel those tectonic plates of the family line shifting, it's scary. People lash out. Afterwards, everyone usually calms down and you can see them benefiting from being free of the wounding. Sometimes, however, there are really hairy moments where there's a flurry of insanity and anger like a snow globe. You simply need to ride out the storm, stay in your lane, not lash out while healing the issue and let the dust settle.

So let's open up Pandora's Box. What comes up from ancestral wounding, aside from everything and anything?

Any story that you or your family members hold onto as a form of identity that isn't particularly helpful, is probably some wound from 'whenever ago'. It could be a money story that your family is always poor or unlucky. Whenever in the ancestral line it started, that story of lack will continue to play out in every generation in some form or other.

Perhaps a grandparent abandoned your family, and that trauma will come down the line. It may play out as your parent being the abandoner, or perhaps they unconsciously set themselves up in a relationship that would end in them feeling abandoned. We seek out familiarity and can unwittingly sabotage ourselves to play out these stories that we know, time and again, simply because we know them and we think that's how it's meant to happen. That this is simply the way it is for us. *It runs in the family after all.*

Sometimes it's not always so obviously played out or it may have been inverted entirely. Imagine as a child, your mother felt neglected and invisible against her siblings. She compensated by smothering you with too much love which felt suffocating. In you, it created resentment and a need for space so you distanced yourself from her, barely having a relationship with her at all. She's still ended up feeling neglected and abandoned but it manifested differently and to the detriment of you.

My friend has an ancestral story about being creative. One of her ancestors from years back, was a highly creative, prolific writer and artist until her lover was taken from her, spiralling her into a despair that she never recovered from. She stopped writing and creating entirely.

In the present day, it's manifested with my friend's father wanting to paint and draw but not feeling allowed. Meanwhile, my friend has walked around for years wearing an invisible label that told her she did not have a creative bone in her body. In unlocking this ancestral story, she has freed herself from the mindset. She has embraced the idea of creativity and begun to write

There is a genetic imperative to embrace the gifts of the DNA line beyond simply neutralising the limitations. In being descendants of this potential, when the crossroad of that potential is once again offered for us to take up and realise, it causes a positive ripple along the ancestral line as a result. By actively embracing the potential and the story of your ancestors, you can heal a whole ancestral line and unlock freedom from limitations that have been placed on the lives of everyone in the line, leaving new possibilities for everyone going forward.

I was very lucky that when Emily turned up in my life, she came armed with tools specifically focused on transforming the memories and legacies in my DNA to assist me in healing some of my family wounds, particularly around money stories.

We worked tirelessly on whatever came up, in whatever order it came up from this life, past lives and DNA ancestry. It felt endless and I often wondered whether I was making any headway. However, one thing that is important to know is that while it *feels* endless, the amount of emotional stuff in your tank is finite. Eventually, you can and will empty your bucket of all the things, but because there have been generations and lifetimes of carrying the weights without dealing with any of them, initially when we start working to heal and release, it feels like there's so much it may never end. Let me tell you, it **does** end. It's not a never-ending porridge pot of emotional crap for the rest of your life.

The thing about this healing journey though, is you never know what is going to be the piece you unlock which makes the most difference. You never quite know what is going to be the thing that dramatically lightens the load. Sometimes it can be a cumulative effect but I believe that often there's one particular thread that weighs heavier and casts a darker, bigger shadow on your life than anything else. When you finally reach it and unlock it, the difference is stark.

The thing that turned the tide for me was completely unexpected.

I don't quite remember when I first felt a sudden darkness weigh upon me but it must have been in my late teens. It felt alien, it felt unlike me and it was dark, very, very dark. This was after I'd become withdrawn and closed off from my gifts. I did keep experiencing the odd supernatural occurrences although I kept writing them off as my imagination.

There was a fear of the supernatural and metaphysical hanging over the house that I couldn't explain. My grandad and I no longer talked about healing, ghosts or anything magical. My mum was terrified of any discussion even remotely in that arena. Talk of ghosts or death had her sobbing and running out of the room within minutes.

The only 'ghost' she could talk about without panicking, was her nan. A psychic, years prior had mentioned to my mum that her nan was her guardian angel and sat at the bottom of her bed. It seemed to bring my mum some comfort. I didn't question it because I felt a chill in my mum's room anytime I dared enter so it seemed to add up. I remember one time when my mum felt confident enough to talk about her guardian angel, she happened to mention how she often saw her nan's face in her mind's eye at night. In fact, she saw other faces sometimes and found it terrifying.

Evidently, spiritual gifts run in the family.

I thought nothing more of it and continued to carry this darkness around with me. Over time, I forgot its arrival and came to think of it as mine. My twenties were plagued with dark thoughts of death, suicide, violence and disturbing fantasies. I felt constantly tormented. Yet because in the interim I'd taken it on as my own, I didn't dare tell anyone. What would they say? I felt like a monster.

One Sunday morning having my regular check-in on the phone with Emily about my unravelling life, I couldn't take it any longer. I needed to tell *someone*. I'd grown to trust that Emily wouldn't flinch at whatever I threw at her and this felt like the biggest test yet. I felt like I was dying in silence waiting for her response on the other end of the phone.

'It's not you, I'm sure of it. I don't know what it is, but it's not you.'

At that moment, I breathed out for the first time in more than a decade. As soon as I heard the words coming down the line, I *knew*. I knew she was right. None of it was mine. Whatever darkness seemed to follow me around, had not originated from within me.

She suggested it being an entity attachment of some kind, not that I knew what that was. After some muscle testing on her part, we discovered it wasn't a random entity but an ancestral spirit, so I settled down to do a DNA meditation from Emily's toolkit.

In the meditation, I saw an ancestor from many generations in the past from the Victorian era. He had suffered from such disturbing thoughts that he had been rejected by his family and the church. With nothing left and nowhere to go, he was contemplating something akin to a lobotomy to free himself of his torment. I don't know what ultimately happened to him but it seemed that in feeling lost and searching for redemption, he hadn't let himself pass over and was stuck in tormented limbo. Instead, he had desperately tried to share his story with his descendants – my family, in the hopes that someone may be able to help release him.

I never asked my grandad if he'd experienced anything, although I remembered my mum's fear of ghosts and the supernatural. I began to wonder if he'd also tried to seek her help, leaving her terrified and closed off. It certainly explained the darkness that had arrived to me so suddenly and gripped me with increasing intensity over the years.

I didn't know what I was doing, but I decided to try and speak to this ancestor in my head. I wasn't expecting a response so my eyes nearly popped out of my head when I heard a very Dickensian voice answer me back. He immediately apologised for the pain he'd caused me and asked if I could help at all.

Redemption was what he sought and it happened to be nearly Easter. Emily extended an invitation for him, via me, to join her and her family for the Easter vigil at her local Catholic church. He was sheepish but honoured. Shortly after the service, I was cleaning out the hearth at home when I heard his voice in my head. 'Thank you' was all he said as I instantly felt the weight of the world lift from my shoulders. I took the deepest breath I could. He was free, I was free, and my entire family was free. It was over.

The darkness that plagued me evaporated immediately. My depression and dark thoughts which had spiralled into me seriously considering suicide on more than one occasion seemed to vanish overnight. I know, without question, I will not have another episode of depression ever again.

During those few days as I uncovered the story and helped release my ancestor, the living family around me threw various strops. By Easter Sunday, absolutely no one in my family was talking to me. However, as the next week rolled out and the lightness travelled through the ancestral line, conversations were had by some, to mend things and we all felt able to move forward once again.

The result of doing the ancestral work has been profound. Not every family member has continued to be a part of my life. Whatever stories we needed to play out, whatever places, spaces and understandings we needed to come to have been played out for the moment. And that's okay. We may intersect again in future but at least we have all been freed from playing out whatever ancestral car crash stories we've been dealing with for however many generations.

For the family that has remained in my life, I've seen massively improved relationships. Things that once divided us are no longer issues. There's more respect for our individual boundaries, we enjoy each other's company in a way we never could before with so many generations worth of pain standing between us.

In freeing myself from these traumas and wounds, I have even noticed more subtle shifts in the mindsets of the family members who have stayed in my life. While from the outside looking in the shifts have seemed subtle, the impact ancestral work has had on them and their resulting actions has been massive. My mum has benefited most of all. She no longer fears the supernatural. I'm able to have conversations with her about all the inner work I'm doing, spirits, angels, anything and everything, and she doesn't run a mile. It's made such a difference to be able to talk about it, not needing to hide it like it was some dirty secret. I'll be comfortable, happy, *proud* even, to let her read this book if she chooses, without worrying what she might think.

My remaining family *feels* lighter and happier. The density we all carried, the frustrations we expressed at being stuck in the same vicious cycles and over the top reactions to things that never really made any sense (until you hear the story from way back when that is), have dissipated. We are happier, harmonious and more united than we've ever been. Whatever we've been through together, I *know* they've got my back.

There were days when the weight of fighting on all these fronts made me wonder why I'd gotten out of bed. It felt like a never-ending porridge pot of pain. I became angry at myself for even starting to dig up all these wounds from everywhere in time. I had to go back and remind myself why I'd chosen to do any of it in the first place. I knew I couldn't stay where I was in misery. I was desperate for things to get better, desperate for change. It was this thought that helped me keep going on those darkest days.

I'm not saying you need to reach a breaking point to start this work though. If you can wholeheartedly choose to free yourself from the trauma and pain that holds you back before you reach rock bottom, then I applaud you.

If you had to reach rock bottom first and you're reading this, desperate for something other than pain, I promise you it gets better. I write this because I can't sugar-coat what travelling through and releasing the trauma is like, to get to that lightness, to that peace and healing. There's no way to bypass it entirely. However, going in forewarned and forearmed will make your journey quicker and hopefully less painful than mine.

This journey isn't something that can be done half-heartedly. This is the reason that I'm so honest in this book about how hard the journey can be at times because you will want to quit on more than one occasion. You will probably wonder why you even bothered in the first place and feel like it's never going to end. It does feel like that when you are clearing out the pain. This is why being able to choose wholeheartedly to make this change is so important. It is not something that can be done by halves. You are either all in or you're not, in which case you'll remain dabbling on the surface.

Know that deciding to and actively taking the steps to heal and release on the deepest of levels initially feels difficult and off-putting. However, there is freedom that lies beyond this when you get to the other side. The knowing of what is possible as you recreate your life makes this part of the journey completely worth it a thousand times over.

People often give up when it gets hard and it serves society's current narrative of suffering to keep you stuck. If people start to ask questions, heal deeply and get beyond the pain, suddenly we're unwilling and unable to conform to society's game of a 'suffering life'.

It is worth doing the work because the rage and the truth under the wounds of the rage keep us weakened and isolated. A woman embodying the divine feminine is powerful beyond measure. Our power comes in embracing our chaos, our intuition, our feminine magic, our rage, our vulnerability, our sorrow, our sensuality, our grace, our pain, our wisdom, our mistakes, our gifts, our guidance and our compassion.

So it's time to start claiming that shit back.

WITH WHAT'S LEFT OF THE RAGE, WE SCREAM

This stage of exhuming all the trauma, pain and suffering isn't linear. There's no telling how long it will take you or how many times you will go over the same incident until you've stripped it down to the bone to find the gold within.

Mary Magdalene's gospel covers the seven powers of what it means to be human. The seventh power is wrathful wisdom. Although it can be hard to find any wisdom within rage because it's so consuming, it is in there. Sometimes you have to go outside of yourself to see it though. Much like how in Disney's *Moana*, the titular character realises that to restore the heart of the nature goddess Te Fiti, she needs to return the heart to the volcanic demon Te Ka, who turns out to be the goddess Te Fiti herself, raging due to her stolen heart.

You can't find the wisdom, you can't learn from what happened and change things, while you're still in the rage. Sometimes this means going over the same incident multiple times as you can gain new awareness. Sometimes you can only look at something by peeling it back in layers because it's too painful to look at it all in one go. It takes time and that's okay. Know that you are dealing with as much as you can each time and keep moving forward.

There is no race or competition to heal the quickest. Everyone goes at their own pace, looking at as much as they can handle each time. That's not to say you are only going to move in tiny increments forever. What happens is that you start to build an energy fitness as you heal. With more experience, confidence and tools and with less in your emotional bucket, you can handle bigger pieces of the puzzle and make bigger strides next time.

Some of the steps forward after healing could look like setting new boundaries, honouring your 'no' or putting yourself first. It may be in allowing yourself, or someone else, to be angry or judgemental and to sit with those emotions. It could be allowing yourself to simply feel, for the first time in a long time. It could mean having a difficult conversation with someone or responding differently. These are all baby steps that you can take; they're new skills that you'll need to give yourself time to get used to using.

Gift yourself some grace and allow it to take as long as it takes.

Sometimes, even when you've found the wisdom within the rage, there is still rage. And it is absolutely valid. Not everything can be or needs to be encouraged to be forgiven. Some people, some actions, some incidents, really are that toxic and traumatising. You are allowed to still be angry and hurt that it happened.

You can decide that because someone has consistently treated you so poorly, even though they've said sorry, you still don't want them in your life. What is important is that this decision comes not from the white hot rage but from a place of clarity. When you're raging hard, you can't think clearly. This is why detaching and going underneath the rage is so important; it takes some of that fire and pours water on it. It allows you to move through that hot rage and see what you're left with.

If you're still left angry, which probably you will be if it comes from everywhere in time and space, then you know what? It's okay to go scream into a pillow. And yes, before you go thinking you can't, you absolutely *can*. We have been conditioned to believe that we can't, that we're not allowed. That it's not what women do. No, it isn't what women are taught to do and are we any better for it? Instead, we're portrayed as silent or moody nags with long memories, resentful of our partners, children and the world.

Seriously, girl, you need to go have a really good scream.

The thing about sacred rage though, is that it has to be felt and transmuted inside of you. To find the wisdom is a guide to how to go about things differently. To change things, make amends, set new boundaries and in doing so, you can release and transform the rage once and for all. Beyond that, if you're still left with rage, it's not an opportunity or reason to take it out on anyone else.

Honour the fact that it happened, that you've done the work to clean it and you're **still** angry. Don't judge yourself. Forgiveness and letting go don't miraculously happen overnight. You are allowed to still be angry.

However, you don't want to carry it around inside of you. Festering, unexpressed rage will manifest physically in the body in all sorts of ways, so it's time to get it out in a way that doesn't hurt anyone. This expression of rage is entirely between you and you; no one else.

It doesn't mean you are never going to be angry at anything ever again. You know what I'm going to say, we're *human*. Things happen and we have a right to feel it all. In letting go of this rage that's built up from everywhere in space and time, when you next feel anger rising, it will be a much cleaner anger.

Next time you find yourself feeling annoyed at your partner for forgetting to empty the bin, instead of then remembering all the times in the last five years that they haven't done what you asked, you'll be able to deal with that one moment. It won't be the tip of the iceberg that contains five years' worth of resentment.

You'll find that you'll be able to move on and cool down quicker from anger too because it doesn't have a lifetime worth of gunk behind it. Instead, you can acknowledge it was awful, it made you mad, and then you can deal with it.

You might still find yourself screaming into a pillow about it at some point, but it won't be about the fifty ways your friend betrayed you, just the most recent thing because you've already dealt with the other stuff.

In the meantime, while all the rage from all the times you've died and been hurt or betrayed are live within you, transmute them while they're right on the surface. Invoke the goddess to help you transform and release those feelings. Get them out of your body and honour the raging divine feminine within you. Embrace yourself as the woman who is unafraid to go into and express her rage. Embrace yourself as the woman who doesn't let it fester, who gets it out of her system so that it doesn't cause more damage.

Call forth Kali and Lilith. Journal and meditate on the source of your rage. Use your tools, whether that's EFT tapping, breathwork, homeopathy, journaling or something else entirely to help you release it. Go find yourself an empty field and scream until it feels like you've razed it to the ground. Call forth that rage from the deepest, darkest parts of you. Gather it all up, scoop all the rage and hate and wrath up into a ball and scream. Scream as if you were calling the Gods from the outer reaches of the universe. Scream as if you were calling forth the Kraken from the Mariana Trench deep in the Pacific Ocean. Scream as if you were screaming on behalf of all the suffering souls in hell.

Scream it out, my friend. Just scream.

BEYOND THE RAGE

Initially, I couldn't believe what I was seeing and feeling. I was feeling pain and rage in my body coming supposedly from other lives, other places and spaces in time.

No, I thought, *this is it. I've finally, truly gone mad.*

In that moment there is a choice we make. Whether we dismiss what we see and feel because it doesn't fit the normal societal narrative or we accept that there's truth in it.

I flip flopped between a state of acceptance and denial for quite some time.

Because to accept that these things might be real is to step into an unknown universe. A rabbit hole that may or may not go to Wonderland. The last time we went there, however, we died for it as witches, remember?

I've had odd, unexplainable things happen to me my entire life. I guess the spiritual, mystical side of me has always been fairly close to the surface. No matter how many times I tried to shut it down, it always popped back up like some supernatural jack-in-the-box. I kept trying to put it back in the box but it never stayed that way for long. Something supernatural would always bleed through.

I remember years ago telling my then boyfriend when my clairalience, which is the ability to gain psychic knowledge through a sense of smell, first started to unlock itself. His immediate response was to tell me I was hallucinating smells out of nowhere.

And yet, I couldn't deny how I'd felt one wintry afternoon a few months before telling my boyfriend about my clairalience when I'd been practising Christmas songs on my piano accordion. There was only me and my grandad, my nan had gone out walking with my mum and all the dogs. In the dim 'big light' of my grandparent's living room, I sat there rifling through the music book looking for a song I hadn't practised yet. I stopped when I landed on one of the songs where you could play the bass more like a melody as it was always a fun challenge.

Ever since I was little, my grandad has always been the one who encouraged me to embrace whatever psychic and spiritual gifts I have. In between my song practice, we'd been chatting about all the weird, wonderful and supernatural. He was reading a book on ghosts of the Norfolk Broads and had been telling me about some of the local haunted sites so I guess we were pretty open to something magical happening. And it certainly did.

I took a breath and threw all my concentration, love and Christmas joy into playing. Suddenly, a few bars into 'Hark! The Herald Angels Sing' the overpowering smell of the coal from his giant stove began to fade. In its place, the entire room began to fill with the scent of roses. The lightbulb which was blatantly many kilowatts too low for such a big room, instantly brightened and I stopped squinting through my glasses trying to read the music.

I could barely breathe for the scent of roses. There was this incredible warm feeling around me, like warm honey dripping down my shoulders. The room felt full of a presence I couldn't see and although I was so sure I was going to trip up over some of those tricky bass notes, I played it note perfectly for several rounds.

Afterwards, my grandad and I sat in stunned silence. I asked him if he could smell the roses and he nodded. We didn't speak for quite a while; instead, we sat there soaking it in. I didn't know what we'd experienced but it felt like a whole host of angels had descended into the room.

Somehow neither of us could tell my mum or nan about it. We didn't *want* to. It was a sacred moment between us and whichever heavenly beings joined us that afternoon. I didn't practise any more songs that day, nothing could compare.

Looking online later, I found out that roses are often associated with angels and I said a silent thank you to whoever had graced us with their presence.

So a few months later, when my then-boyfriend told me I was hallucinating, I knew that I wasn't. I *knew* I'd experienced something different only a few months before. Something that was so incredibly profound that I haven't talked about it since, until writing it today.

Although I was so afraid of what embracing these spiritual gifts meant for me, no matter how hard I tried to pretend it wasn't real, that it didn't really happen, there was a tiny voice in my head and a tug on my heart that couldn't let it go.

The soul *knows* when it's seen the truth. The soul remembers. The soul always knows. It will keep leading you back to it time and again to see if and when you're ready to make a different choice.

So although these past lives were unravelling before my very eyes and I was desperately trying to tell myself I was making it up – I'm a storyteller with a vivid imagination after all. When I finally took a moment to get quiet and feel into it, I found only myself. And what I heard myself say was, 'you know it's all true, Camilla. I see you are scared. What do you choose?'

I wanted to run away, far away. Forget it all, pretend it hadn't happened. However, I'd done this rodeo enough times to know that it wasn't going to go away. Besides, this time I had a practitioner armed with teaspoons and tools ready to help. This was my best chance at dealing with it. Dealing with it meant not denying it any longer.

Does that mean that there weren't ever any days afterwards where I wondered if I was crazy? Of course not. Does it mean that there weren't ever any days where I wondered why on earth I said yes to working on healing all of it? Of course not!

As you heal and are moved into becoming a bigger version of yourself, you find the questions asked of you also get bigger. Your soul mission, the thing you feel called to do in life, gets bigger. It isn't to say that what you feel called to do becomes more scary, heaven knows by this point you've already climbed many a mountain in your journey of healing. You have the evidence of what you've already overcome, you have more knowledge, tools and awareness which means even when the question asked of you gets bigger, you know you can handle it.

Sometimes you look back and see just how far you've travelled away from the normalcy of who you were and wonder how you could ever go back. Then there are some days where you long to go back because it was all a lot simpler than the jumbled mess of emotions that you sometimes feel that you have become when your emotional bucket has been shaken.

However, you're not in Kansas anymore Dorothy, and you don't have any ruby slippers. Glinda the Good Witch is not going to send you back to what you were because that version of you rapidly ceases to exist. I found that in the excavation of my rage and all that lay behind it, I couldn't call forth the previous version of me. Even part way through the process I hadn't fully healed and I hadn't quite arrived; even then I knew I wasn't who I once was.

And as you shed the layers of the rage and hurt, the fear, the suffering, you will grieve the old you. You will grieve the roads that might have been but now will never come to pass. You will mourn the lost possibilities, the missed opportunities, the roads taken, the roads not taken. You will grieve for the sacrifices and the outcomes, good and bad. You'll grieve it all in layers.

As you accept the path to heal your wounds, as you embrace the weird and wonderful and let it all be *just so*, you will grieve like never before. Grief isn't where we stay either, even if once again, it feels like a never-ending porridge pot of pain. There's no sidelining your grief, it is important to feel it, honour and release it. Know though that although you may grieve for the lost opportunities and closed doors, you can eventually move towards love and possibilities. All that you have been, seen and done has led you to this point, into being who you are now. As we heal, we release those things from defining our entire futures and invite the new into our lives. In continuing to say YES on this journey of healing and transformation, you are saying yes to the most powerful, loving and empowered version of yourself who is free to choose going forward.

When you can see past the anger and indignation, there's a grief that comes for all the pain and suffering you experienced at the hands of others. The pain and suffering you witnessed by the hands of others. Finally, and this is often the hardest of all to reconcile, you'll find grief for the pain and suffering you inflicted and caused others.

This grief is profound. It grips you in a way that anger doesn't come close to achieving. The grief holds you with an insufferable ache. It clouds your mind and everything is tinged grey. The colour of the world drains away. It feels like there's a black cloud, the looming spectre of your grief trailing you day and night. There's no escaping its hold, the only way to deal with grief is to go through it – remember though, you don't need to do it alone. This is where your support system, practitioners and friends are so important in the equation in helping you to choose the road of love and possibility whenever the grief rises within you.

At first, it'll feel like wading through treacle. It will feel like it never ends and will consume you whole. Here's the thing though. Unlike Artax the horse from *The Never Ending Story*, you will not die in this swamp of sadness. It may feel like you're sinking into the depths and it may last longer than you ever anticipated. But you are not on this journey alone and you will get through it.

What you need to remember is the weight of the grief is all the heavier because it's not coming through from just this one life. It can come through from past lives, ancestral trauma, the lot. It weighs heavy because of how much of it there is, not because it's impossible to move through.

Grab your teaspoon and your support team; you're going to need it.

Because that's the only way you can do this in the beginning. One tiny teaspoon at a time.

Unfortunately, I cannot tell you how to navigate the grief. There is no handbook to tell us the best route through. There is only *your* route. Grief is so individual. There's nothing good anyone can say, I can only hold you in grief.

And in solidarity, I will tell you about the days I grieved for love that I've lost through my own fear. I will tell you about the days I've felt like my heart had been ripped from my chest over children I've lost across lifetimes. I will talk about my pain for all the horrific times I've died and all the people I couldn't help or save numerous times.

While the specific details of my story may not particularly help, sharing my grief with you shows you that grief knows no bounds and comes in many different ways. The individual stories and details of our grief may look different but the things we grieve over, whether that was a lost love, bereavement or lost opportunity, are things we all grieve in our own way. Grief and loss eventually come to us all. The most important thing is not wallowing in it and instead finding a way through and back to love and possibility.

I once read grief being described as 'like water', but my experience of grief is not like that. Instead, I feel grief is closer to fire. This poem I wrote explains why.

Cinder In My Veins

They say grief is like an ocean of relentless, crashing waves.
I say it is not water—it is *fire*.
It is the sun that blinds you, fading the world to white.

Sometimes it's a summer day;
I think of you and feel the warmth of your embrace.
I'm left with a glow where your arms should be long
    after sunset.

Some days it is a candle; gentle heat on my skin.
Too close—might catch light of my sleeve.
Take hold and swallow me whole.

Rage into a towering inferno.
Consume everything until there's nothing but ash—
remnants of who we used to be.

In dying flames, the evidence on my skin remains.
Forever changed by the ember memory of you.
Grief is not water that washes over but leaves no trace.

No – missing you is like fire.
Scars etched on my skin—a patchwork of all the times
    I've thought of you;
testimony of a life I've tried to live without you;
grief is a fire that *burns.*

———

No two fires of grief are alike. To try and extinguish it would
be to try and diminish its existence. It is actually in acknowledging and honouring ourselves exactly where we are that we
move through it.

The best thing I've found for dealing with grief is to practise non-judgement of yourself. Intellectually you may think you're crazy for grieving things that happened a time long ago. Don't do that to yourself. Your grief, wherever and whenever it comes from, whatever or whoever it's for, is completely valid. It's a process we all need to go through once we realise that the road is closed and there's no going back.

In French, to say I miss you, the phrase is 'Tu me manques'. The actual translation of it is to say 'you are missing from me' and I think this beautifully sums up why we grieve. It's about *us*. It's about the loss we feel, not so much about the other person or thing that happened.

It's the loss of ourselves that we grieve the most. Who we are as a result of the grief can feel alien and not be the person we expect to become. Too often, we grieve the hardest due to the disappointment of unmet expectations and unrealised potential.

Practising non-judgement of your grief and acceptance of the existence of the grief will help it to pass more easily. Grief is hard enough to move through without berating and beating yourself up in the process.

Know that grief isn't linear or logical and there's no schedule for it. Days or even weeks can pass and you feel like you're getting a handle on things and then the smallest thing could catch you entirely off guard.

On those days when the grief was truly breathtaking and my heart felt like it was being crushed... sometimes all I could do was breathe. Sometimes it was the only thing I could do.

Easier said than done, I know. But taking it one step at a time was all I could do.

I remember a conversation with my dad when I was at school. I was stressed, depressed, overwhelmed and struggling with anxiety over my exams (and the fact that it felt like everyone hated me). The doctor eventually signed me off from even attending school, it got so bad.

Talking to my dad one day about it, he offered me a quote that said, 'by an inch, it's a cinch, by a yard it's hard.' That conversation changed everything for me. It was a reminder that part of the overwhelm was in looking at the whole picture at once; that in breaking things down into manageable chunks, you can inch forward.

I practised this to the nth point years later in my third year of university. I was contemplating quitting as I was having a hard time with a tutor I didn't get on with and the fun had been sucked out of design work.

I'd been put on beta blockers for my stress because I'd developed constant itchy skin due to anxiety. The last straw was when I was almost hospitalised due to my blood pressure dropping too low — I should not have been put on beta blockers in the first place. Something had to change.

I remembered what my dad said, so I tried to focus on making it to half term. When that became too hard, could I get through the week?

When that wasn't enough, could I make it through the day? Could I get through to lunchtime and then go home?

Could I make it through this hour?

Could I make it through the next ten minutes?

Could I make it through this one minute?

Could I make it through the next breath?

I wish I was exaggerating but I'm not. It did get that bad. The only way I got through it was to take it one breath at a time. It kept me present. It stopped the overwhelm and allowed me to focus on the pain right in front of me, in that one moment. And that's exactly what it's like to deal with grief.

I made it through the final year of my Bachelor of the Arts. I somehow even managed to get a First in the process. I never could have gotten there without staying in the present moment, the only moment in which I could breathe. Thanks, Dad for the one piece of advice that truly saved my life that year.

This brings me to my final piece of advice for dealing with grief. Don't do it alone. Grief is truly isolating in its individuality. We turn inward, consumed by the grief. We feel like no one can relate to or understand us in our grief.

At the beginning of grief and bereavement, people often rally round and check on you. However, when you're doing this kind of inner work, no one knows what you're grieving unless you tell them. *So tell them.* Find your support team and keep them in the loop before it gets too complicated or painful a story to explain. Make it clear to them what kind of support you need.

Lean on them as your life depends on it. Let your friends, family, practitioners and professionals, whoever you choose to confide in, let them be your sanity and anchor point to help you come back to earth once again. Let them be a beacon to bring you back to shore.

Break the societal conditioning of your belief that you have to do it alone; you don't. It's a story you've been sold to hinder and isolate you. We are far more powerful together. Make the journey a little bit easier to bear by getting yourself some support.

Because on the days where I felt I was losing my mind in pain, in grief, in whether I'd gone mad and was making this shit up. On those days having Emily keeping me sane, believing in me, encouraging me to keep going... having her turn up with her teaspoon to sit with me made all the difference.

So go find your teaspoon buddy. The one who won't question what to do but will get started bailing you out straight away. They are worth their weight in gold.

And you?

You are going to be just fine because now; we heal.

Healing

HOPE

At the temple you have come undone.
Golden water turned black;
like tar it oozes
from your very core
and your heart bleeds
tears stream, staining your face.

The pain of a thousand lifetimes
has awoken in you.
Breathless,
crushed in suffering;
you beg for mercy.
Sweet release from your personal hell.

She comes to you now
in billowing white,
wiping away your tears.
Holding your face in her hands
with a voice like honey that says,
'come now, it is time.'

Across marble floors and endless corridors,
always almost out of sight
yet never far away.
She guides you through the labyrinth

into a light and luscious courtyard;
Your healing garden.

As you settle yourself beneath the ash tree
calm embraces you.
You breathe a little deeper
knowing all is well;
that here is where you will find peace
and truly heal your soul.

NURTURING SEEDS OF HOPE

Hope is where healing begins. Within grief is the seed of hope, sprouting roots from your tears.

Hope is the moment you choose a different ending to your story. It is the moment you recognise you cannot stay and wallow in grief and despair. It is the moment when, for just a moment, you look forward, not back.

It is the moment when you catch a fleeting glimpse of the future and remember it exists. It is the moment when the spell is broken and you see that life goes on, the world still turns, with or without you in it.

Hope is when you make a choice that says YES.

Yes, I'm choosing to live. Yes, I'm choosing myself. Yes, I'm choosing love over loss. Yes, I'm choosing love over fear. Yes, I'm choosing love over suffering. Yes, I'm choosing love over regret.

The moment you allow yourself to hope, however briefly, is a chink in your armour. A tiny crack appears for light to shine in. Hope is where the tide begins to turn for you. It is what spurs you on to live. To see a glimmer of hope is to witness the beginning of your resurrection and rebirth.

Hope is not the final destination, for to live in a constant state of hope is to push things out into an unreachable future. But in those early days when the wounds are still fresh and you feel raw from the battlefield, hope is the best thing you've got.

Cultivate it. Nurture and protect it. Hope is the evidence that you are capable of living again, of healing. Do not allow anything to diminish your hope; it is the most precious thing you can hold.

Hope is the battle cry that rallies the weary. Hope is the Hail Mary in the face of what feels like a certain defeat. Hope is an incomprehensible lightness that cannot be stolen from you.

Keep your hope. Hold it in your heart and fan the naked flame until it roars. For when it roars... when you unleash uncontrollable hope, fear has lost. Pain has lost. You have won the first battle. Now it's time to win the war.

When I think of the presence of hope in the healing journey, I'm reminded of the Greek goddess Iris. I first came across her back in 2018 when I was running a Facebook group on the divine feminine, where I channelled goddess energy into daily and then weekly readings. Iris is a messenger of the Gods; she is associated with communication and most commonly, the rainbow.

While she doesn't have much of a mythology of her own due to her often being a messenger, I have personally come to associate Iris with hope. For the rainbow comes after the rain, much like hope reveals itself in the depths of pain. A rainbow is a sign to look up and follow it. The rainbow itself isn't the answer but in following its guidance, you will find the pot of gold at the end.

In despair, hope is that moment you look up; it is seeing that faint glimmer of a thousand colours shining bright and following it toward the gold. Whenever I feel lost in pain and need to re-centre myself, whenever I need a reminder as to why I'm on the path or whether it's all worth it, Iris is the one whose energy I feel. Call upon her and let her send you a sign too, as a reminder whenever you need it.

Healing often happens alongside the exhumation process. Some things that you dig up, you can get to work healing straight away. Others need to be lifted from the depths and unravelled in layers. Know that you can heal parts of yourself while the rest of you still bleeds. You don't have to wait until you have excavated everything to begin to heal.

Healing is not a linear process. Some days you will feel like you're winning. Some weeks may feel like plain sailing. Other times, a moment could throw you straight back into the depths. Like a game of Snakes and Ladders, while there may be days where you feel like you'll slide back down the snake to square one, there will also be days you can climb a ladder and skip ahead.

The key isn't to avoid the backslide. It happens. Something; a song, a smell, a phrase will take you off balance and transport you back to someplace else in your memory. This is unavoidable. As humans, we are constantly making connections in our minds. Our brain and ego are always trying to return us to what they know to be familiar, regardless of whether it is any good for us or not. The train of thought may be random but it will suddenly click into place and you're back there again.

Accept that this will often be the case. We're not trying to transcend it. This is part of what makes us human after all. The key to healing is how quickly you can get yourself out of wherever you find yourself. To land in a moment of pain and remember that you don't have to stay there. That you can choose to step out of it and back to where you were.

Remember that your suffering does not have to define you. You can choose what story you write for yourself — is it a story of love or fear? Is it a story of hope or pain? You get to choose at **every** moment.

To be healing is to not get caught up in the wound every time you land there. Instead, you see it, recognise it, honour it and choose not to remain there. Take whatever action is needed to transform it. Take it to your practitioner or therapy sessions. Journal or meditate on it. Whatever moves it for you rather than wallowing and stagnating in it. That is healing. That is the goal.

When you are filled with chaos, when you can't see past the fog of memories, how quickly can you step outside of it and return to who you have chosen to be? How quickly, how easily can you return to divinity, to love over fear and suffering? What tools and support do you have access to now that will help you release it?

At first, this isn't so easy or quick. Trust me though, stay the course and it does get easier.

Accept that the journey will be like a rollercoaster; there'll be ups and downs and sometimes you'll loop back on yourself. Some days might feel like a slow climb where everything creaks as you stretch yourself beyond what you ever thought you could be. Other days will feel like a stomach lurching freefall or an exhilarating and jubilant rush of adrenaline as you ride the waves and loop the loops. Either way, you find that life, instead of feeling like you're stuck in the doldrums, becomes an exciting ride. It becomes *your* ride. You can take control and ownership of your journey *and* destination and embrace every minute of it knowing this is what it is to be human.

It isn't to be some Zen master who never gets swayed, never lets emotions get the best of them and never feels anything. It's about daring to feel it all, good, bad and ugly and knowing you will make it out alive. It's knowing you don't need to live with those bad, dark, ugly feelings. You know you can return to joy and love and fun. You know you can return to the true you, the you who is not defined or controlled by any of it. The new you, the you that you didn't know you were capable of being when you started on this journey.

You know you can choose to shift whenever you want. That you don't need to remain stuck. To be human is to feel and experience it all and know every piece of it is transitory.

When you can accept that the experience will be like this… a theme park of rides that are yours for the choosing. It'll be fun and illogical and sometimes downright crazy and maybe more than a little scary at points, but it's yours and you can shape it as you choose.

When you can accept your rollercoaster of healing without judgement, the journey gets easier because you stop battling yourself. There is no need to fight yourself internally on what you think the healing process should look like. Getting out of your own way by accepting how it flows does help make a difference.

So where do we begin with healing? As with most of the journey in the beginning; baby steps. Many small actions build a cumulative effect which is how we build momentum, confidence, trust and freedom in the process. And as you go along you'll be able to take bigger leaps, empty your bucket quicker and face some of the tougher, deep-rooted issues head on.

But for now, on your wobbly Bambi legs, it's all about taking just one step forward.

FOUR PHASE FEMININE HEALING

With Cypriot heritage on my dad's side of the family and being born on Halloween, I have always known about and sometimes feared the Greek goddess Hecate. Ancient goddess of the crossroads, the moon and witchcraft, she has often been called the crone. As the term witch became derogatory throughout history, visual representations of Hecate have turned her into a ghoulish hag.

Later periods saw Hecate turned into the triple goddess, a concept that has prevailed in the rise of New Age Spirituality and the Divine Feminine. The triple goddess, meant to represent the three aspects of the feminine; maiden, mother and crone, has resonated widely across the board.

For me, the concept of the triple goddess felt incomplete when I first heard of her, I could not fully connect with the idea. It felt like there was something 'off' with the picture. I remember thinking of my mum and other family friends I knew. None of them embodied the crone, but all of their children were far too grown for these women to fit neatly into the mother stage either. It wasn't until I discovered a missing phase that it suddenly felt like it made sense to me.

Maga, her rite of passage is menopause. She is not yet the crone but her children have grown. She's still full of life and vitality yet shoulders responsibilities that the crone will shed. Jane Hardwicke Collings introduces the concept of maga, the phase that sits between the mother and the crone in her book *The Four-Phase Feminine Way*. It is this evolution of the triple goddess into four aspects, a quadruple goddess as it were, that I felt resonated in so many ways.

The original triple goddess was conceived back when humans' life span was considerably shorter than it is today, averaging about 45 years. It made sense as women were becoming mothers in their teens and grandmothers in their thirties, there was no need for anything other than these three aspects of womanhood. However, as life spans have increased, this triple goddess has fallen short.

Consider how so much of the feminine is tied to the number four; our menstrual cycle has four phases; menstruation, the follicular phase, ovulation and the luteal phase. These phases are also known to correspond to the seasons, with menstruation being your inner winter moving through spring (follicular phase) to your inner summer (ovulation) and into autumn (luteal phase).

Women, the feminine, yin are linked with the moon which cycles through four primary phases; new moon, first quarter, full moon, third quarter and four intermediate phases; waxing crescent, waxing gibbous, waning gibbous, waning crescent. The moon cycle and average menstrual flow occur over a 28 day period – which is four weeks.

Although it is widely known that pregnancy has three trimesters, the fourth trimester immediately after birth until the baby is three months old, is often overlooked and certainly less commonly named. Yet again, there's that number four popping up again. We are inextricably connected to the number four so it simply makes sense for there to be four phases of the feminine.

We can use the wisdom of these four stages and connect to the corresponding goddesses in our healing. It doesn't matter what life phase you are currently in, whether you have yet to reach a phase or have passed it, there is wisdom that we can all embrace from each life phase regardless of our age and current phase of life.

While Hecate has often become the triple goddess with three aspects, in her singular form she embodies the crone. It is widely considered that Persephone (Greek goddess of spring and Queen of the Underworld) is connected to the phase of the maiden and Persephone's mother Demeter (goddess of agriculture) sits within the mother aspect.

So who represents maga? As she is a new aspect, this has not been standardised yet. In my considerations, research and allowing myself to be intuitively guided in writing this book, Carpo (also spelt Xarpo or Karpo) is the Greek goddess of autumn, harvest and the ripening and seems a likely and perhaps most obvious candidate.

I also considered Gaia, Mother Earth herself for her early depictions of being worshipped alongside Demeter. For me, Gaia represents wisdom and unconditional love much like that of any mother goddess, but Gaia has detachment – she allows life to grow and evolve beyond her. She understands the intricate harmonies and balance of the ecosystem she has created and doesn't interfere. To me, this speaks of maga; still a mother but with older, more capable children who do not need constant input or motherly care.

Finally, I considered Tethys. She is a Titan goddess of fresh water, daughter of Gaia and married to Oceanus. I felt the case for Tethys was compelling the more I researched her. Goddess of fresh water, she was considered to be the source from which fresh water entered the world – if that isn't considered the ultimate giver of life, I don't know what is.

Her name is derived from the Greek *têthê* which translates to grandmother or nurse, which befits the role of maga in our lives as she becomes a grandmother and acts as the midwife of life experience for the generations that succeed her. This coincides beautifully with maga and her grown up children starting families of their own and is reinforced by Tethys birthing at least 6,000 offspring including the 3,000 Potamoi (river gods).

What I also find to be a compelling argument in why Tethys represents maga, is in both her visual depictions and absence. Despite having so many children and grandchildren that were prominent in Greek mythology, there are minimal stories featuring Tethys and even fewer that depict her in an active, key role.

The visual representations show her as relatively plain and occasionally with a winged forehead, unlike some of the better known and extremely beautifully depicted goddesses like Aphrodite. It's also important to note she isn't shown to be hideous either but rather forgettable, much like this entire aspect of the feminine that has been overlooked.

There is so much rich wisdom to be gained in each of these four phases and how they apply to our own healing. So for this journey, I'll be connecting the phase of maga to the titan goddess Tethys, as we honour every aspect of the feminine.

Let's begin.

PERSEPHONE

She offers spring flowers
and the promise of hope;
with cherry red lips and
cheeks flush with the pink of youth.

She holds a fiery passion;
in love with the world,
seeing the beauty
and wonder in all things.

With wide eyed innocence
she meets you as you are,
without judgement
and all mistakes forgiven.

Let her guide you in quiet rebellion
of love, trust, innocence and faith.
In reclamation of your power
with a youthful heart.

HEALING THE INNER MAIDEN

The goddess Persephone represents our inner maiden and is often overlooked as a seat of trauma. While many of us would recount tales of challenging childhoods, trauma and abuse we experienced, there is an emphasis on looking at the trauma and not the maiden as a concept, life stage or energy herself. To heal her, first, we must understand her.

The story of Persephone in Greek mythology is well known and overall, her story is quite standardised and singular. While out picking flowers, Persephone was abducted by Hades, god of the underworld, ruler of the dead and taken to the underworld to be his wife. Her mother Demeter is distraught and searches for her alongside the goddess Hecate. Demeter's despair plunges the world into famine. She finally learns of her daughter's abduction (which in some accounts was done with the approval of Zeus, the Greek god of the sky and known as king of the gods). Persephone is returned to her mother and the world is restored.

However, it is discovered that Hades tricked Persephone into eating pomegranate seeds whilst in the underworld. Having eaten food from the realm of the dead meant that she couldn't leave the underworld. A compromise is made by Zeus, that Persephone may spend part of the year above ground with her mother and the remainder with Hades in the underworld. The length of time varies across accounts between half a year in each or two thirds above ground and the rest in the underworld. Whatever the case, while mother and daughter are reunited, the earth flourishes but the moment Persephone returns to Hades, her mother's grief causes winter across the land.

There's a lot to unpack with the maiden in the divine feminine journey. When I think of my own maidenhood, my teenage years and early twenties, it is the area of healing where I have spent the most time working. Perhaps in part, it is because I haven't reached the other life stages yet so this one is most fresh and relevant to freeing myself to move forward, (although that doesn't mean there's no wisdom for me to gain from the other life phases right now).

However, in general, the maiden spans our most formative years and so can hold a lot of trauma. It is often the time when we are told we can or can't do things and unintentionally take it as gospel for the rest of our lives. I spent a lot of time working with Emily to uncover and heal the impact of my first relationship for example. This is a wound many of us will need to heal from the so-called 'Bluebeard', which I will explain later in this chapter.

Authentic self-expression and body image are rooted in the maiden because this is often the first place where we are told we are 'wrong' for being different. Food turns from being a source of love provided to us by the crone through our grandmother's baking and cooking. In maidenhood, food becomes weaponised and instead of being associated with love, it is inverted to control us. We begin to hate food, hate our bodies or have a disordered relationship with both. My ability to express myself in the clothes I wear and my opinion of my own body are both things I spent time working on, alongside the first instances of the persecution complex being activated for me due to childhood bullying.

We overlook just how pervasive trauma from the maiden is, how it colours and bleeds into the rest of our lives. Regardless of your age and life phase, the impact of the unhealed maiden can be massive on the rest of our lives which is often why the majority of trauma from this life can be traced back to childhood and teenage memories.

Once healed, so many of the issues that sit with the mother, maga and crone phases are much easier to clean up and heal when you've got to the root of the trauma in the first place. Otherwise, we end up much like the robotic art installation, *Can't Help Myself* by Sun Yuan and Peng Yu.

The premise of it is simple, a robotic arm is programmed to continually try to contain the hydraulic fluid that is leaking and is required to keep the robot running. At first, the robot manages to contain the spillage well, but over time the leak becomes uncontrollable. The robotic arm continues to try and contain the hydraulic fluid but it's fighting a losing battle. You can imagine eventually it will run out of hydraulic fluid, come to a standstill and metaphorically 'die'.

But here's the real kicker for the art piece, it was run on electricity – the hydraulic fluid wasn't the crucial component that determined whether the robot 'lived' or 'died'. Regardless, the programmed robot spent its entire 'life' trying to save itself for something that it didn't actually *need* to survive or continue to function.

This art installation is the perfect metaphor for humans. We continually spend time fighting small fires in our lives which are caused by deeper trauma, conditioning and limiting beliefs and we never go deeper to the underlying cause. We make our existence meaningless by focusing on the superficial, and unimportant and wonder why we're never satisfied or happy.

I get it, I really do. This stuff is painful to look at whether it comes from somewhere else in space and time or your childhood or teenage years. In going straight to that source, wherever it is in time, we create freedom for ourselves in our present and future. It also brings forth some of the wisdom from the maiden that we may have forgotten or discarded over time.

When I think of the story of Persephone, I'm reminded of the concept of Bluebeard which Clarissa Pinkola Estés described in *Women Who Run With The Wolves,* as a rite of passage for women. Indeed, while the menarche, the first menstruation may be the physical rite of passage for the maiden, I believe Bluebeard serves as the emotional rite of passage. Tied up with the concept of Bluebeard can be so much trauma and deep seated rage that it is hard to move through.

In short, the concept of Bluebeard is that he is the first man, the first relationship a woman enters just as she is rising into her power. At that precise moment where she is claiming herself, embodying the divine feminine, he will swoop in to cut her off from that power and potential that of the maiden and our claiming of Persephone. She may not realise it has happened and may continue to think she has some semblance of control and power, but eventually, she will find she has been undercut.

We know Persephone did carve out her own space in her new role in the underworld as Hades' wife, being both feared and respected and given names such as 'The Pure One' and 'The Venerable Goddess'. She demonstrated authority within the underworld, rather than being a trophy wife. Persephone is cited in numerous accounts as being the decision maker over mortal lives such as Orpheus and Eurydice, and Heracles and Cerberus. She found ways to become influential and powerful within her position regardless of the hand that was dealt to her.

Before Persephone was abducted by Hades, she was the goddess of spring. The herald and fertile life giver after the depths of winter. In her abduction, her story was irrevocably changed. She retained her title of the goddess of spring although it was entirely overshadowed by her marriage to Hades and her new title, Queen of the Underworld. Her story and trajectory are permanently rewritten.

Now we might not know what Persephone could have become without being abducted by Hades, but we can learn from her and her story. We can see how she continued to hold her own. We can see she used her position for goodness, rather than letting herself be consumed by darkness. We can heal and embrace that inner maiden and bring forth her vitality and newly awakened power and wisdom into the rest of our lives.

We can reclaim the parts of us that were lost. We can celebrate our stories that our bodies have previously been deemed unpalatable, and unclean by society. We can reclaim the power stolen by Bluebeard and rewrite that rite of passage so it doesn't need to exist at all for our daughters. We can reclaim and heal our sexuality. We can transform that naivety into wisdom. We can transmute the rebellion and anger of youth into healthy, focused change. We can embrace our sense of wonder and imagination. We can reignite our passion, our fire, our vitality, our zest for life. We can reclaim our confidence, our power and our divinity.

We might not know what Persephone could have become. We don't know what our trajectories might have been either, but our stories are not done yet. We are not myths or legends, forgotten, discarded and lost in another time. We are living, breathing women. We are here now. We can heal, now. Our stories have not finished being written yet.

THE LOOK THAT CHANGES
EVERYTHING

It has become an insult to be silly or childish. To express our-selves so fully without care is like a rare jewel rather than a com-mon occurrence. We have suppressed ourselves so much and convinced ourselves that there is nothing of value in whimsy.

Persephone herself becomes the cautionary tale. For we do not chide her in her abduction, we empathise with her. The moment a man sees her and wants her for himself, he simply takes her – so many of us can relate to that.

When we reach the part of the story where we find that she cannot permanently return to her mother because she has eaten food from the underworld, that is when the tone shifts for women. In the story, Hades tricks Persephone into eating pomegranate seeds, knowing once she does, she'll forever be tied to him and never be allowed to leave. She eats them unwit-tingly, not knowing the implications or what it means for the rest of her life.

And while there's hate and backlash towards Hades, after the initial anger directed towards him, we feel a flash of anger towards *her*, too. We wonder how she could be so foolish and naive. How could she be so gullible and stupid? In our hindsight and wisdom, we feel she has ruined her life with her selfish ways and wonder if she was thinking of anyone except herself in the process.

Truthfully though, the maiden is far more impulsive than the other live phases. She thinks with her heart and acts in response to that moment rather than considering the implications and consequences of her actions. She was a hungry, innocent teenager after all and had no idea what eating those pomegranate seeds would mean in the wider world. She was an unwitting pawn in a much grander plan.

Again this similar cautionary tale is shown in Adam's second wife, Eve. The woman of original sin. The Bible has convinced us that it is her fault we live as we do. She ate the apple and committed the crime, causing damnation for us all as a result.

These stories have built the narrative that women are stupid and everything wrong in the world is our fault. We've grown to believe we are poor and helpless and that we need men to guide us, save us and look after us. Women are led to believe we have no power, nothing of value and nothing to say. We grow up thinking we are nothing other than an endless source of temptation for the poor men of the world and everything would be so much better if *we* could behave.

We've been conditioned to believe that the qualities that these maidens exude; curiosity, naivety, wonder and innocence are dangerous and make us liabilities. That those qualities have no place in our world and add no value to our personalities or lives.

We've been conditioned to believe that to be innocent will mean you are taken advantage of by everyone you encounter. That to be naive is to be blind and ignorant to the horror of the world. That to be full of wonder and imagination makes you childish like it's a bad thing.

We've been conditioned to believe those qualities are not good for us to discourage us from finding and embracing the wisdom within them. In doing so, we never experience the beauty of an innocent and loving heart with clean intentions. We never get to appreciate the ability to see the good in people, be open and trusting even when we've been hurt and not close ourselves off in response. We never get to experience elation and joy at the wonder and magic that lives in the world. In rejecting these qualities, we reject both the good and bad possibilities that the maiden can bring into our lives. Instead, they've been twisted to encourage us to reject and fear them, leading us to self-regulate and control ourselves without even realising.

The qualities which are beloved and accepted in children suddenly become irresponsible in adult women and warrant instant rejection, ridicule and shame. It comes at us from all sides. The rejection of these qualities in us is one of the first things that the sisterhood wound targets. It's certainly what happened to me.

Here in the UK, we wear school uniforms daily so when we get to have a non-uniform day, it's a big deal. Everyone spends weeks planning their outfit. Weekend shopping trips are undertaken to buy something new and amazing to wear. Groups of girls coordinate to make sure no one commits the fashion crime of the century by wearing the same outfit as someone else. It's a *whole* thing.

I was never particularly interested in fashion and I certainly wasn't cool at school. But I do remember the day when I was allowed to go into the *Etam* shop and go upstairs to *Tammy*, what a moment. *Tammy* or *Tammy Girl* was *the* place all the teenage girls wanted to shop. When my mum said I was finally old enough, I was ecstatic. It was like walking into wonderland.

With a non-uniform day coming up and my first purchases from *Tammy*, I knew exactly what I wanted to wear.

The day arrived and I walked into school feeling *cool as*. I had these flared jeans on with an extra triangle inserted in the legs to make them flare even more. I'd worn them the weekend before on a family trip out to Cromer in Norfolk. I'd been minding my own business walking down the street with my dog with the rest of my family behind me, when two old ladies sitting outside a shop had tutted at me and called me a delinquent because of what I was wearing. I said nothing, smiled and carried on walking, determined not to give them proof they were right.

To go with my delinquent flares, I was definitely a 'borderline hooligan' in my zip up cardigan; knitted rows of very bright rainbow colours. The zip had a tassel. It had pockets and flared sleeves and a hood that was shaped like it belonged on an Elven cloak with a tassel on the tip of the hood. It was SO fabulous, I loved it. I thought I was the bees' knees in that cardigan.

My dad still talks about it to this day with disdain whenever he mentions my 'weird rainbow' phase where I wanted to wear every colour under the sun, all at once. I'm going to be honest; I was totally naive to the connotations of rainbows at the time. It was shortly after this rainbow wearing non-uniform day when the untrue rumours of me being a lesbian started. I had no idea where *that* idea came from until much, much later.

Back to non-uniform day; I was walking around with my head held high feeling great. I walked past the girl who I'd healed several years prior and she gave me **that** look. You know the one I'm talking about. The one where they look you slowly up and down with an expression of horror and disgust. The look that says, *'What on earth were you thinking going out dressed like that?'*

'*LOVE* the rainbow, Camilla! It looks *SO* good on you!' she called after me enthusiastically dripping with sarcasm. Suddenly, I felt about an inch tall. It's not that I wanted approval from the cool, popular girls. All I wanted was to *not* be noticed by them. On the other hand, how could I have not stood out to them in my glaringly vibrant hooligan rainbow cardigan with tassels and jeans flared to delinquent levels? I might as well have walked into school holding a neon arrow above my head. Pretty sure I'd have been visible from space in that getup. It was *that* noticeable.

All it took was one look, from one girl to make me want to crawl up under a rock and hide for the rest of the day. I contemplated feigning illness so I could go home.

No one else said anything to my face about what I wore that day; they didn't need to because the damage was done. If someone had handed me a match, I'd have burnt the rainbow cardigan there on the playground. I kept hoping someone might hand me a shovel so I could dig myself a hole to hide from the world.

From that moment on, it wasn't just my personality and mannerisms that became invisible at school. *I* became invisible. I wore nothing outrageous, nothing that would garner any kind of attention. Nothing objectionable. Nothing too cheap or too expensive. Nothing that made it look like I was trying to fit in and be cool. Nothing that made it look like I was trying too hard to be the antithesis of cool either.

I became an expert at blending in and devoid of all personality. Anything that made me, *me*, was quickly suppressed or hidden away for when I was at home.

As a result, when I finally started on my healing journey, my appearance rapidly came up as a pain point. As I transformed the pain and started to heal layers of this narrative, my clothes very rapidly didn't fit anymore. As in, they weren't *me* anymore. I hadn't miraculously lost ten kilos overnight. Instead, I had lost the ability to blend in. I had begun to reconnect to the parts of me that loved wearing delinquent flares and rainbow hoodies. While it didn't mean I was necessarily going to take up wearing those clothes again, in unlocking the possibility I could look at the question again and ask myself what clothes *did* feel like an authentic expression of me in the present time.

I'd started to awaken myself. I could feel the change occurring within me. Even though I didn't want to talk about that transformation publicly, I still wanted to acknowledge the transformation on the outside.

It was like shedding a skin. Overnight I felt the desire rise within me to buy a whole new wardrobe. Chucking everything out and starting over wasn't feasible though. What I *could* do was to let go of the worst offenders, the things that felt the least like me and replace them with something that *did* feel more like me.

I wanted to bring in what felt fun and joyful. I bought dungarees, pinafores, fedoras and leather look leggings. I mastered the winged eyeliner I always loved the look of, and wore red and dark purple lipstick. I wore my hair in space buns and added in subtle streaks of red, because I could, just to see what it felt like. For the first time in a long time, I experimented with what it felt like to show inner me on the outside and it felt great.

When I went out to celebrate my birthday with an afternoon tea, I confidently strode in wearing an outfit that made me feel *cool as,* once again. This time, I did get a look. I got several. The look this time said, *wow, look at her, she looks amazing.* Not only that but they meant it and I accepted the compliment.

However, the look did have something reminiscent about it. When I stopped and really noticed that look from other women, I realised they both had the same essence. Those looks were *wistful.* They saw me, expressing myself as I wanted to, with complete confidence and those looks said, *I wish I could do that too. I wish I could be that confident. I wish I could express my whole, raw, authentic self.*

All because we've grown up being conditioned to believe that it isn't safe or sensible to do so. That we need to consider what we wear, not for whether we like it, but whether it will offend, entice or repel other people. That we need to consider our hobbies and interests and make sure we choose things that conform to societal norms and don't make us stand out.

That we need to consider our behaviour, to be demure but not too shy, sexy but not too sexy, fun but not funnier than him, pretty but not so pretty that we're out of their league. Confident but not so much we have a diva complex, attentive but not to the point of obsession. Generous but only to our partner, not mute but not too loud either. Well isn't that all a crock of shit?

In rejecting these qualities of curiosity, innocence, naivety, wonder and imagination, we harden our hearts. We become impenetrable fortresses that cannot relate to anyone. These qualities bring a softness, vulnerability, trust and openness that we have once lost.

Instead, we became angry, rebellious maidens who felt hurt by the world. We became mistrustful, disconnected, unimaginative and bored. We became frustrated and insular, isolating ourselves and pitted against one another.

The beauty of the maiden lies within that innocence and light. She is the life giver, the herald of spring. She is possibilities and dreams; she is passion, love and joy. She is ready to take on the world. She'll try anything once, believing with total conviction that she is invincible and quite rightly so.

Return to your softness and innocence. Be curious, be naive and open. Allow fun, whimsy and passion back into your life. Embrace the silly and childish; let it embrace your wounded soul. Let it be your medicine. These are the wisdom the maiden offers to heal our hearts.

MEETING MYSELF AT THE CENTRE OF MY UNIVERSE

There is something about that youthful energy, that zest for life that we lose rapidly as we get older and the burdens of life weigh us down. It seems to creep up, quietly, gently. There's no warning it's coming until one of those days when everything culminates into you losing your shit entirely.

Sometimes it's a loud realisation in a fiery blaze or lands like a nuclear bomb after the tension that's been building up for days, weeks, maybe even months. You scream at the kids, your partner, the dog, and the house, that you're fed up with all of it and you're running away to a desert island.

Other times it's a quiet realisation, like the sun inching over the horizon. You realise you feel flat, bored, uninspired, *unhappy*. You feel depleted, worthless, depressed and isolated. You wonder where your love for life has gone and how you came to be stuck here in this place. Yet you don't quite know how to extract yourself from the hamster wheel. So you push those thoughts down and pretend it's not happening because you simply don't have time for it or don't know where to even start looking for happiness again.

The maiden, however, in her youth, in seeing herself as the centre of her universe, is where we learn to rekindle our own flame. She has a love for life bound up in so much energy, confidence and a go get 'em attitude that means she does what she wants because she wants to. So often, adults around maidens, around teenagers, accuse them of being selfish but actually, there's a cleanliness to the maidens intentions that we can learn from.

A maiden only says yes, when she really means yes. If she doesn't want to help you take out the rubbish, she'll say no. If it's not cool to go shopping with mum because she'd rather be doing anything else, she'll say so. It's clean and clear cut.

As we get older, we lose this ability to focus on ourselves. With burdens, responsibilities, jobs and families, life gets messy and looking after ourselves slides right down the list. For the maiden, she is her number one priority. Not in a narcissistic way, she simply owns who she is because she knows she can't be anyone else. The maiden works hard to shape her life within the confines of her caregiver's rules because her life, how she spends her time, how she looks, and who she spends time with; are the *only* things in her control.

Her world is relatively small in comparison to when we get older as it revolves around being either at school or not. Since school is often a place where there isn't much choice, her time and life outside of school are everything to her and her self-expression. The maiden ensures she makes the most of it and squeezes every bit of life into that time as she can.

She's fearless, bold and goes after what she wants. Of course, with maturity, age, hindsight and experience, we could think of her as reckless. The wisdom in the maiden is her ability to try something, fail and pick herself straight back up and carry on. Nothing stops her in her tracks. She's fiery and passionate. We often try to dampen her, to diminish and constrain her using the reason that we're worried about her selfish, reckless behaviour.

Truthfully though, we do it out of jealousy and fear.

Because the maiden has something that we have lost; passion and fire. That zest for life.

Instead, here we are stuck in jobs and lives we hate. A hamster wheel of endless routine. We're starved of excitement, adrenaline, spontaneity and joy. We, in our active sisterhood wounds, hate that she has access to what we have lost, particularly as we never seem to know how or where we lost it.

All we know is eventually life wore us down and beat us into submission. Now we're stuck and it makes us want to lash out at anyone who seems to have access to what we want so badly for ourselves.

For me, this realisation came in August 2021. I have struggled with summer in recent years, despising the heat and spending most of it holed up inside in the shade trying to keep myself and my dogs cool. Being cooped up inside meant I spent lots of time at my desk trying to chip away at building my business, or should I say, trying to figure out what my business was.

It came to a head over a few days. I was starting to feel constantly exhausted and fed up. Everything felt too much. I felt like I couldn't cope, I felt trapped, and bored. If this was what my life was going to look like for the foreseeable, I didn't want it.

Watching TV one evening with my husband, I started crying. I couldn't even tell you what I was crying at, whether it was a comment he made, or an advert on TV, who knows. I've never been one to cry much so to cry for no reason was… weird. My husband looked confused and surprised but didn't make a big deal of it.

The next night, the same thing happened. Out of nowhere, tears were streaming down my face and I had curled myself up into a ball. The third night in a row when this happened, my husband looked concerned and turned the TV off. When I was finally able to see his face through tears and breathe again, we started to talk. Gently he suggested that maybe I was burnt out. I didn't argue. It felt like someone had named something that I couldn't.

He suggested I take the whole week off and I simply nodded. I didn't have it in me to argue whether it was possible, I was beyond caring by that point.

The next day I went to my desk and fired off a bunch of emails telling people I needed some time and would get back to them in a couple of weeks. I made a short list of the very urgent things I couldn't ignore and powered through them as quickly as I could. Then I logged off and went to bed.

I slept a lot for a few days.

When I started to feel a little more like a human being again rather than a zombie, I started wondering how to get myself out of this mess. Google searches for recovering from burnout felt unhelpful. No amount of bubble baths and face masks were going to solve *this*.

After a week, I went back to my desk out of habit and looked at my 'to-do list' and emails. Ugh. None of it felt interesting or exciting. How had everything gotten so boring? I sat, fighting with myself for what felt like hours. Paralysed, I couldn't get myself to approach a single task.

I dashed off a whole new set of emails – *need more time, sorry I can't help right now, I'm referring you to…* anything to free me from the urgent requests.

It was then that I sat with myself and went deep. Sleeping and rest had helped but hadn't fundamentally changed anything.

Sure my feet were now smooth as a baby's bum thanks to the foot masks, and my nails were all pretty but that hadn't changed anything either. What *would* change things?

I thought of my younger self, how she spent hours doing 'silly' things like making graphic blends and blinkies on the computer because it was fun to her. Suddenly I had an idea and tentatively asked myself... *where is the joy for me today?*

I'd love to tell you it was an instant answer but it wasn't. I thought about my 'to-do list.' I thought about my younger self and all the things she loved doing. Was there anything she loved doing that I could match up with on my 'to-do list'?

It felt like a long shot until I saw two words on my list 'Sheltie Annual'. Lightbulbs went off in my head.

I've owned Shetland Sheepdogs (aka Shelties) since I was seven. They're not a particularly well-known breed but they are wonderful family dogs, smart, eager to please and super cute. Think like the big Rough Collie Lassie from the films and then shrink it to half the size and you have a Sheltie.

As a child, I wanted everything Sheltie. Keyrings, mugs, t-shirts, pictures on my wall, you name it. However, as they're not so well known, they're hard to get hold of and they never feature on anything. Every time I walked into a shop that had things with dogs on, whether it was calendars or bookmarks, I'd scour the rows looking for a Sheltie but with no such luck. To say I was gutted was an understatement.

I decided that one day I wanted to change this and put Shelties on everything. Mainly for me because I wanted all these things but also because I wanted everyone else to know about this amazing breed too. I didn't know how I was going to do it but I knew I wanted to do it.

Fast forward roughly twenty years and with my design skills I realised I could make this reality. I set up a side business, more of a passion project than anything else, called *I Love Shelties*. I had big dreams for it but it always seemed to get swallowed up by having to do 'real work' that paid the bills.

I remember my mum chatting with me about all my ideas for it back in summer 2020 and I mentioned my idea for an annual that never seemed to get off the ground. As a child, I loved receiving my Christmas Annual books of *The Beano* and *Dandy*. I envisaged doing a similar book featuring photos and stories of Shelties, but I never seemed to have time and didn't know if I could get the online Sheltie community behind it.

My mum challenged me though and said, 'Why not just try it? There's still time to make one this year.' I thought, well, *why not*? I jumped into it and the first edition of the 'Sheltie Annual' was published in November 2020. It raised £300 for Sheltie rescue in the UK. Everyone loved it, so the next year I planned to do the same again. I had opened up submissions and people were sending me photos and stories from all over the world but I hadn't gotten started on designing the book yet.

And so, scanning my 'to-do list' for where the joy was for me, I found myself staring at the *Sheltie Annual*. It was a no-brainer. Who wouldn't enjoy looking at photos of gorgeous dogs all day? Suddenly I was in action, motivated and inspired. I spent the whole day working on it, and the next, and the next…

Every day I sat at my desk and asked myself, *where is the joy for me today?* Some days I didn't even ask myself the question because I knew it lay within those pages of beautiful dogs. Days turned into weeks working on it. I'm sure my family and friends got sick of me talking about it because it truly was my only topic of conversation, but to me it was *everything*. It was joy, it was fun. It was my lifeline.

Most of all, it was energising. I found myself waking up in the morning with a spring in my step, eager to get started. My mood had lifted dramatically, I felt purposeful, I felt like I had something to live for, and I felt excited by life again.

Weeks later when I finished working on the annual, I felt bereft. I didn't know how to translate that joy and energy into anything else. I remember telling Emily in a session, that I initially had no idea how to translate what I'd done with working on my Sheltie annual to other aspects of my life. To help me make the transition, we worked on both an emotional level using the tools I had been introduced to as well as on a practical level. I looked hard at my business, every inch of it. *Where was the joy?* Unsurprisingly, it was almost completely absent.

I took inventory of all the tasks I did in my business and their function. Did they bring me direct income? Was it necessary admin? Could I automate or outsource that? Why am I doing that, it's not fun and doesn't further my business at all, can I ditch it entirely? Although I couldn't afford a virtual assistant, even just knowing I had ditched things and had a list of actions I could outsource as soon as I was able, helped immensely. I looked into automation and did what I could to streamline so much of what I'd been doing manually for years. I started to feel lighter.

But the joy wasn't quite there yet.

I entered 2022 and decided to make 'joy' my word of the year. I put the whole concept under a microscope. Was it fun? Did it make me feel alive? What could I do to bring in more joy? I started in small ways; changing my morning routine to make a small window of time for me to write, throwing out clutter, buying myself a book for the first time in ages, exploring new places to walk with the dogs, blu-tacking postcards to the wall above my computer to inspire me. I went back to the basics and started looking for joy in the small things.

Slowly, very, very slowly, I did see life start to change for the better. It wasn't perfect but I didn't hate *everything* anymore.

Eventually, I started to make the question bigger. How do I want to spend my days? What does a joyful life look like? Who am I when I'm not trying to simply survive?

As more and more parts of my business fell away, I felt wobbly. I called upon every spirit and higher being I could think of for support and leaned into trusting everything would all work out. I stopped trying to make everything make sense and fit into neat boxes and instead, went exactly where I felt the joy. I stopped the endless daily Zoom calls with everyone and anyone who asked for my time. I bought roller skates. I shared my poetry for the first time online and decided to work towards publishing it as part of a poetry collection

Nothing I was doing made much sense for building a business and nothing has since. What *has* happened is I've fallen more and more into alignment. I've fallen more and more in love with myself and have built total trust in my feelings and my intuition. My boundaries in my business and how I spend my time have become clearer and more aligned with joy. It hasn't been done with ruthlessness or unkindness but as each day passes I become much clearer about what lights me up, and I have got very good at letting go of the things that don't.

Have I become selfish? No. I still care, I still love the work I do and I still have a desire to help people. I have also decided to put myself at the centre of my universe again for the first time in a long time. Because unless I'm energised and happy, nothing I do comes from a good place. It instead comes from a place of lack, obligation and resentment. It has meant that there have been times when I've had to have difficult conversations laying out my boundaries in relationships and situations to allow adult interactions that do not cost me, rather than being forced into a child or parent role. There have also been plenty of parts of my life and business that have needed reshaping or letting go of entirely which wasn't always easy. However, by this point, I had access to more tools such as EFT tapping to support the transitions and make the journey easier.

I've found that it's made it all the more difficult to describe the work I do or want to be doing. Niching once you start to follow your joy becomes a nigh impossible task. I do however feel more me, more whole, more true to myself. And yes, I do feel more joyful!

The spring in my step has returned. There are things to look forward to. And while some of the biggest changes in my life that I desire haven't yet occurred, like finally moving house, I can see the smaller steps being taken towards the bigger things. Life has become not just bearable but enjoyable.

Often you see in books, movies and TV that people have this kind of crisis in life and their way to resolve it is to pack a bag and move halfway across the world in search of themselves. For me, this wasn't a feasible option and it wasn't one I wanted either. I love my husband, my dogs, and my family and I didn't want to leave them, despite being unsatisfied with so much of my life. Instead of immediately running away, I stayed with the uncomfortable feelings and changed what I could, as I could.

I didn't need to set fire to my entire life to find the burning passion within me and neither do you.

The one thing you do need to do is ask yourself what you truly want and actually listen to the answer. Put yourself at the centre of your universe once again and let the world revolve around you for a change.

THE FREEDOM WE WISH
WE COULD SPEAK

The maiden's fiery passion and determination to do what makes her happy often puts her at odds with her caregivers. It can be the source of arguments, and her passion can quickly shift into anger and rebellion.

Suddenly it's not about doing what makes her happy but about undermining and rejecting the authorities that bear down upon her. She becomes increasingly inventive with her workarounds, exploits and take-downs of anyone who dares cross her. This is the dark maiden. A maiden in the shadow. A maiden who has lost touch with her true nature.

For the maiden, in her true aspect, evokes the sense of carefree fun and lack of responsibility that we long for. As the goddess of spring, Persephone brings light to the darkness. She breaks the cold, dark winter days, calling forth new life and with it, hope. She demonstrates to us humanity's ability to self-destruct as well as humanity's potential.

It is in those moments when we don't get our own way that we decide which path we will choose. Will we choose one of maturity and responsibility beyond our remit? Will we take on burdens, responsibility and blame beyond what is rightfully ours? Will we choose one of angry rebellion and abdication, disregarding the consequences of our choices and actions? Will we lash out in a desperate attempt to unleash our anger at our lack of control? Or will we choose one of stepping into our power and the capacity to choose for ourselves? Will we respect and accept the consequences of what happened and the actions we may have unwittingly taken and use this wisdom to make powerful choices for ourselves going forward? The maiden walks this fine line with us.

I didn't know this when my parents divorced. I was seven years old. All I knew was my dad wasn't there and my mum was constantly crying. I woke up one night feeling thirsty and went downstairs to get a drink. We'd moved into my grandma's old house only six months before my parents split up. I started walking down the stairs when I heard my mum in the kitchen. She was sobbing into the phone.

I sank onto the stairs, holding the bannister railing. She was crying too much to say many words but it was about my dad and how he could have done this to her, to *us*. The whole house felt like there was a heavyweight, a dark cloud hanging over us.

I went back to bed thirsty. I didn't sleep that night.

At that moment, I decided I didn't want to cause additional hassle. I didn't want to add to my mum's upset and stress. So when we had to sit our SATs (Standard Assessment Tests) that year, I didn't tell my mum. When I took my result papers home and she asked why I hadn't told her I was doing tests at school, I shrugged. In the grand scheme of things, it hadn't seemed that important. It was my small way of not adding to the load. I kept these things to myself and took on responsibilities that weren't mine in an attempt to be helpful.

I got so used to not telling anyone what was going on that I even forgot to invite my mum to my Brownie Promise Ceremony. I'd practised my Brownie Law religiously. I was so nervous. When I got there I saw all my friends with their mums,

I realised my mistake but it was too late to call my mum now. The ceremony went ahead, I joined the Brownies and I didn't trip over the Brownie Law or my own feet, but I had to do it alone.

It was a horrible feeling. I'd somehow fallen too deep and couldn't get out of the habit of not telling anyone anything. I simply didn't know how to do it any other way.

Whether you recognise yourself in this because you stopped sharing, or maybe you shared something of the burden you carried and were not believed by the adults around you. The wisdom the maiden offers you is the opportunity to choose differently at this moment and speak your truth.

A few years later when someone I knew was going through their parents' divorce, I reached out because I knew what it was like and offered to be there if she wanted a friend. She spat back in my face that she didn't need anyone and certainly didn't need me.

I watched from a distance as she became very angry at the world. I'd listen to parents gathering, tutting and talking about the girl who had 'gone off the rails'. She had taken the other road of angry rebellion.

There were days though, when I wished I could have been more like that old school friend. When I wished I could have screamed and shouted. I wished that the turmoil I was in would be noticed by someone and supported in healing the wound.

I'd retreated so far within myself that I'd lost the ability to speak about how I truly felt at such a young age. I'd become old before my time. I was like a swan, looking graceful above water yet below the surface, I was paddling furiously, trying to make sense of it all.

Instead, the adults all rounded on me saying, 'But *you* didn't. You did so well. You turned out alright. You took it all in your stride, didn't you?' What they were really saying though, was that I had made the choice that made them most comfortable, as my behaviour didn't challenge their world.

Over the years I've worked to heal this wound. Part of it was to tell my parents how I'd felt back then. I'd spent years growing up listening to both their sides of the story as they attempted to blame each other. I'd dutifully listened each time once again taking on a responsibility that wasn't mine, until one day I'd got tired of being talked at and told my mum that if I blamed anyone, I blamed both of them or none of them at all. I didn't want to take sides. She didn't dare to bring up the subject for a very long time after that.

I first started to tell my dad about the impact on my first trip to Cyprus as a teenager. I was sixteen and I'd opted to visit the motherland rather than go to my high school prom. It was my first trip abroad and my first time spending an extended period with just my dad. It felt like we were having to get to know each other all over again.

One night, we were exceptionally late heading out for dinner. I was hungry and therefore grumpy. The conversation had been stilted all evening until the subject worked its way onto my parent's divorce. Suddenly I snapped and let him have it. I told him what it had felt like for me, what impact it had left and how all I'd wanted throughout it all, was just to have my dad.

It felt like a release to be able to finally speak the truth. I didn't need to throw chairs or smash anything. I hadn't needed to cause a scene. It hadn't turned into a massive argument. I'd been heard. It felt good. I felt myself let go of the breath that I'd been holding onto for nearly a decade. In speaking my truth, I'd released myself, I'd *healed* myself in a small way in that moment. It was the first layer of healing this particular wound.

I had not filtered what I said for fear of what my dad might think. I had not held back or changed my truth in any way, shape or form. What I had done though, is handed back a responsibility that I'd taken on when I was far too young. I'd handed back the fact that I was a child having to deal with things that were well beyond my understanding. I'd given the responsibility back to its rightful owner.

It has taken many conversations over the years with both of my parents to fully unpack how I've felt, how they've felt, how everyone has behaved and the impact it has had on all of us. It's something we continue to work on when new understandings and realisations arise but each time we do, a part of us heals in being able to have the conversation, rather than shying away from it.

The healing has come over time, in layers. Some of it has meant having conversations with my parents to clean things up. Other times I took things to my sessions with Emily and used her subconscious tools to heal and release parts of it. With the healing came new learning and awareness that added to the picture and I kept going. With each layer peeled off, the pain diminished.

It's a fine line we walk as we decide how we're going to respond to things life throws at us. What dealing with the fall-out of my parents' divorce from a child's perspective has taught me the most, is that before I react, before I decide to take on something that isn't mine, before I decide to act in angry rebellion for things outside of my control, I need to know the truth.

I need to know *my* truth and sit with it. Before I say or do anything outward, I turn inward and know what my heart says and feels.

The angry maiden acts out of anger and spite. The dutiful maiden reacts in silence and burden. The true wisdom of the maiden is to find the balance and truth of her own spirit and act accordingly with her own integrity.

Persephone found herself stuck in the underworld through no fault of her own. Instead of being angry or resentful, she got clever. She built authority in her position and used it wisely, for good. She handled it with grace to become feared yet revered. She took her lack of control and carved out her own role, claiming her own power in the space of unchangeable, unspeakable things. She reclaimed her voice when it had been stolen from her. And she didn't reclaim it in a scream, nor a whisper, but with a calm truth that she knew for herself better than anyone else.

THE BODY UNKNOWN

The female form is in itself, a paradox. Loved, adored and desired; yet repelled, suppressed and rejected. It is an object of desire for the male gaze and we are encouraged to play up to our sexiness. We are pretty, perfect dolls. Our natural bodily functions such as menstruation and breastfeeding are seen as obscene and we are unclean unless we're perfectly shaven.

We've become alien and disconnected from our bodies. It is an unwelcome foreign object that we must endure.

Patriarchal society has sought to control and suppress our bodies and by extension, women at every turn. In a dictatorial fashion, we've been conditioned to believe it is our sole responsibility (and sin) to handle the consequences of sex. That we should take contraceptives containing hormones that cause a myriad of unwanted side effects on our bodies as a service to humanity.

We should hide every imperfection, agonise over every wrinkle, cover our greying hair, and cake ourselves in makeup and moisturisers to look as young and appealing as possible. That we should dress for the male gaze and always be receptive to their advances without having any urges or desires of our own. We should be quiet, beautiful and subservient. In short, I think what the patriarchy really wanted was maids, nurses and blow-up dolls rather than *actual* women.

As a result of the narrative that we've grown up with in society, we've been conditioned to hate our bodies unless it is viewed through male desire. Everything else is obscene and unwanted, so we remove it and hide it until we are the perfect human woman. It's been the source of so much body dysmorphia, mental and emotional trauma and illness, stress, anxiety and general unhappiness to women and it is so ingrained in all of us that we don't even notice it is an issue.

Shortly after rainbow-cardigan-gate, I became increasingly self-conscious and obsessed with my appearance. Until then I'd happily been dressing as I wanted in all kinds of outrageous things and experimenting with zigzag hair partings and glitter makeup thanks to my subscription to the Sabrina The Teenage Witch's magazine collection, *Sabrina's Secrets*. It featured a purple glitter cosmetics case and every week there was some new piece of makeup that was most certainly full of glitter to be applied to your hair, face or body.

After the non-uniform incident at school, suddenly dabbling with makeup and glitter was not okay. I needed to fit in. Not try too hard to be cool but the fear of rejection and need to be accepted kicked in. I looked at myself under the microscope and hated what I saw.

I had big bushy eyebrows although not quite enough hairs to make it a monobrow but enough for me to notice. My arms and legs were full of dark hair too. I had thick, frizzy hair that stuck out in a beautiful triangle shape when it was long and unlayered. I had a highly noticeable moustache that had once caused a girl to stick a Post-it note on my back telling me to shave it. I'd spent years pretending the moustache didn't exist because I was too ashamed to say anything or ask my mum for help. The Mediterranean DNA from my dad's side of the family shone through in me and at school I stuck out like a sore thumb.

I stood in the mirror one day and seeing all of this for what felt like the first time, the person I saw staring back at me, wasn't me anymore. It was *Gorilla Camilla*. Yes, that's a real nickname they gave me at school.

When I saw *Gorilla Camilla* myself for the first time, I was horrified. I was too ashamed to talk to my mum. Being very much an English rose she didn't have the dark hair in super noticeable places quite like me. I didn't know how to even bring it up, let alone hope she'd understand or be able to help.

To bury my feelings, I ate. A lot. I piled on the weight. No one in my family mentioned it, like it was some kind of unspoken rule not to talk about my appearance.

My one saving grace is that I never had so much as a single spot. I made up for that by having a deathly pale complexion, thanks to what was most likely anaemia due to the menorrhagia (heavy periods) that seemed to run in most of the women in our family.

The more I ate the bigger I became and it got even easier to hide in shapeless layers. It was too late; I had seen *her* and there was no way I could unsee it. I hated myself and withdrew even more.

I retreated online, a safe place to hide my true self. I struck up friendships all over the world that seemed to accept me and my eccentricities. I even met my first boyfriend online who I got to accompany me to school on one of his trips to visit me, in an attempt to not only prove to my friends that he was real, but to also quell the rumours that I was a lesbian because I was already clear about my sexual orientation. I hated the idea that not only was sexual orientation being used against me as a weapon but that I felt I needed to 'prove' myself to stop at least one hurtful comment from flying around the school.

Initially, things looked on the up and I began to feel like I could be myself again. I stopped eating for England and bought some clothes that were just a touch more like me again. I had real friends, even though they were all online. School wasn't so bad because I kept my head down as much as possible. I had a boyfriend who seemed to accept me as I was... Well, he did at first.

What I didn't know was that I had just met my Bluebeard. At first, he made me feel loved, important and special. Over time though, his self-righteousness, and controlling attitude shone through. One day when I wore some eyeliner, he told me I looked like a deranged Bambi. He didn't care about how overweight I was, 'but that maybe I wanted to try eating more healthily,' he said with an air of elitism. As I became more self-conscious about my appearance, suddenly I was accused of becoming self-absorbed and narcissistic. I was too emotional all the time; maybe I could tone it down a bit? '*You have changed,*' he said. '*Why can't you be like the person you were when we first met?*'

Over several years of our friendship and relationship, I kept being pushed back into the box of someone I didn't want to be. The more I tried to find myself and my confidence, the more I was receiving a message that I'd only be loved if I continued to be the broken, unhappy, unconfident person I'd once been.

Truth is, we do all sorts of things to be loved and accepted. It is built into us, coded into our DNA to want to be part of the pack. In the past to be rejected meant certain death. This shit is hardwired in us. So of course I did what any teenager who felt abandoned, rejected and just wanted to be loved would do and I went along with it. I accepted it. Perhaps *I* was being the unreasonable one. Maybe I really was crazy and he was doing me a favour by putting up with my insanity?

As time went by, I became more and more disconnected from myself. My body was screaming at me that this was wrong. That it wasn't what love was supposed to look like. That there was nothing wrong with me.

I stopped crying myself to sleep every night due to school misery. I stopped crying at all. In fact, I stopped feeling anything at all, that way nothing could be twisted. To become numb was to keep myself safe. As I shut down the access to my feelings, I metaphorically died and became a walking corpse. I reasoned that if I felt nothing then at least I couldn't be hurt.

I stayed that way, comfortably, uncomfortably numb for over a decade. And when I finally started my healing journey two and a half years ago, from the moment I started I knew time was running out on being disconnected from my emotions and body.

As I dug into painful memories, I remembered why I'd cut myself off from feeling in the first place — the pain was raw and real. It was all consuming and there were days when I thought the pain would swallow me whole. The pain felt endless.

Over time, working through the memories and in healing, the pain lessened but I realised I felt nothing in its place. Positive feelings; joy, happiness, love, and excitement, were distinctly absent. At celebrations, I was going through the motions. I knew how I should behave when I felt say, proud, but I didn't have any physical reaction to accompany it. I started to feel broken and wondered if I'd ever be whole or feel anything again.

I sat down and used my EFT tapping to tap in phrases like, 'I am in tune with my body,' and 'I am allowed to feel positive emotions daily.' At first, it seemed like nothing had changed. Slowly, I began to feel flickers of a feeling when something good happened. My heart felt a bit warmer. For a split second, it felt like it had grown twice the size. Something *was* happening.

What I've found is that after being numb for so long, the good feelings can be fleeting and quiet. They're not always loud, they don't grip you tightly quite like sadness or anger.

The good feelings are like butterflies. You need to get quiet inside before they'll land on you. When they do, if you try to catch them, they fly off. And if you do manage to catch one, hold it too tight and you'll crush it.

Instead, the best you can do is silently thank it for coming and smile to yourself in acknowledgement. Go gently with yourself, treat the good feeling with reverence and it'll come back to you again.

Learn to appreciate those moments however fleeting and then practise anchoring and amplifying them within your body. This is the first step in reconditioning yourself and rehabilitating your emotional state.

Because it's not about becoming a tidal wave of uncontrollable emotions like an emotionally wrought maiden — it's about finding the balance and holding duality. Allowing yourself to feel it all, good and bad and knowing all of it will pass. The world is cyclical in its design, absolutely everything comes and goes. You can't hold onto the good any more than you can hold onto the bad. It all moves on with time.

Part of the maiden's lesson is to embrace this transitory nature of things. Learn to love your body however it shows up each day. Honour every emotion as it arises, then let it go. Explore your impulses, urges and hunches. Be everything and hold onto nothing, it is where you will find abundance and infinite flow.

Stop viewing your body, your emotions and your intuition as foreign objects to be looked down upon and suppressed, but as vessels of divine wisdom. Women hold magic and the key to creation. Start owning it, it's yours.

DEMETER

Words cannot capture her essence;
she is felt by the vastness of her love
lullabies that call your name across oceans;
a love that stretches beyond time and space.

You will feel her on the wind
and in every corner of the world.
When you're on your knees in prayer
or walking through the forest dense.

She never stops, never rests.
always reaching, forever waiting
to wrap you in the safety of her arms
and her heart that is home.

You will find her smile in the candle flame,
her warmth beneath a grand oak tree,
her presence in every single breath.
Forever by your side in the life you make;

in boundless love

MOTHER WOUNDS

You do not need to have birthed children to resonate with the lessons of the mother phase of the feminine. The rite of passage to become a mother is not to have birthed a child from your body. As I write this, I am not a mother to children; however, I've been a proud mum to my two dogs for the past seven years as their primary caregiver. To be a mother is to leave a legacy, a mark on the world whether that is through your own children, furbabies, being the cool aunt, your business or creative works, it **all** counts.

Regardless of the outcome or tangibility in the world, you have laboured, 'birthed' something and transformed yourself in the process. To become a mother in any form changes you fundamentally. You will stretch and grow, physically, emotionally, spiritually and mentally. Life will change and never look the same again. It can't. You can't go back to who you were before you made it.

Just like a caterpillar becoming a butterfly, to become the mother is to go inward and transform. While in your cocoon, like the caterpillar, every inch of you will dissolve entirely to be rebuilt, and reborn.

Metamorphose complete, you burst forth as the butterfly and enter a whole new world of life, knowledge, learning and possibility. It can never be undone. To have birthed something leaves a permanent mark, not only physically but in your heart, in your soul. Suddenly a piece of you lives on, outside of your own body and it is up to you to be the steward of both your soul and the soul of your charge. This is to truly become a mother.

It's ingrained in society that the only way to be a mother is to birth children, anything else is not valid. Somehow, if you choose not to or are otherwise unable to have children, you become a pariah to society. *Surely you will change your mind, you still have plenty of time,* they say.

The expectation is that of course, every woman will have and/or want children. It's assumed and initially not directly spoken about. Anyone who doesn't conform, regardless of the reason, is invalidated as a woman. Somehow in not having children, this air of suspicion builds around us. We're not part of the pack because we haven't bought into the mentality. Motherhood it seems has been weaponized and turned into the ultimate elite women's club.

For me, the question was finally asked directly to my face on my wedding day. At the reception, mere hours after the ceremony, a relative came over excitedly asking when I was planning to get pregnant as if it was something I'd scheduled into the diary. Their face dropped five miles when I said I didn't have any plans.

Late last year when I met up with another relative and we caught up with each other on our lives, I was thrilled to be sharing that I was going to be published in a book for the first time. I made the mistake of starting the sentence with, 'in April next year…' and saw their face drop when I mentioned the book. Evidently, they'd been expecting another kind of announcement.

Unfortunately for women, pregnancy and marriage are often the only types of announcements that we have been programmed to believe have value. There's no celebrating ditching the toxic ex or leaving the job you hate. There's no party with your friends for publishing a book or starting a business. There's no ceremony for healing your trauma or letting go of your limiting beliefs. The world for women revolves around being a mother and the steps it takes to get you there.

The truth is, we weren't *born* to be mothers. We were simply *born to be*.

Keeping us preoccupied and overly concerned with being perfect and trying to attract a mate that will lead to the ultimate prize; the child, stops women from coming together to rock the boat about the bigger issues. Divide and conquer. Distract to control.

Autonomy over our bodies and personal choices has been swallowed up by this obsession with creating every woman as the perfect mother. A role that has been carved out for us by patriarchal society and in no way represents what motherhood is like in reality. A vision that has stripped the warmth and wisdom from the experience.

Mothers are often presented as wounded souls, martyrs to the cause. They are asked to carry so much, especially in the modern world. The mother herself becomes largely forgotten, her identity swallowed up by being 'mum' which can lead to resentment, isolation and martyrdom.

Women starting side hustles call themselves 'mumpreneurs' and 'boss mamas' wearing it like a badge of honour. They cling onto this title like it's all they have left and sadly, often it is. They can't relate to anyone who hasn't had children, their hobbies, interests and social life fall away to be replaced with a myriad of playdates, after-school activities and an obsession with gin or wine. Physical intimacy with their partner becomes a joke to be laughed at some time in the future.

These types of mothers become non-existent unless they are viewed as extensions of their children. It is only much later in life, as the nest empties that they reach a crisis point. Not knowing who they are outside of their children and the life and routine created by their children's existence. With an identity so wrapped up in children and trying to juggle the demands of our busy lives, mothers simply don't have time for anything else and as such, the wisdom and joy of alternative manifestations of the mother, outside of birthing children and loving them, has been lost to the ages.

Demeter is the ultimate depiction of this wounded mother soul. Demeter is the Greek goddess of agriculture and grain. The main story by which she is known is that of her daughter Persephone's abduction by Hades to the underworld. Distraught, she searches tirelessly for her daughter's whereabouts. She calls upon the goddess Hecate to assist her in the search as she finds she cannot locate her daughter alone. In her despair, she plunges the world into famine until they are reunited. Demeter asking for help from Hecate is our permission slip to seek out help for ourselves. An eternal memorandum from the goddesses to know that we are not meant to do any of this alone. In the depths of despair, seek help.

Due to Hades' deception of tricking Persephone into eating pomegranate seeds from the underworld, Persephone cannot leave the realm entirely. Zeus creates a compromise whereby she can reside above ground with Demeter for some months, but must also return to the underworld for several months of the year. As Demeter pines for her daughter who is the goddess of spring, the world descends into winter each year until Persephone returns to her mother.

This story has become ingrained in our psyche that our world revolves around the children we bear and that without them we have no identity or function in the world. For there are no stories about Demeter as well-known as that of her being the desperate mother looking for her child?

I'm not trying to diminish the pain or loss of a child at all. It's another subject entirely. It's a pain unlike any other. What I'm trying to illustrate is how society has created a world for us where you become invalid and invisible unless you are someone's mother. That you have no value, that your character is entirely swallowed up by your ability to conceive.

Once you move out of the mother phase, even the next step of maga has been hidden from us, instead sending us straight into the supposed haggard, unsightly, unwanted crone. If you never get initiated into the mother phase, you're forever a reckless maiden, a barren spinster who has nothing to offer the world. It invalidates masses of society who do not walk the path of bearing a child. This mode of thinking diminishes the importance of other projects and creations we can birth and disqualifies any other kind of caregiving unless it is that which has come from your own body.

So much trauma and wounding is wrapped up in the mother phase. However, we are too focused on the children (or lack of) to see it and far too busy juggling all the balls of life to have the time or energy to do anything about it. Being a mother is far from all we are and not anywhere close to all we are meant to do on this earth. The creation of life is only the beginning of the journey for us as women, not the end of our existence.

YOU ARE NOT ATLAS

My family on my dad's side is Cypriot. I'd love to say I've been immersed in and grown up with the culture but that wasn't the case. Unfortunately, through no fault of my own, I didn't get to spend time with much of my Cypriot family growing up for many years and for many reasons.

However, I've always been drawn to the culture and history and did what I could to learn about it. One of the things I did pick up over the years was *the shrug*. There's this way that they shrug, with a lightness in their shoulders, a nonchalant expression, and a raise of the arms that instantly turns mountains into molehills.

They live life in the slow lane. Why do it today when tomorrow is good enough? There's no hurry, no stress, no worrying. This is a civilisation that has learnt to shrug off the weight of the world.

This expression of carrying the weight of the world upon us comes from Greek mythology. In the stories, Atlas was a titan who was punished for his participation in a war against Zeus, king of the gods. He was condemned to hold the heavens aloft for all eternity. The fate of the world genuinely rested upon him, for if he faltered, the sky would crash down onto the earth.

In modern times, no one carries the weight of the world more than the mother in her martyrdom. Responsible for so much, not only do we still live under the spectre of being the perfect housewife, but we hold down jobs as well.

The concept of the housewife has no place in modern society when many of us cannot afford or don't want to stay at home and live on our partner's wage. Or worse, single mothers have no one to rely on, so what can they do other than get a job to pay the bills, feed and clothe the children and keep a roof over their heads?

There's no way we can do that while trying to be a domestic goddess that has the cooking skills and sexiness of Nigella, be Mary Poppins and occasionally Florence Nightingale for our children and build an empire to rival Oprah, all while looking as polished as Dita Von Teese. *No messy buns here, please.*

It's a hard pass from me.

Although more and more of us are rejecting it, the concept persists. The responsibilities, burdens and simply *trying to do all the things* stack up until we're permanently exhausted, burnt out and resentful at life, the universe and everything in between.

Now here's the thing, we're not the titans that pissed off Zeus. I mean, we can and have pissed off that womanising king of the gods for a whole host of other reasons I'm sure, but this time it wasn't us.

We're not Atlas. I'm not Atlas. You are not Atlas. Shrug for fucks sake! Let it flow. You are not responsible for solving the world's problems before bedtime.

You are not being punished for being a witch in another life by kids that run around screaming like little gremlins hyped up on sugar.

You have a choice as to how much you take on at any one time. Yes, you do! Read it again.

There's no such thing as not having a choice. We have a choice; we simply don't like all the options or the subsequent consequences of the choices. I like to call them choiceless choices and it feels like there is no other alternative.

Admittedly, in some situations, there *isn't* an alternative or the options available are extremely limited. But what I mean when I say there's no such thing as 'not having a choice' is that sometimes, all the options we have available are unappealing and we can feel cornered or completely stuck. And that although the choices available are awful, it can sometimes be a case of choosing between the lesser of two evils, and none of the available options will bring us happiness at that moment in time.

It also creates a mindset of thinking in extreme consequences. So we think that by choosing not to do the dishes or clean the house, it will pile up and within hours we'll end up living in a pigsty. That if we go on strike, no one will pick it up for us and nothing changes. That everything rests solely on us because we can't rely on anyone else to do it for us. This is the world we've grown up in. Having pitted us against each other, separated, divided and isolated, it takes this concept of being the independent woman and holds it aloft like a badge of honour for us. We've lost our support systems, our community, our camaraderie, our tribe and our sense of kinship.

It used to take a village to raise a child. No one was ever overspent because everything was shared and done on rotation. Now the onus is on us and solely us. Everything starts and ends with Mother. If she doesn't do it, no one else will, that's the mentality we've become accustomed to. It's built up resentment, weariness – no, not weariness. We're goddamn tired, fed up with it all and on some days, we really couldn't give a flying fuck if we never did anything else for anyone else, ever again. Going on strike becomes more than appealing.

This idea was taken to its nth point in a book I love, conveniently called *Atlas Shrugged* by Ayn Rand. In it, the 'prime movers' of the world went on strike and disappeared. The book showed the struggles, scrambling and how everything ground to a halt as the key players, the 'prime movers' as Rand calls them, refused to take on anything that was beyond their responsibility and left the world to its fate.

Now I'm not suggesting you stand by and watch your house go up in smoke because you stopped making dinner every night, and waited to see what would happen, only to find the kids have just blown up the microwave trying to cook a pizza.

The choice isn't to say or do nothing. The choice is to draw a line in the sand and vocalise it. To educate. To hand back responsibilities. To assert boundaries on what you will and won't do and ask that those around you pick up their fifty percent. You are not here to be a cook, cleaner, nurse, maid, chauffeur and general dog's body to all and sundry.

You have a choice to say... no. No, I don't want to do that. No, I don't have time for that. No, it doesn't feel good to me. No. No. No. No. No.

That doesn't mean you're going to spend the rest of your life saying no. You can say yes too! The difference is that you have a choice of yes or no. It's not an automatic yes at your expense. You get to choose when you say yes, when you say no and what parameters and conditions you place on both. Instead of letting everyone else dictate the terms and conditions of your life, you can take back control and practice saying *yes with these conditions* or simply, no thank you because I am already over-stretched. You *choose*.

Initially, you'll feel like a prize bitch. We've been condi-tioned to believe that women should be there to do everything and anything. We *love* to help, we *love* to serve, and your every wish is our command. *Really?* We're not fucking genies sum-moned from a lamp. We're human beings just like the rest of them. We're not perfect, there's no such thing. It's a myth the men created to keep us busy trying to reach it. We're human beings, not human-(constantly)-doings.

We're human beings who are learning how to say no and hold the line. We're learning to take on only what is ours and let go of the rest. We're human beings who are learning how to give responsibility for things to someone else.

We're human beings who are learning to communicate our needs. We're human beings who are realising, perhaps for the first time, that we actually *have* needs and that it's okay to put ourselves first. In fact, it's vital.

The thing about motherly love is that you would give your last dying breath to your child to save them; such is the extent of your love. Is giving so much of ourselves away that we feel constantly depleted an example we want to set for our children? That you need to drain yourself for the sake of everyone around you? That you should be overly generous to the point of your exhaustion? Is this what we want to perpetuate for the rest of time?

When you keep spinning on your wheels too long, you start burning rubber. Once you've burnt through the rubber, you get worn down to just metal and it grinds on the ground. Day in, day out. It'll grind until there's nothing left and you come to a standstill. There's nothing left to give.

Before we get to that stage, or to get out of this dark mother phase, it's time to claw it back. No one in this world is going to think you're important unless you do. We set examples by leading. So go first. Be the example.

This isn't about selfishness. It's about seeing your value as a human. You are more than worthy of having support, love, rest, fun, and happiness. You deserve it as much as anyone else.

When my parents divorced, I was seven at the time and struggled to understand the reasons why. At the time there was nothing I wanted more than for my parents to get back together and for us to be a family again. I spent hours thinking about ways that I could engineer a scenario that would bring our family back together.

Underneath it though, I didn't want my family back together and for everything to go back to the way it was. What I wanted, what I truly wanted deep in my heart was for us to be *happy*. What I wanted was for my parents to be happy, whatever that looked like. That happiness was never going to come from them bleeding themselves for my benefit.

Don't get me wrong, my mum has always given me everything she could. We didn't always have much growing up but she gave me the best of what she had. I instinctively knew not to ask for a PlayStation when they were first released because I knew we couldn't afford it. I saved my pocket money to buy PC expansion packs for *The Sims* myself rather than ask for them.

It was a huge deal when I could finally go to the shop and buy it for myself.

Truthfully, it wasn't ever really about the material objects. So many think they need to go overboard buying stuff, doing stuff, giving too much of themselves when all our children really want... is you.

Sure there were some presents I received that I've never forgotten like the fluffy white cuddly cat that 'Jack Valentine' left at my door one year. Jack Valentine is a character who goes around giving gifts on Valentine's Day (or sometimes on Valentine's Day Eve). It seems the tradition of Jack Valentine solely exists in my home county of Norfolk, England but it was a fundamental part of my upbringing to await a mysterious knock on the door and find he had left me a gift. It left such an impression that I still have the fluffy white cat he sent me one year!

Another gift I clearly remember receiving was the first digital camera I got as a Christmas present from my dad which was bright blue. It sat in the palm of my hand with about two buttons on it and started a lifelong love of photography. Those vivid memories though, are few and far between.

What I *really* remember is the night my grandad came home from work with a giant hamper he'd been given as a Christmas bonus, and we all sat around oohing and aahing as we pulled things out of a box so big I could have fit in about five times. I remember my mum bundling me into the car to drive me to the nearest town to see the Christmas lights. I remember laughing till we cried at my mum turning into Miss Marple trying to figure out who was the murderer playing Cluedo because she got *so* into it.

What I also remember is sitting up at the table watching my mum iron, waiting for her to finish so we could play a board game together and she kept saying, 'Maybe later when I'm finished'. So I'd scoot on next door to my grandparents' house. Grandad was watching Formula 1 on TV and my nan was in the kitchen hovering over the roast dinner like it needed her total attention. I would ask if they'd play a board game only to be told, 'In a little while'. I didn't have siblings so there was no one else to ask.

Eventually, I got the message that they didn't have time, so I stopped asking to play games together and stopped asking for the games to even be bought in the first place.

What I *really* wanted from my family was their **presence**, not the elaborate presents they perhaps could or couldn't afford. In a world where we've been taught you only have value if you're working yourself to the bone, they didn't have the time or energy. They had nothing left to give me, not even their presence, attention and smile. This is how the dark mother wound continues to perpetuate because we pass on this mentality that we drain ourselves in all ways, leaving no space for what is truly important.

And the most important thing… is you.

You don't win any prizes for how exhausted you are. There's no recompense for giving your life and time away to people who do not value them. It's not a competition for who can be the biggest motherhood martyr. All you're doing is missing out on building memories and building a life that has you as more than just a recurring background character. You're missing out on carving out your own identity and reclaiming your energy to begin to enjoy the life you're building.

I love watching *Escape To The Chateau*. It's not really about my secret wish to own a castle (although that would be cool)! What I love about it is the pace of life being slower, and more mindful with a balance of inward and outward focus. Angela and Dick Strawbridge aren't just building a business and restoring a Chateau, they're building a life for their family that has both of them *actually* in it.

Some of the most charming moments of the show are when they've finished building or decorating a new room or feature and then everyone dresses up, food is made, drinks are poured and they, as a family, spend time together enjoying it.

You are not Atlas, the titan fated to hold up the heavens for all eternity. You are a human, having a human experience on earth. You do all of it without any superpowers. The truth is, you don't *need* to do it all. You can let go of some of those reins and give other people a chance to step up to the plate and take responsibility.

In learning to say no and yes and setting boundaries, there will be people who kick up a fuss. These are the people who benefited from you having no boundaries and doing everything for them. These are the people who do not value you as a person; they only value what you can do for them. These people have no respect for you regardless of whether you set the boundary or not, so respect yourself enough to protect yourself from being drained by them.

In saying no, in making yourself a priority, you will lose people. It's important to go in knowing this. It won't be easy at first. You'll feel awful saying no. You'll feel awful asking people to do things that you've done without question many a time before. Start with the interactions and situations that feel like the biggest drain because solving these will give you the biggest lift.

One of those times I had to hold the line was with my mum. Since I moved out she had a habit of calling me at random times every day and multiple times a day too. If I didn't answer, she would continuously keep ringing. When this started to interrupt Zoom calls, workshops, classes and sessions I was attending online, eventually something had to give. When I first tried to explain how it was affecting and interfering with my work, it blew up into an argument immediately because she refused to even attempt to hear it. Instead, she accused me of never wanting to talk to her, not having time to talk and not telling her anything. She hung up on me and said she'd never call me again. It hurt to be shouted at. I cried a lot that day while also holding my Emotional Stress Release (ESR) points as instructed by Emily to help alleviate the stress and upset.

For days she didn't call. When I felt calmer and had a free window in my day, I called her. I explained again why the random calls were a problem and offered suggestions of how to remedy it, like messaging me to check I was free first. Eventually, we agreed that when I was available, I would call her.

What it did was open up our relationship. I only called when I knew I had time. Our short, sharp conversations of less than five minutes became longer, chattier and happier. Our overall relationship improved dramatically because it demonstrated that I could hold a boundary on something that was costing me, and the result didn't damage the relationship but improved it. To this day, 99% of the time, I call my mum first and our conversations are great. We laugh and enjoy talking to each other. I don't worry about scheduling my day around when I think she *might* call, I don't worry about being interrupted during work. It's given me back so much headspace and doesn't drain me anymore.

After you're done wondering if everyone hates you, what you're left with is a tiny bit of headspace. A little pocket where you don't have to think about or deal with their stuff. It's not yours, it's not for you to solve and that's okay. The more you can hand people back their stuff, their problems, and their issues and not take it on as yours, the less resentful and drained you will feel.

You will have more of you and for you. More energy, more time, more headspace, more room to breathe and more time to think. You'll notice how much it costs you physically and emotionally to say yes to something you don't want to say yes to doing.

It doesn't mean everything has to be a blanket no forever. It means you get to *choose* how much you help and how you help. Instead of inconveniencing yourself and bending over backwards for everyone else, you can give people options that work for you, not against you or at your expense.

The burden isn't all of the things we've taken on; it's in thinking we have to do all of it by ourselves. We've been taught asking for help is a sign of weakness. However, it is an act of strength and bravery. To ask for help is a power move that takes us out of the isolation and illusion of independence society has conditioned us to live by. To ask for help is to acknowledge that you don't have all the answers and resources and allow yourself to access the solution via other people's knowledge, skills and strengths.

Asking for help is a power move because it brings us together, it gets us working together towards common goals in collaboration and shit gets done. So book in with your practitioner for an extra session if you're having a wobble. Ask a friend if they could look after the kids or pick up a couple of groceries on their way over. Ask work for a pay rise or a discussion on flexible working. Be brave and ask for what you need.

Demeter didn't search for her daughter Persephone alone. She knew that enlisting help would mean more ground was covered, so she had Hecate and Helios also join in the search. I'm sure it meant they found out what had happened to Persephone in half the time. And that's the key here.

We only have a set number of hours in a day. Stop giving all of yours over to everyone else and leaving yourself with nothing. An empty cup is simply that, an empty cup. No one will be replenishing it if it's empty. By allowing yourself to claw back some of your time and energy, you will be able to help and look after others better because you won't be running on empty. You'll be firing on all cylinders.

It doesn't matter if you have children or furbabies, run a business, birth creative projects or anything else in between. You do a better job when you've filled up your own cup first. You're more creative, more patient, more focused, attentive and productive. All of those things start with making yourself important again and handing back responsibilities that were never yours in the first place. It doesn't mean you don't care about anyone else, it just means you care about yourself just as much, rather than viewing yourself as a second-rate citizen or a background character in your own life.

So Mother Atlas lay down those burdens that are not yours. Stop carrying the weight of ten worlds. Hand back responsibilities that are not yours. Fill up your cup with love and care for yourself. Without so much on your plate, you have more energy and headspace available for both yourself and others. No one will fill your cup for you, but the benefit to you upholding and honouring yourself as important will mean you can stop martyring yourself, start enjoying your life and heal yourself.

THE WAYS WE DESTROY OURSELVES

While a group of outraged and triggered mothers who are operating from their wounds can be vicious towards the object of their anger, the most dangerous is the mother who listens to the world and begins to hate herself.

There's nothing underhand or backhanded about her internal hatred of herself. Her internal monologue will pour out a constant stream of vitriol night and day. Eventually, she'll believe all of it and sabotage herself to fit the narrative she has created based on society's expectations for women.

Society expects us to see ourselves as worth *less*. Worth *less* than the men who objectify us. Worth *less* so we'll conform and do what we're told. Worth *less* so we don't rock the boat. Worth *less* because we're *only* a woman.

Worth *less* because we are only a mother. Worth *less* because we're a stay at home mum. Worth *less* because we're a working mum. Worth *less* because we have only one child. Worth *less* because we have ten children. Worth *less* because our children have different fathers. Worth *less* because our children have absent fathers.

Worth *less* because we're childless. Worth *less* because we've lost a child. Worth *less* because our child is sick. Worth *less* because we can't conceive. Worth *less* because we chose not to conceive.

We're trapped in a state of being, not being, being not. It hurts us to *be* a mother. It hurts us to *not* be a mother in our choosing to not have children. It hurts us to *be not* a mother through inability when we desperately want to be a mother.

We've been set up to fail whichever way we turn. We have been sold this dream of motherhood and yet, the dream has been engineered by society to put us in a prison of being worth *less*, of never being good enough or perfect enough or having it all together enough.

The only way that you can 'win' is to become a mother. However, in doing so, you once again find yourself on the back foot. Scrutinised under the gaze of society and of ourselves, and held up against the vision of the perfect mother of which you will always fall short. It's a game that has been rigged against us. *The house always wins.* We are playing a game inside the framework of society where the deck is rigged against us no matter how we play our hand. How can one expect to be happy within these circumstances?

The truth is, we simply can't. So we wound ourselves thinking we've somehow failed as mothers, not being mothers and being not mothers. Whichever way we cut this cake, we've failed. Society does and will judge us. Beyond that, we internalise all of it too. We judge, berate and destroy ourselves in our innate knowledge that we can never 'win'. That somehow we will always be seen as a failure whichever route we take. This is the hold that the patriarchy and society have on women in a game that conveniently, men never have to play for themselves.

Our inner critic does most of this work for us. We're not doing enough. We haven't spent enough time with our kids. We're not cooking every single meal from scratch using only the most organic ingredients. Our kids have too much screen time. We lost our patience and shouted at them and therefore we're the worst mother in the world. This monologue is ongoing and endless and it's the one that by far does the most damage because it's so constant. There's no escape from the voice in our head telling us that we're the worst person in the world.

Trying to win the game of being a mother is the source of our stress and anxiety, being constantly pulled in different directions. Whether we are being a mother, actively deciding to not be a mother or are being not a mother due to being unable to conceive, there is a psychological imperative for us that has been engineered by society for us to 'be' a mother. This psychological imperative builds up against our individual choices and creates a conflict we struggle to resolve. This inner conflict is the source of depression and feeling like we've failed. It is the source of our strive for perfectionism, trying to live up to the Jones and their seemingly perfect lives.

We judge ourselves by everyone else's highlight reels on social media while looking behind our curtain at the mess backstage. We see these perfectly curated photos on Instagram of smiling kids with piles of presents under a Christmas tree and then feel inadequate at what we feel is a meagre offering for a magical Christmas for our children.

The conflict of whether we are being, not being or being not a mother, against the narrative of society to 'be' a mother is the source of our paralysis – we're tired and feel like failures. We feel like we simply can't win whatever we do and don't know what to do for the best. It is also the source of our self-doubt, *what were we thinking? Are we cut out for this?* We can't ever be good enough. We need to do what everyone else is doing, we don't know better than anyone else.

The inner conflict is the source of our burnout. If we just keep doing more and more, maybe one day we'll crack this code that suddenly makes it easy makes it all perfect and keeps everyone happy. We're constantly striving in the mother phase, trying to win a game that has long been rigged against us.

The only way forward for us is to stop playing the game. There's no point playing, you're set to lose anyway regardless of what you do so... don't play.

To step outside of the narrative, you need to observe, stop and transform the negative self-talk first. This inner critic telling you that you are shit needs silencing if you are ever to heal this mother wound that afflicts us all from various places in time and space. For this to be successful, you simply can't hope to talk yourself into a more positive mindset. It starts with observing the thoughts. Then you can challenge the truth of these thoughts, either in your mind or journal on them.

To successfully make the shift from negative to positive self-talk, the negative needs to be released. I like to use EFT tapping for this, you can find whatever tools work for you or whatever your practitioner offers. All of this happens before you can even think about putting in the positive. Without releasing the negative first, there's no solid foundation for your positive thoughts to exist upon. They'll be swallowed up and twisted by the negativity putting you firmly back at square one.

The mother wound has become so wrapped up in self-loathing that to turn it into self-love, or even neutral self-talk, isn't something that happens overnight. It's a practice in mindfulness and the first step is to start to observe your train of thought and listen to your inner monologue. What is your inner critic saying to you?

So you dropped the dinner on the floor and started telling yourself that you're useless – how quickly can you stop that thought in its tracks? When was the last time you challenged that thought to see if it was true? In challenging the thoughts, you can uncover the lack of truth within these spiralling negative thoughts. In asking your brain to assess the truth of the statements, you create a pause in the thought cycle where you can stop and choose whether you want to continue that train of thought, challenge it or actively replace it with something more positive. You have a moment there to decide whether you want to continue letting yourself 'believe' it or start telling yourself a different story.

Are you useless because you dropped dinner on the floor? Or are you stressed and trying to do fifty million things at once? Are you useless or are you too adrenalised and feeling jittery because you're stressed and hyped up from drinking too much coffee because you're tired? Are you useless or are you just needing to take a minute to breathe in your body and slow down your pace?

Are you useless or is it what society tells you that you are and you've come to believe it? And now, because it is who you know yourself to be, you need to sabotage yourself to maintain the narrative that yes, you are in fact, very much a useless human being who can't even take a dinner out of the oven without dropping it all over the floor.

You're not useless because you dropped the dinner. Society has made you think you are to keep you wounded and therefore controllable. So we choose to stop playing the game.

You wouldn't tell a child they were useless for dropping something. We'd say, 'Oops, butterfingers! Never mind, let's clean it up!'

Sometimes to change our self-talk, we need to start talking to and caring for ourselves like we would a child or our best friend. To take a moment to pause and challenge what we're thinking and ask ourselves, is this true? What is the evidence for this? Even if until now it has been true, do I choose for it to stay true or do I want to change it? Who says this is true about me? Who doesn't say this is true about me? What do those who love me unconditionally say is true about me?

Give yourself a little bit of that love for just a moment; you've more than earned it. At the moment when you stop the train of thought in your head, you may want to actively choose new positive thoughts to replace them. This is the conscious side of changing your negative self-talk and silencing the inner critic. The real success comes with a multi-pronged approach where you work on it both consciously and subconsciously.

Consciously you can use journaling, mindfulness, challenging your thoughts and replacing them with new positive ones. Subconsciously, it's time to use whatever tools you have access to, personally and with your practitioners. Release those negative thought patterns, work on your subconscious self-image and you'll find that the conscious work of interrupting the negative thought process is much easier to do. Connect to your inner goddess, the most powerful version of you – who is she? What does she say about herself? Use this vision of yourself to help you form a new narrative for your self-talk. Eventually, when you have completely rewritten how you see and feel about yourself, the inner critic falls away naturally because you know yourself to be a different person.

To love ourselves is to stop playing the game. We've been taught to loathe and destroy ourselves at every turn – so don't. Self-love isn't radical, it's something we all innately deserve yet deny ourselves to maintain the narrative of society. And that is exactly how the house that is the patriarchy wins the game. With us all divided and hating ourselves.

If we can transform the depths of our self-loathing into the deepest, most profound and unconditional self-love, suddenly we are outside of the game. Suddenly we are not playing by their rules. Suddenly we can tune into ourselves, trust ourselves and create our definitions of motherhood and life that work for us.

The quicker more of us can do this, the quicker the game falls apart. The quicker society has to transform to accommodate us. And it starts with self-love and self-acceptance.

This shift in how we talk to ourselves takes time; it's not something that happens overnight. Initially, neutral self-talk may be all you can manage and it may be fleeting, but at least it's not detrimental. To stop that thought process in its tracks, to stop yourself mid-thought and create a pause in the process is where we can start creating the change. In doing so we create space to release the negative because we are seeing it is not true and creating space for something positive to be reinforced there instead. Connect to the goddess within you, and call upon Lilith who helps us transform and unleash our authentic selves so you can start to see your true self. To be able to see yourself in a loving light takes time. Give yourself the gift of grace in the process.

It's time to see yourself for who you truly are, not what society has told you that you must be. The woman is the font of the creation of life; that in itself is a miraculous thing. To see ourselves as anything less than divinity for what we can create is more than a disservice to ourselves. It is an outrage. It is an injustice.

It is time to honour your ability to create – whether you choose to create life, a business, art or anything in between. You are a vessel that channels creativity energy. We have spent far too many years, lifetimes and generations dimming our light and yet, we are still here doing what we do with love in our hearts.

The divine feminine's capacity for compassion and love in the face of oppression goes some of the way to showing the true strength of our character. Embrace this. You are not broken, you have not failed, and you are not worth *less* for anything you do or don't do. Cultivate a sense of your inner goddess.

Sometimes you don't always see your inner divinity through your own eyes at first. More than a decade after seeing *Gorilla Camilla* in the mirror, I finally saw *her*, Camilla, the Goddess, reflected at me through my husband's eyes.

Although I've written plenty in this book about the patriarchy and the men who have twisted what it means to be a woman, this isn't the whole story. Some men don't fit the description and don't agree with or condone the narrative society has conjured for women to endure.

These are the gentle men. The men who embody more of their divine masculine, rather than wholly masculine energy.

The men who don't identify with being an 'alpha male' or try to desperately convince themselves that's what they are. The men who struggle to fit into a society that has told them who they are and that they're not allowed to feel anything other than anger all the time.

These are the men who are not afraid to cry at a movie or wear pink. They don't feel emasculated by their wife earning more than them. These are the men who accept you and love you entirely as you are. These are the men who are your energetic match, feel like one half of your soul, a twin flame, a sacred union. These are the men who innately understand what a sacred union is, even if they don't have the words to vocalise it.

These are the men who see your divinity and treat you with the sacredness and respect you deserve and reflect it to you. These are the men who even in the worst of your self-loathing, can see the divinity within you and treat you with the reverence you cannot give yourself.

My husband has always understood me and seen me on a soul level. We communicate in a way that rarely needs words. He can tell me more in a single glance than he can in a sentence.

Now, over the years of our dating and then marriage, he's looked at me plenty of times with love, admiration, happiness, lust, pride, concern, caring and so many other things in between. It wasn't until this year, however, that I was finally able to see the look that changed the way I saw myself forever.

It's not a look that says *I can't wait to get into your pants*. It's a look that says... you are the other half of my soul. You are the embodiment of divinity in human form. You are where I am safe. You are where I am whole. You are where I am held and seen. You are where I can be all of myself. You are completely perfect.

You are the one I've been searching for my entire life. You are home. You are the most incredible vision of beauty and intelligence to have ever walked this earth. You are the most magnificent shining light. You are the embodiment of love. You are perfection in a single soul. You are where I find the meaning of life. You are the greatest gift life has ever bestowed upon me.

It's a look that says... You are a walking goddess; can't *you* see it?

When we're in our state of self-loathing, we cannot see this look from another who holds our heart. We cannot look at ourselves in this way for it would be too exposing, too painful so instead we mask it with self-hate, self-harm and self-sabotage.

The moment you can look at yourself and know and feel those truths for yourself, whether that is through your own eyes or the eyes of another reflecting it back. The moment you can look at yourself and that's what you see, you are forever changed. You step outside of the game, outside of the paradigm that says women are worth *less* and you know yourself to be worth *more*.

You know yourself to be *utterly worthy*. There's a reverence with which you see and treat yourself that no one can take from you.

In acceptance of your divine worthiness, everything changes. The way you treat yourself changes. You are kinder to yourself, more forgiving and accepting of yourself. You stop judging yourself by external standards. You stop contrasting and comparing yourself. You stop feeling jealous, envious or competitive.

In knowing you are worthy, your standards rise. The treatment and behaviour that you will and won't accept changes. You become intolerant of being treated like dirt. You set standards for yourself because you know you are deserving and worthy.

You stop accepting poor treatment. You set boundaries for how people can interact and engage with you and can hold the line. You stop worrying about what anyone thinks because the only opinion that matters is your own. You build up your trust in yourself and belief in your internal authority to such a state that it becomes unshakeable. You become your internal compass, guiding and driving yourself forward.

You stop listening to the masses and start doing what feels aligned and good to you. You stop playing society's game and play by your own rules. You stop being able to be controlled and free yourself from the expectations and judgements of everyone else.

The way you stop destroying yourself is to love yourself and become utterly devoted to yourself. Let this extraordinary, unconditional love and the truth of your inner divinity into your heart into your body and your life. When you can do that, you can do nothing but honour yourself, your needs and your desires. In honouring yourself first and foremost, you have more capacity to love and be loving to those around you.

In aeroplane safety talks, they always tell you to put your oxygen mask on first before you try to help anyone else. Why? Because you can't help anyone else if you're unconscious or dead.

So give yourself the kiss of life. Breathe now, for yourself, for just one moment. And then breathe for yourself again, and again, and again. Breathe first for yourself from a space of love and then you can help everyone else. Help yourself first. Everything else will follow.

MOTHER KNOWS BEST

It's hard to know what came first; whether we became disconnected from our bodies and therefore lost touch with our intuition, or if we stopped listening to our intuition and therefore disconnected from our bodies.

As we have lost touch with ourselves, we lost trust in ourselves. It's become a perpetual cycle that we now obsessively seek validation and reassurance outside of ourselves because we can't access it from within.

Intuition is those hunches you get. That inner knowing. The gut instinct. That otherworldly knowing. The sixth sense that you get a flash of on occasion. Maybe you'll think about someone you haven't seen for years and then bump into them later that day. Or the phone rings and you know who is calling before you even reach the phone.

It's that feeling that something is wrong and you can't explain it, and then you find out that someone you love was in an accident at exactly the time you felt the knot in your stomach and your heart skipped a few beats.

Intuition is a highly feminine state of flow that we've been discouraged from tuning into because it's beyond logic and reason. It's something that cannot be controlled or sometimes even explained because when you trust it, it will guide you far outside of societal norms to bring you back to yourself.

Back to yourself is a place society would rather you didn't reach because then you're out of their game. You cannot be manipulated or controlled because you know yourself, you know your heart, you know your soul and what all your aspects want.

To come back to yourself is to come back to the primal, raw version of you that is untamed. The version of you that doesn't settle, doesn't accept everything you've been told blindly. Back to yourself is to come back to you who asks too many questions and makes men feel uncomfortable as you bring a lens up to their objectification, manipulation and oppression of women.

Mother knows best when it suits the patriarchy.

In ancient times when women were the wisdom keepers and governed themselves, they knew instinctively how to give birth with ease. Squatting in childbirth allows for the baby to come down the birth canal with the flow of gravity and in the natural direction. As men have taken over science, medicine and reason, this information has been disregarded in favour of putting women in stirrups to give birth. While it allows doctors a clearer view to assist and monitor the labour, it goes against women's instincts and doesn't support the natural flow of a baby *down* the birth canal.

Instead, we've been given options and allowed to make a 'birthing plan', giving us the illusion of authority and control over our bodies but it all exists within the parameters handed to us by men. Our decisions and options are handed back to us, filtered through patriarchal knowledge of what makes the process easy for the men who, I might add, don't have to push any living being from their bodies and so look at the entire process from an outside and alien perspective.

We've been conditioned to stop trusting ourselves and each other. This distrust has isolated us from our communities and support systems. What began as communities raising children together have become women struggling to survive alone while raising children.

We have the banner of the independent woman flown before us like this is something to aspire to, but it is only independence allowed on their terms. We can be strong, independent women as long as it doesn't offend or encroach on the patriarchy and we are taught to be *grateful* for the opportunity. That society is doing us a favour, a kindness even. *Why thank you ever so sir, for letting us be independent on your terms, it is such an honour. We're very grateful and glad to be so proudly independent!*

Deep down though, there's this gnawing feeling that something is wrong. Something is not quite right with this picture. We're hungry for something other than our false independence.

It creeps up on us and manifests as unhappiness, loneliness, anxiety, stress, and weariness at the world. We overeat because we're hungry for something that isn't food. We lash out at each other in spite and anger at how we've had the rug pulled from under us and turned against one another. We know deep down, it isn't meant to be like this. We don't know how to get back to what we lost when we're so angry, jealous, fearful, insecure and alone in the world.

What we're hungry for is our community, our trust and love for ourselves and each other. Not chocolate.

We've been conditioned to believe that to ask for help is a sign of weakness. We've been taught that to be weak and vulnerable is to become a target so we conform. We sew our mouths shut and hide our bleeding hearts as we smile sweetly that we're *totally fine and we've got it all under control.*

We haven't though, have we? Let's be truly honest. We're barely keeping it together under the weight of the world that we've been told we need to carry because it keeps us busy and quiet. Inside we're simmering with the rage of the generations of our ancestors who know the truth of our souls. And the truth is that we're meant to be together, we're *meant* to be connected, we're *meant* to support each other. We're *meant* to love each other, we're *meant* to raise each other up.

There are no prizes for struggling and doing it all alone. There's no one to cheer you on or celebrate with you at the finish line when you're proudly solo and independent.

Wars are not won; revolutions are not built on the shoulders of only one person like Atlas. It takes the many, it takes a team.

We have forgotten how to ask for and accept help. We've been taught to feel shame for needing and asking for help but truthfully who is keeping score? Honestly, no one cares. Everyone is too wrapped up in their own lives and problems to worry about yours and it'll stay that way if we keep all of it invisible.

In standing up and owning the fact that you can't do it alone and aren't meant to do it all alone, that you need help and are willing to be helped, you start to turn the tide.

It's in our inherent nature to want to help someone in need. It makes us feel good, gives us a sense of belonging and gets us out of our heads and away from our problems. Helping someone else gives us perspective on our own lives. But we can't help each other if no one says anything.

So get loud. Ask for help. Tell your friends you're having a tough time. Book a session with your practitioner. Give help when it feels good within your boundaries and doesn't cost you energy. Open yourself up to trust. Stop eyeing all your sisters with mistrust and start rebuilding your community and tribe. We are stronger together.

If you feel resistant to ask for and accept help, question yourself why and dig deep for the answer. There's usually some kind of secondary gain that we have to do or not do, even if intellectually we know it would benefit us, so what's yours?

When I thought about seeking professional help to heal my issues, there were a multitude of reasons that made me want to hide under a rock instead. I was certainly afraid of what lay underneath and what I might uncover if I went digging. I worried I was crazy, that other people would think I was crazy or that I was genuinely beyond help and too broken to be fixed. To go digging into my emotional baggage and to heal it felt like a somewhat selfish thing to even consider. Initially, I had this perception that it was a luxury I couldn't afford both monetarily and in terms of time spent in sessions and continuing to work with the subconscious tools I was learning outside of sessions.

Then there was the overwhelm of so many options and not knowing where to begin. While I've always been spiritual, there are so many modalities and holistic practitioners out there that I had no idea what might feel aligned for me. I felt sceptical that anything would work because I had tried things before – how was this time going to be any different?

This shift in being able to trust yourself and that others won't turn on you takes time. Trust is not instantaneous, it's built, it's earned.

Start small. Start listening to your gut feeling. If you're about to go out for a walk and you have a tiny niggle to wear a thicker coat, honour it. If you choose to go against the feeling and are then cold in your flimsy jacket, take a moment to acknowledge inward that your original instinct was correct.

Apologise to yourself for not listening rather than pretending you didn't hear yourself in the first place. In acknowledging that you did hear the nudge, ignored it and have since been proven right, you create a space for your intuition to try again. Your body is always listening to you, so acknowledging you heard it even if you didn't follow through is enough to show that you're at least listening and can start to lay foundations of trust within yourself.

If asking someone for help feels like too much of a stretch, ask the universe, source, spirit, god, angels or whatever you resonate with for help. This is how I started. Parking stresses me out so when I knew I'd be going somewhere busy and parking my car might be a challenge, before I left I'd ask the universe to find me a car parking space. Crucially I'd say thank you when I found it on my arrival. Expressing gratitude is important. Gratitude shows your acknowledgement of the solution being provided and reinforces the foundations of trust that you are building – that you can ask and will receive. Thanking the universe for what you receive creates a cycle of gratitude and receiving that grows exponentially. When you trust that you will receive what you ask for and are grateful for the outcome (even if it looks a little different from what you expected but is exactly what you needed), it opens up your intuition and receiving flow.

Over time I was more specific in what I asked for help with — I'd like to find a space further up the road or by the church. It was *always* there when I arrived. This slowly built up my trust in something outside of me looking out for me. It built my trust so I could ask for help with different things.

Here's the thing about asking for help — you need to trust and be open to receiving help in return. If you ask but don't trust your request will be fulfilled, then you won't receive the help you desire and you'll find yourself back in a space of martyrdom and resentment.

Trust is a two-way street, you need to give it, to get it in return. There's a surrender in trusting that you don't have all the answers and that something out there; a friend, a higher power, a relative, a group, god, the universe, source, spirit or angels can hold you in your not knowing and support you.

Although we are all individuals with our own lives, personalities, skills and experiences, no life story is unique. Our experiences are made up of common moments and landmarks that we share the world over. Getting married, for example, is highly individualised to us, however, the concept of a wedding is an event that happens across the world all day every day. It is our humanity that colours and individualises the experience for us. We're never truly alone in anything we experience because although we might feel like no one understands, so much of life is repeated patterns and experiences, coloured with the flavour of us as individuals.

To think that no one would ever have the skills, knowledge, experience or compassion to help you is arrogance. You **are** and **are not** that special all at once. You're special enough to be unique; there truly is no one else like you in the world. No one else exists who has lived the exact same life in exactly the same way. No one else exists that thinks exactly like you, has your exact same perspective on everything, has your personality, skills, and knowledge… no one but you. You *are* special.

And you're also *not* special. You are not some rare little flower that exists who cannot be helped in any way. You are not so special that you cannot be healed. You are not so special that no one can extend empathy or compassion towards you. You don't know everything; you haven't experienced everything there is to experience. You have gaps in your world, just like we all do. You have flaws and imperfections and the things you hate to do, are someone else's joy. That is what it means to be human. Allow yourself to admit and accept help when you need it. There are no prizes for trying to do it all alone. Engage with practitioners and get help on the journey.

I believe that if humanity's basic needs were entirely met the world over, and no one needed to worry about food or shelter; if everyone felt safe and clean, fed and watered well enough to spend time doing what they loved doing and exploring their interests, we'd find much like nature itself, that humanity can create a perfect balance for itself. Allow for that perfect balance. You don't have to have all the answers and do everything yourself. We're quite literally not designed that way.

When you can trust that someone else has an answer, resource or simply time to help you, you invite abundance into your life. Instead of sending out this vibe that says 'Leave me alone, I've got to do this all on my own,' in asking for help you're sending out a wave that says you trust in the power of the collective. You trust in something outside of yourself *as well as* within yourself to provide for you.

Not everything has to rest entirely on your shoulders, does it, Mother Atlas? You don't have the solutions to the world's problems and you know it, that's something you can own with ease. To be able to apply that to your own life, your problems, hold up your hands and say, 'I don't have the solutions, who can help me?' is to reclaim the power we've lost. Because of patriarchy, society has taught us that it is not how things are done. That to stand alone is to be a powerful, independent woman but all it does is lead to a bunch of tired martyrs who hate their lives. While that might suit society to keep you quiet and under control, it doesn't serve us in any way.

There is no shame in asking for and accepting help. It's a power move that the patriarchy won't see coming. They're too smug and too convinced that we're too deeply divided to come and work together. We won't be able to affect any real change because we spent too much time hating and being jealous of each other.

Do the work. Do it together and not in a vacuum. Heal your wounds and liberate yourself. Work with practitioners to fully release what doesn't serve you. Work on your subconscious mindset as well as the conscious to make the shifts in who you are in the world. Tune into your intuition, let it get really loud because we do know best. We know what's best for ourselves far more than a group of men who've never had to bleed every month or go through labour to birth a baby.

We do know what's best for us. When we're able to trust ourselves that we won't abandon ourselves or each other, we start to pool our resources, our experience, our love, our tenacity, our intelligence and our grit. We create abundance collectively so that when one of us wins, we all win. However, first, you need to learn that it's safe to ask for help. It's safe to be helped. It's safe to trust others. It's safe to trust yourself.

TETHYS

She dwells in the shadows
where no one dares to tread;
a discarded relic
trapped in her own personal hell.

Her name has been forgotten,
a story lost to the midst of time.
You'll find her place in history
through those she gave life.

Now her star is rising,
she is remembered once more.
As we embrace the wisdom and lessons
and write our stories in honour of her name.

THE INVISIBLE WOMAN

The triple goddess has been long established, well known in Greek mythology as Hecate and in pagan mythology as the maiden, mother and crone; they are life phases and wisdom we can embody.

As lifespans increased, there was a gap between mother and crone. A woman who no longer needs to tend to her children so constantly as they've grown up, yet she has not become the crone in her golden years. There's a stage long forgotten and hidden and her name is maga. She is the invisible woman.

Maga represents those women who have become menopausal yet are still sexually active, sexually empowered and lubricated despite the current narrative being one of a dried out, withered hag. She passes into this phase where she's lost her single function in society; to reproduce yet has not found her place in the world. She is overlooked — passed over for job promotions, discriminated against and sidelined until she becomes invisible. Men of this age become lauded as the 'silver fox' while the women struggle to hide their wrinkles and grey hair, trying to retain their youthful appearance to help them stay relevant. These women don't get a title like the silver fox. They are simply over the hill. Too old and out of their prime, but not old enough to have retired and become the crone. They are held in limbo, in this 'in between' state of being.

It is where the 'midlife crisis' kicks in. Having spent years with life on hold while raising children, suddenly those children have flown the nest and we're left standing in the ashes. Who are we when we are not being the mother? Can we reclaim what we lost, what we were forced to give up on becoming the mother? Does any of that old skin still fit anymore? How do we find a skin that fits us now?

I remember once reading about why wasps are so annoying. They spend the majority of the summer in worker mode, busily gathering food (protein) to feed the larvae in the hive. In return, the larvae create a sugary secretion that feeds the worker wasps. The worker wasps are like drug addicts, solely focused on feeding the larvae to get their sugar fix.

As the summer wears on, more larvae grow into adult wasps and the ratio of larvae and adult wasps shifts. Suddenly there are too many worker wasps and they're essentially out of a job. But they're still addicted to sugar. Enter the human with the fabulous smorgasbord of barbecues and summer picnics and the wasp has somewhere to go and get their fix, much to human annoyance. We wave them off, scream and run away as they buzz around us because we see them as pests, not furloughed addicts who've lost their place in the world.

Maga in the shadow is the wasp of the women's life phases. Society has no place for her, all doors are shut. Too old, not old enough. No wonder women get to this stage and question all of their life choices. If this is where it's led them and when they get to their supposed liberation and find there's nothing there waiting for them, who wouldn't question it all? This is where we often find women in the maga stage of life turning to addictions like alcohol and overeating to dull the pain of their dissatisfaction with life.

In the shadow, they spend time wallowing in regrets. It could be mooning over the one who got away, the things they didn't do, the life they could have lived had they just taken the leap. If maga in the shadow had a motto, it would be a bitter 'what if'. She lives life once more in hindsight, looking at those previous choices. This is where maga stands at her crossroads between her light and shadow aspects. It is her power to choose whether she laments what is lost or whether she can choose YES and go forth renewed. In the light maga reclaims the power of her inner storyteller and navigates the future as she sees fit, rather than let life 'happen' to her. For maga in the light, her motto becomes a curiously excited 'What's next?'

For maga, menopause is her rite of passage. Losing her ability to conceive children creates this void that she then questions how it can be filled. In a society that places a woman's ability to have children as her highest function and disregards any other form of birthing, labouring, mothering or nurturing. A woman in the maga phase of her life can be left feeling out of place. Not only this but she resides in a phase of silent suffering of the physical symptoms of the menopause which are understudied, misunderstood (if they are understood at all) and it becomes a taboo subject. Maga herself is so taboo she barely exists.

For many people reading this, the concept of maga may be familiar but the word itself may be new. Even if you are aware of the idea of the triple goddess and the feminine life stages, maga isn't widely discussed, let alone understood. In fact, she doesn't even have a clear goddess attached to her essence, unlike the maiden, mother and crone. Maga has always stood alone, outside of the pack but not anymore.

As I said back in the chapter *Four Phase Feminine Healing*, I took it upon myself to research this. Maga as a life stage deserved a face and a name. She needed an energy that we could understand as her starting point so we could become familiar with her, her energy and her role in our life, but let me tell you, this is not where she ends.

I mentioned earlier that I've found in my explorations and work with the divine feminine that goddesses often arrive in sets or pairs. This is due to how they often have built upon each other's work, modernised and expanded it. For me, my choice of Tethys to represent maga is to put her in as patient zero. My intention is that as you come to meet and work with her, you take her lessons and move them forward. To embody the divine feminine fully is to understand how we once again, embrace the free sharing of wisdom. How we learn from each other continuously. Nothing is ever finished or complete, there is always more to learn, more to do, and more we can be because of what we know and how we live.

Tethys, titan goddess of fresh water, encapsulates maga as she has been for the last few decades – where she has lost her place and story in the world. She has become the invisible, forgotten woman. Despite having birthed thousands of children, Tethys still did not feature prominently in any Greek mythology. There were no real stories that could be called her own. We saw the beginnings of this in Demeter, whose story is inextricably tied to her search for her daughter, the maiden Persephone. We see it now compounded with Tethys.

Tethys hasn't quite gained the notoriety or fear that is evoked by the crone, Hecate. Instead, she has become somewhat of a plain Jane. Not really offensive and mainly a background character in everyone else's lives. Her part of being a mother is mostly complete and no new role has been carved for her unless she is thrust into being the matriarch, an often overbearing figure that no one seems able to escape from the grip she holds.

That doesn't mean there's no wisdom to be found in maga. If the maiden embodies what it is to be carefree and at times irresponsible, and the mother represents the responsibility and sometimes weight of the world then maga strikes me as a blend of these two. She still holds some responsibility but can employ a more carefree attitude to the world. Jane Hardwicke Collings who wrote about maga in her book *The Four Phase Feminine Way* called this stage 'carefree responsibility'.

In exploring the healing wisdom that maga offers us as a life stage, I hope we can embrace the importance of maga. Remove the fear, smoke and mirrors that seem to surround her essence and return her wisdom. Maga is a rather joyful stage of new possibilities. It's an opportunity to re-examine your life and make new choices. A whole new chapter to write. Let's meet maga and hear her wisdom.

UNRAVELLING THE THREADS OF A LIFE NOT LIVED

Maga's wisdom starts with the ability to unravel her life and find herself again. This is the moment for the first time in years and decades that she chooses YES and she chooses *herself*. This hand might be forced upon her through her children growing up and the resulting empty nest shows her how unhappy she is. It could be in a divorce or relationship breakdown, family dynamics changing with older parents needing more care, burnout or exhaustion. Either way, it comes to a head somehow and maga has finally had enough.

She finds the world has transformed around her and it's up to her to decide how she deals with it. Whether she comes from a place of fear and desperately tries to pull her life back together, clinging to what she knows. Or whether she can embrace this new chapter and write herself a new story. Maga's response to this change of circumstances and the crossroads she finds herself at is the deciding factor on how or if she can move confidently forward. Does she say YES to herself? Otherwise, she'll find herself in limbo where she is stuck in a life she doesn't enjoy, living a form of indentured servitude to anyone who will accept her in their orbit. This is the ultimate rejection of herself and her wisdom. In saying YES to her wisdom, we accept and invite the light maga into our lives.

For maga has built up experience, skills and wisdom through the avenues of her life, alongside a maturity and detachment that neither the maiden nor mother possesses.

Society has turned the 'midlife crisis' into a joke to remove the power of the transformation that maga can access when she decides to finally move and choose for herself. The midlife crisis has been built up as something to be feared and avoided, lest it turns you into a has-been, try-hard or a desperate cougar that gets taken advantage of by men.

They've stripped maga of her power and told her that there's no grace or dignity in this phase. That when her world crumbles to dust, it has been entirely at her hand. Blame and responsibility are forced upon her; she is cast out as a pariah. Responsibility is weaponized against maga in the shadow as she is seen as the destroyer of the family unit, not a trailblazing seeker of her happiness. She is the one that makes others truly uncomfortable because in the loss of her life as she knows it and her willingness to embrace the power and wisdom of this new phase, she becomes a liability. A loose cannon that cannot be controlled.

However, responsibility is an important component of maga's wisdom that we can reclaim and bring into the light. By taking responsibility for herself and her happiness, she can create a new chapter in her life. It is the power of maga's ability to respond and create for herself instead of letting life happen to her and around her that shifts the notion that she is negatively responsible and always at fault, into one of maga's self-empowerment and personal choices to create the life she desires.

She reawakens the ancient woman; she calls forth a primal instinct, raw anger from the depths that sees the world for what it truly is. Maga takes her blinkers off and sees the world for what it is and how it has treated her and wants no part of it. This makes her the most dangerous because she has the time, energy and wits about her that the mother lacks because she's too tied up in childcare. She has the wisdom of her life experience that the maiden doesn't have and has much more energy and fight left in her, unlike the crone.

Maga can make waves. She is a serious threat to society, so the patriarchy has made her invisible. They've made her something to be avoided at all costs. An entire wellness, weight loss and beauty industry has been built upon the idea that you are successful and have more value if you are leaner. If there is less of you and you are closer to the maiden (both energetically and in body shape), we avoid maga and hark back to the maiden who doesn't have the power and wisdom. It's a state of being where you won't cause any hassle.

Much like Lilith, maga when she's embodying the light has been buried because she's too outspoken and too revolutionary. She's too much of a threat to the status quo of society to have ever seen the light of day before now.

But reaching the life stage of maga is to know she can be rebirthed. To become maga is to look back at your life only once and not with sorrow, but with curiosity. It is to look forward at one's life with the courage and curiosity to choose what you *really* want at your crossroads. It is to turn inwards, return to the deep centre of the heart and ask yourself, 'What do you *really* want?' and to wait for the answer that comes after all the obvious things. Wait for the answer that comes after you've rattled off the list of things you think you want but somehow still leave you unsatisfied because they are a list of the things you've been told you should want. Wait for the answer that comes after your list of socially acceptable things.

Wait for the answer that comes after a long silence and comes out as no more than a whisper. Wait for the answer that makes your bones ache and your heartbreak. Wait for the answer that makes you skip a beat and sweat from orifices you didn't know you had. Wait for the answer where your brain stalls and your tongue trips over the words. Wait for the answer that makes you wetter than you have ever been in your life. Wait for the answer that wants to make you scream until the universe shatters. Wait for the answer that makes you cry rivers and oceans into existence. Wait for the answer that splits you in two. Wait for the answer that makes you see divinity in colours.

Ask the question and wait for the real answer. The one you're afraid of. The one you can't unsee once you have seen it. The one you can't unknow once you know it. The one you can't unhear once you've heard it. Wait for the answer that speaks from your very soul of an ancient dream that you recognise the tune of but forgot the words long ago. Wait for *this* answer; it is the one you *actually* want.

Maga's reflective nature makes space for new wisdom. She is not afraid to sit in uncomfortable feelings and will do so for as long as it takes. She does not shy away from the pain but faces it head on. She knows life cannot go on like it has, she knows she is walking into unknown territory and therefore needs to be armed. Everything life has ever taught her is the fuel for her fire going forward. Maga transmutes her pain into wisdom and her passion into creation to manifest the next chapter of her life.

Women spend so much time before maga thinking of everyone else. The maiden is preoccupied with the world around her; fitting in, avoiding being judged and attracting a mate. The mother thinks of her children above all else, sometimes at the expense of everything and everyone around her. Maga has found her entire world crumbled and there is no one left to care for and no one left to care for her, except herself.

While there is so much fear in this stage of having to start over so 'late' in life, to me, maga brings a sense of liberation and freedom. To have the opportunity to think and choose for herself allows her to revel in being 'selfish'. She can finally indulge in herself and build a world and a life more aligned with her true values.

There is this joy in self-discovery to be found in her. To return to the hobbies, interests and expressions of your authentic self that have been lost under everyone's expectations and try them anew, as if trying them for the first time once again. Or to explore entirely new things to see if they fit your new skin. Maga is the chance to see and live life again through your own eyes, not anyone else's.

As I've peeled back the layers of my authentic self, everything I've ever done has once again come up under the microscope to decide whether it fits with who I am now. In terms of the clothes I wear, there were certain things like pinafores and dungarees that I loved in my youth and I'll happily wear them again now. And then there are other things like those 'delinquent' flared jeans that are not coming with the version of who I am now.

Being able to choose what comes with this new version of me and what I discard has created space for me to invite new things in. I remember spending time scrolling photos of outfits on Pinterest, pinning them to a board and then looking for common threads in what I had pinned. It is how I discovered my love of fedoras and bought one for the first time in my life a couple of years ago (and I now have a variety of colours!)

Similarly, with my hobbies and interests, there was a period of assessing the old for its continued merit and inviting in the new. I realised I still love roller skating, so I have bought some skates to practice indoors while I look for a suitable venue to skate at nearby. However, playing the piano accordion that I took up as a child is something I currently don't feel inclined to pick up again. It may or may not be forever and that's okay, I'm allowing it to be what it is.

On the other hand, a couple of years ago I tried paddle boarding and loved it. Even trying paddle boarding was huge for me because I've spent most of this life with a deep fear of water which activated after a near drowning incident as a child, and no doubt features in some other places and spaces in the history of my soul too. To try paddle boarding and *enjoy it* was revolutionary for me. It was a marker of how far I had come in my healing and how much I have rewritten the narrative of my life from one of fear to curiosity and choice. Now I can choose to go out on the water when I want to without being afraid and have fun in the process. This is the power of maga and her ability to choose for herself and rewrite her next chapter in life.

In the unravelling of the old like a skin that doesn't fit anymore, there's a softness that arrives. We see our bodies anew, scarred from the battlefield and instead of berating ourselves for not 'bouncing back' to our pre-baby bodies or wishing we'd spent more time at the gym in our youth, there's an acceptance that starts to seep in. Acceptance of the evidence of a life lived, yet with a knowing that you still have plenty more life to live on your terms.

The ultimate lesson here is to learn how much it costs us to stay in the place that drains us. How much does it cost you in time, energy and unhappiness, to stay stuck in your box or play small? We're taught to believe that we're tired all the time because life is busy. That we're drained because we're too stressed, don't eat well enough or don't get enough good sleep.

What if being so tired was because you are deeply unhappy or unsatisfied with your life? That the tiredness comes from the weight of carrying burdens that aren't yours. That the tiredness comes from the emotional trauma you carry that you haven't healed and let go. Maga's wisdom arrives in healing her wounded soul and letting go of the things that no longer serve her.

In doing so, she can truly see what the cost is to her happiness. How staying stuck playing a part in a story that wasn't ever truly hers to begin with, is like a black hole slowly draining her life force. The key for her is to allow the old to fall away. To not fear the change but to embrace it. To know that to remain fearful is for this to be as far as you go. Nothing changes if nothing changes. For the sake of your own ego's comfort in the familiar, how long are you willing to remain unhappy?

Our ego tries to keep us safe by keeping us in situations and playing out stories where it knows what happens. It doesn't judge whether they are good or bad, it doesn't care whether the story is toxic to our own happiness. The ego just wants to stay in the safety of the familiar. Maga's biggest question is what is most important... to stay with what she knows, even if it's detrimental, even if it costs her to stay. Or whether her own happiness is more important than whether she's scared of the change it will bring or not. The truth is, maga still has plenty of life left to live, too much in fact, for her to spend it deeply unsatisfied with life.

She can no longer remain silent and invisible. It is her time to embrace a strength she didn't know she had and set the tone for the rest of her story. Maga's wildness is her true strength.

LINES IN THE SAND

When you see the world for what it is, and people for who they truly are, there's no going back. Whichever life stage you are in, to tap into maga's wisdom is to be awakened. To see the truth you were blind to before.

There's an accompanying anger, grief and fear that comes with learning your truth because once you know it, you can't unknow it. You can't go back to a time when you didn't know, it's too late. Pandora's Box has been opened and you can't return the truth to the box.

To sit with the uncomfortable truths of the things that cannot be changed and accept them for what they are while bringing forward the wisdom of hindsight is maga's power. Maga in the light accepts that she didn't know then what she knows now. She knows that she can make new choices going forward, regardless of what happened in the past. She is unafraid to get uncomfortable exhuming and healing her wounds for she knows that while the transition may be difficult, it is only passing through.

Maga's power when she embraces her light is to heal her wounds at speed, rather than wallow in the pain of the past. She knows that to get to your happiness and carve out a life that is for you, sacrifices will need to be made and she is unafraid. In being willing to destroy everything and create her new life, she can make up for lost time and open herself up to new possibilities for the future. When she utilises the wisdom of her previous choices, actions and roads both travelled and not travelled, she embraces hindsight not as a device of sorrow but as a tool of wisdom, love and growth for her path going forward.

People who have previously benefited from your lack of boundaries and overly generous nature will hate you clawing it back and drawing a line in the sand. They'll be angry because your lack of boundaries doesn't benefit them anymore. You'll see they never really cared for you in the first place, only what you could do for them.

Embracing the wisdom of this phase and carving out something for yourself for the first time will mean you lose people who don't love and respect you. They may have loved what you did for them, but they didn't love *you*.

You are allowed to grieve the losses. Don't hold it in and pretend it doesn't hurt; it does. Grieve and let them go with as much love as you can muster. Know you are making space for the people who *do* love you. The ones who do will respect your boundaries and love you. They'll love you *because* of your boundaries. They'll see you starting to love yourself as much as they do.

Keep going when your world starts to crumble. It's not the end of your life. It's the end of feeling stuck, unhappy and living life on someone else's terms. It's the beginning of living life for yourself.

Boundaries manifest in all sorts of ways, whether it's what you're comfortable doing or helping with, how you want to spend your time and energy and with whom you spend it. Anyone who can't accept and respect your boundaries needs to be released from your orbit with love. It can feel hard, it can feel impossible, but you do have the choice to walk away from anyone. You may not *like* the choice, but it is always there. Initially, you may need help recognising the choices because society has programmed you not to see what doesn't serve the self-sacrificial narrative.

The most difficult ones to walk away from are family. We've been sold this cliché of 'blood is thicker than water' by Christianity to trap us into staying with our pack, our family unit, no matter the cost. It guilts us into staying in toxic situations, with toxic people who don't have our best interests at heart. Relatives may also be acting out of and repeating their own inherited toxic patterns from their ancestors in their relationship with you.

What's worse, the quote is not the original quote, it's been cannibalised to suit the Christian agenda. The original quote is in fact, 'the blood of the covenant is thicker than the water of the womb'. That is, the bonds we choose to form with friends, the sisterhood and brotherhood we create with people are stronger, more important and more potent than blood relations.

The original quote shows us that you do not need to feel guilty or obligated to keep people in your life just because you share some DNA. You are not obligated to stay or keep them in your orbit, especially once you start clearing DNA-inherited epigenetic patterns as I did with Emily. Go back far enough and we all share common ancestors anyway. Genetics is not what you need to hang your hat on. Instead, it's the bonds you form with others who truly love and accept you that matter most.

This is your permission slip to walk away. Walk away from anyone who makes you feel *less than*. Walk away from anyone who makes you feel shit. Walk away from anyone who drains you. Walk away from anyone who doesn't respect you and your boundaries. Walk away from anyone who makes you feel uncomfortable. Walk away from anyone who makes you feel unsafe or two feet tall.

Just walk away. Even if you don't have many people left to walk *with*, it's better for your own peace to release what makes you unhappy.

That's not to say it's forever. What you're saying is, that until they can honour who you are, they don't get a seat at your table. Some people may never come around. Other people will slingshot back into your life because they've learnt something about themselves, healed and can value you and love you fully now. Don't attach yourself to any probable or possible outcomes; it's out of your control. What you **can** control is who gets access to you. Focus on that.

This is about taking back your power and liberating yourself. Every interaction is a transaction. We spend so much time interacting with people in a diagonal — parent to child, child to parent.

This isn't just applicable to your blood family; anyone who doesn't respect you can push you into the position of the child or force you to parent them. To set boundaries is to pull them up on this and refuse to interact unless it's adult to adult. Not everyone likes it but what you gain as a result is more peace, more energy and more time to devote to yourself and the people who do love you.

Maga's power is in her discernment without judgment. Everything goes through the filter of how it makes her feel with priority and space given to what makes her good. She's fucking earned it.

Truthfully, we know what hurts us. We know where it hurts to stay, where we feel guilty, obligated and inextricably tied. We know when it costs us our peace and our sanity. Society has told us that this is what love looks like, that this is how we're meant to behave and how we're meant to be treated by the world, so we put up with it. Why should we settle within our own lives?

For every person in our lives, we have a soul contract with them. Some are more complex than others. Maybe they are a family member with lessons for both of you to play out, learn and heal over decades. Other times they are acquaintances or friends with a transitory role in our lives. Perhaps it was some karmic debt that needed to be played out, a lesson to be learned, a promise to be kept. It can span across lifetimes and millennia.

It's why when you start doing past life work; you sometimes see the faces of people you know, popping up time and again. Of course, they didn't have that same face in the past life – this is simply to show you it's the same energy, it's the same essence of that soul that you're working with once again. Sometimes we hold onto those contracts longer than is healthy for us because we need to navigate the past life contract powerfully this time. In navigating it differently and closing the contract, you can walk away empowered and let yourself be fully healed by the experience. Let yourself be free from those karmic and genetic contracts to move on and build something new for your life.

How do you know that the contract with someone is closing? You feel that sense of peace and relief. Whatever happened, whether it was a relationship that ended with a bang or one that faded away, you don't feel the need to go back. It's done, it's complete, it feels clean. You feel relief. You feel light. Mother Atlas has shrugged.

I knew my first relationship was truly over before it actually finished. My boyfriend had come from overseas to visit and we were saying goodbye at the end of his trip. We said our goodbyes and he boarded the train.

Normally, I would have waited for the train to leave and wave him off but something in me felt finished. I turned on my heels and walked to the car somehow knowing I'd never see him again. Our relationship limped on for a few more months before it ended in drama, but as I knew in my heart that day at the train station, we haven't seen each other in person since. Neither of us had visited each other since that moment I'd walked out of the train station with my head held high.

Sometimes people will turn up again months, even years later. That moment can serve as the final acknowledgement for you that it's over, like the time a friend from university checked in with me and I knew it was done. We'd been very close during the course but as time went on, I felt controlled and isolated.

The final straw for me was being told not to speak to some other people on our course and not be friends with them. Now I've never been one to be told what to do, I have my own mind. So upon hearing this, I was straightforward, 'I'll talk to whoever I want' and I walked out of the room. It was an instantaneous closure for me even if I couldn't name it as such at the time. Fortunately, this happened in the last weeks of the degree so I didn't have to interact with them much after that, although even if there'd been another year to go I suspect we wouldn't have interacted much, if at all because there simply was no need. The contract was closed.

After graduation, we didn't speak. I removed them from social media and genuinely didn't think about them again until several years later when they sent me a friend request online which I accepted. Nothing happened for a few weeks before I finally received a message. However the message was intended, the energy it arrived with made me feel like ick. I still didn't want to tell this person anything about my life. I knew that engaging with them would result in them trying to pull me back into their vortex of control. I didn't want that so I let the conversation drop and quietly removed them as a friend. It was finished for me, it didn't feel like there was any need to cover old ground and repeat patterns of the past.

When you know it's over; you don't think about them. If you happen to see them in person or a post of theirs online, it doesn't cause a reaction. If they're spreading lies about you or even arguing to your face, you will know that the contract is closed and you're done when you have nothing left to say to them. The real knowing is the moment that during an argument, when they're spewing hate and spreading disinformation you don't feel the need to say anything back. It's not worth your time or energy to correct them or prolong the interaction.

When you're truly done, you can walk away mid-sentence. When you can get on with your day without having skipped a beat. When they don't enter your thoughts and you don't spend time mulling over your last conversation for the things you wished you'd said. It's when you don't even feel the need to write them a final letter to set the record straight because **you** know the truth and that's enough. That is true power and freedom from attachments and toxicity. That is the moment when you've matured and transcended, when the lessons have been learnt and the wisdom of the contract and wisdom of maga has been integrated into your being.

Sometimes it happens in an instant and you can feel that contract energetically close. Other times it is done in layers of your own healing. When you know... *you know* and there's no going back.

And I feel it's important to say that the healing can be done without the other person being present. You don't need to have a final conversation with them to liberate yourself. You don't need the other person's presence for forgiveness, understanding or anything else. You *can* do it for yourself. The main motivation needs to be for yourself and not for anyone else's benefit. Because sometimes people do things that there's no coming back from, sometimes it's too broken or too toxic to salvage what's left.

There's this concept that perpetuates that we need to forgive everything. To be enlightened is to forgive everyone who has ever wronged you. It's important to highlight here that forgiveness is not acceptance. In forgiving a person we are not sanctioning their actions or behaviour. What we do when we choose to forgive is free ourselves from the power this person has over us. We can forgive the actions we may have unwittingly taken at the moment. When we choose forgiveness, we stop our wound from metaphorically bleeding. We stop carrying the wound and allowing it to affect us. That doesn't mean we've forgotten or pretend something didn't happen, it means we've learnt the lesson and will not allow it to continue hurting us.

Sometimes the lesson is learned in acknowledging what happened and the consequences instead of glossing over them. Other times it's about walking away or holding a boundary. It could be saying a prayer and sending them off with love. The healing of forgiveness for oneself can be in knowing it was awful and it hurt like hell and you're never going back that way again. The lesson is that you won't allow that to happen in future.

However you approach forgiveness, it's important that it feels right for you above all else. Never mind what the expectations are or what you have been told to do.

We find the path to our inner peace and happiness by carving it ourselves, not by following someone else's path. Trust your feelings, trust yourself, trust what you know. It never serves you wrong.

I've found in my own experience that you know when you've fully healed and integrated the wisdom on all levels when your instant reaction matches the one you would make if you were given time to think and carefully plan your response. When that gut feeling matches your intellectual thinking, that's when you know it's fully integrated and completely aligned.

The biggest tell for me is when it happens in the dream space too because dreams are when our unconscious is in control. To know you've integrated is when your subconscious and conscious thoughts and choices all line up.

Over the years, my first boyfriend has turned up sporadically in dreams and the next day I would always feel like ick. I didn't want him turning up in my dream space to start with but what was worse was always my reaction. In the dream, I'd talk to him like nothing had happened. Sometimes the dream would put us back in a relationship again and you know what I mean when I say I *really didn't want to go back there*.

In this journey over the last couple of years, I've done a lot of work around that relationship. For a while, an image of him would still occasionally conjure up and remind me all over again the next day why I wanted to heal.

The turning point was one morning, waking up from a dream. He'd appeared out of nowhere and had been telling me he missed me and wanted to get back together. My first reaction was… no. *No, I don't want to. No, I don't want you here. Leave me alone.* When that was my first reaction while dreaming, I woke up knowing that I was no longer connected to the pain because I'd begun to truly integrate the healing. It was a triumphant day for me. I was elated because it was a small yet significant marker on the road for me. It demonstrated that all layers of my conscious, subconscious and unconscious mind were all singing from the same hymn sheet. That the healing had permeated through to my very soul.

For me that demonstrates the power of maga that we can tap into. She is the master of letting go of anything that no longer serves you. Her intuition and discernment are so nuanced that nothing gets to be in her life unless it feels right for her.

After spending so many years not featuring in any stories other than as a side character, this is maga's opportunity to clear the deck of the narcissists and toxicity. It's her opportunity to make room for herself, to make room for love, for joy, for the new. This has been maga's most transformative lesson for me. Let her wisdom now guide you towards making the choice that is most powerful for you too.

THE VISIBLE WOMAN

To become maga is to take the hand that life has dealt you over the years, all of the experiences, choices, regrets, and lessons and not become bitter and twisted. This is after all, what society **expects** us to do. We're expected that once we're past our prime and beyond our function, we turn into the wizened old hag. The one that lives in the woods and frightens children. That she has become bitter, soured by the cruelty of the world and reflects it back to us.

We're taught to fear her, that nothing good resides in her. That there's no value in her and she should be discarded.

Tethys, the goddess I chose that embodies the spirit of maga, represents what she was, nothing special, no one of note, nothing to write home about. *The invisible woman*. This is where her story began but it's not where it ends. What happens next is we take forward her lessons; we embrace her wisdom and juiciness. We let her be loud and proud and take up space in the world.

It is our turn to write the stories that Tethys never did. In writing our own stories, we embellish her mythology, we create our own legends. The tales of the women who would not fade away. The stories of the women who wouldn't be quiet. The women who wouldn't accept the world as it was or what had been decided for them by others. The women who lead themselves.

The most compelling lesson we can glean from maga isn't a lesson she has taught. It's the one we learn from the *absence* of her. We know the maiden, the mother, the crone. No one knows who maga is, so make them listen. Make them know her, through you.

The concept of the triple goddess was, in my opinion, always missing something. Truthfully, there was no space for a fourth stage due to human life spans. However, even as we started living longer, society shelved the concept of a fourth stage and perpetuated the triple goddess because maga was an inconvenient truth.

She's inconvenient to the world because they see her as destructive. Lilith is another goddess who is also inextricably tied into the concept of maga for she wouldn't accept the role she was asked to play. She was neither naive nor duty-bound. She set off, out of the Garden of Eden on her own adventure and carved out something new for herself. She demands to be heard, to be seen. She demands a seat at the table and the time has come for us to listen to her because she has much to say.

To embody the energy and wisdom of maga is not to become angry and rebellious in the traditional sense. This isn't about angry disruption; it's about quiet self-assurance. It's a confidence that comes through when you know your worth; you know your inherent value and will accept nothing less.

Society has taught us women are worth *less*. Maga brings us the lesson, not that she is worth *more* or worth *more than*, but *worthy*. With no comparison, justification or validation. By simply breathing, by *existing*, she is worthy and she lives in all of us.

To fully integrate her wisdom and healing is to see your worth and the worth of your fellow sisters. It's to know there's no need for competition. Instead, there's a need for collaboration. It's knowing your strengths and weaknesses and allowing other people to fill in those gaps.

We are the community we didn't believe we needed. We are the ones who hold each other when the world crumbles and offer a hand to help you stand up. We are the ones who are not afraid, who will not let the stories the world has told us or told about us, define who we are. We are the ones who do not let the past or our conditioning, hold us back.

We are the ones who can honour the truth of our souls and share that wisdom freely. That's the epitome of maga's healing wisdom. To not be afraid of each other, to learn that we can let down our guard and that there's nothing to fear from each other. We are all people doing our best at any given moment. And we're wise enough to know that we could do even better if we allowed ourselves to help each other and be helped.

The world continues to turn as it does because it suits the ones who made it. And it will continue to do so for as long as we play out the story they gave us. History has long been written for us but they missed one vital piece of information; how persistent and determined we are. Maga is where we make our choice – do we stand up for ourselves and our truth or continue to play small? Do we fight for our happiness and carve out the life we deserve to live or continue to keep others happy and comfortable?

Truthfully, most men don't know what to do with women who have unleashed themselves and embraced maga or Lilith's power. Lilith left the Garden of Eden after she refused to be subservient to Adam. The unawakened men don't know what to do with women like that because the wisdom of her isn't in their bones and blood. They recognise her as Adam once saw her and then they pull up short because they don't know what comes next. This makes them uncomfortable, hence why they're so preoccupied with cutting us off from this power. In keeping control, they know what happens with that version of the story.

Although throughout our history and ingrained on a cellular level, we may not have a solid template for what it *does* look like, the difference between the unawakened man and the man embodying his divine masculine is the fact that although we don't have a clear template to follow, it doesn't frighten the divine masculine. It doesn't challenge him in a way that makes him want to control or suppress the divine feminine. Instead, it challenges him in a way that makes him want to rise up to meet her in divine union, writing the new template together.

Maga has been quietly rising for a while. Everywhere I go; more and more people are awakening to her and her wisdom. More and more people are sharing the lessons she has taught them and helping others embrace it for themselves.

This is how we start the change and gather pace. For every unafraid woman, who can break out of her persecution complex and stand tall in her truth, those in her orbit will feel the impact. You cannot help but notice these women who have already embraced her; they shine out like beacons of light. Take heart from those who have gone before you that it's possible to break free of everything holding you back, no matter how painful or frightening it may seem. They are your evidence that it's possible.

Embrace the wisdom they share and then turn inwards and find truths of your own. Share them with your family, friends and community, whoever will listen. The more people that come to know maga, the more visible she becomes and the more her message of persistence and strength will shine through. Allow yourself to shine, take the pen and write your name in history. It's what maga and Tethys would wish for us all.

HECATE

Feared and revered,
moving within the duality of life and death.

With wisdom of the ages,
awaiting your imminent arrival.

Guardian of the crossroads, she will
reveal the ministry of your feminine magic.

She will walk you gently
where your heart fears to tread.

REGENERATING THE CRONE

We come to the final feminine stage; the crone, the most feared by far. To have reached the crone is not what it once was, a revered position of wisdom and power. Instead, society has turned her into an unwelcome hag. She has soured even more than maga to become narrow-minded and stubbornly set in her ways.

Her heart is closed off by life and her experiences, she has been isolated from the world and eyed with suspicion and fear. She is seen as decrepit, retired and past it, of no use or value having served her usage long ago. She has nothing to offer us and no warmth resides within her, it has been consumed by hatred, fear and bitterness.

Or so we've been told.

We've been conditioned to go to extreme measures to retain our youth and avoid becoming the crone, the disgusting, demonic hag that society despises. She's the weird, creepy, old woman who lives alone in the woods creating potions and casting spells. Witchery has been absorbed into this image of the hag to reinforce the message; *stay away from her.* Do whatever you can to avoid becoming her.

In our avoidance, we spend fortunes on diets and beauty products to keep us youthful, thin and beautiful. Plump, vibrant and juicy like the maiden. Fertile and abundant as the mother. We inject chemicals into our skin to smooth out the wrinkles, to erase the evidence of the life we've lived. We'll do anything to avoid her because we've been conditioned to believe that to become her is bad.

She's here to show us her truth. She is here to show us she is ancient but not decrepit. She holds a wisdom of the world that in our youth we couldn't comprehend. In ancient times, to become the crone was to be elevated to the highest position within the community. She was the wise woman, the elder, the way shower. The medicine woman, the oracle, the high priestess, the matriarch, the seer. She had been there and back again a thousand times, now ready to guide **you** on your path.

To be the crone was not just to be revered; it was to hold everyone in reverence. It was having the openness to feel and the detachment to not be wounded. It was to revel in peace and joy, to radiate love wherever you went. To be the crone was to be someone exuding adoration and receiving it from everyone in return.

The crone was the highest honour, evidence that you had survived. Living in ancient times was far more perilous than it is now, so to reach such an age and status having not succumbed to disease or not having been broken down by pain and fear was a great achievement.

When she is embraced and embodied, becoming the crone is a loving experience full of grace, wonder and acceptance. She has walked in duality; she has tasted both life and death and fears neither. We have nothing to fear from her. Instead, we have an opportunity to embrace her, her wisdom and her life experience. If we take the time to listen to her, she has much to share with us; otherwise, her knowledge will be lost to the ages. In receiving her wisdom, we can embody it. In embodying it, we can understand the need to preserve it. In understanding the need to preserve it, we can share it with others. In sharing it with others, we can shift the paradigms of women's narrative and wisdom in society.

Hecate is the Greek goddess of witchcraft, magic, the moon, the night, doorways and death. She held power over heaven, earth and sea and was known to bestow wealth and blessings. Her three faces allowed her to preside as the goddess of boundaries and crossroads. In later representations she embodied the triple goddess entirely; maiden, mother and crone. As a singular deity though, she most closely links with the crone.

Her story is wrapped up in that of Persephone and Demeter, for she heard Persephone's cries when she was abducted and assisted her mother Demeter in the search. After the compromise is struck for how Persephone will spend the year, Hecate chooses to become her minister and companion for the time Persephone spends in the underworld each year. The phases of the feminine come full circle when the crone can embrace and guide the maiden in this way. It is a reminder once again for us that this journey is not meant to be undertaken alone. That it is so much easier when we lean on others and more is achieved quicker when we work together. Hecate choosing to be Persephone's guide is our reminder and call to action to seek out help for ourselves and engage with those practitioners who can act as the midwives for our healing journeys, as we are healed and reborn anew.

Hecate's name means 'worker from afar' which encompasses the true identity of the crone. Having lived her life, she is now detached and carefree (responsibly carefree as described by Jane Hardwicke Collings). The crone in the light has lost the density that the other feminine phases carry within them. She moves through the world with a lightness, having shed the density of burdens and responsibilities. This is such a stark contrast from the symbolism of the goddess Hecate herself who is often portrayed as dark and fearsome. However, this truth of Hecate in the light is a demonstration of her duality – her ability to tread in both the light and the dark with ease.

Her ability to transcend both light and dark stems from her parentage. A child of Titans Perses and Asteria, she moves freely between the physical and underworld and shifts between being a titan and a goddess within her mythology. She retained her control and influence against Zeus and was also known as a protective goddess of the home and household.

Often depicted with hell-like hounds and winged creatures, she was a fearsome yet beloved figure who guided and supported pretty much everyone. I think the gist of what I'm saying is; she held extraordinary and incredible powers and was basically a really badass bitch. Who *wouldn't* want to embrace being as cool as her?

And yet, Hecate is also tied up in witchcraft and magic, things we've been told not to touch unless they're associated with the bright orange, purple and green commercial holiday of Halloween. That's fine because it's goodhearted fun and lines the pockets of the fat cats in charge. *Then*, it's okay. Except we know it's not.

The only way we regenerate and reclaim the crone's rightful place as a revered and honoured figure in society is to become her. To let go of our fears and embrace her and her wisdom. We are not the Sanderson sisters from Hocus Pocus, trying to regain our youth. And although we do not eat children, our incessant quest to retain our youthful looks makes us no better than those witches depicted in Hocus Pocus. It's a thirst to regain being the maiden, mother and maga that we will never quench. In accepting that those phases of life are over, in healing the wounds of those phases and bringing forth their wisdom, we realise we're in a whole new phase. This allows for joy and wisdom to settle into our being.

Society has taught us there is no joy in the crone and so we believe it... that way we never seek the truth for ourselves. If you only believe what you're told, of course you'll never discover the truth for yourself. The crone embraces this self-rediscovery and learns to see through her own eyes to that which she was blind before. She sees with a wisdom beyond her physical eyes, she sees through the wisdom of the heart.

Invite her in, settle down with a cup of tea by the fire and listen with your heart. She has much to share, regardless of your age or life phase, which you can apply to your life right now.

A LESSON IN LOVE

When you can look at what you fear most through the lens of love, you are free. The crone knows this. She holds in her heart compassion for all things, even those that would hurt her for she knows they are but a reflection of the parts of herself.

To embrace the crone is to come home to yourself in love. It is the ultimate paradox. As the body degrades through time, you need to learn to love her more, not less. Love the body that has carried you through existence. Cherish the body that has gifted you the experience of humanity.

Honour the body that is the vessel for your soul, coming together once more through the aeons to allow you to walk the earth. She gives us the briefest of moments, no more than a drop of ocean in the grand scheme of the universe. For that one moment, that lifetime is your entire world.

It is when we finally face our fear instead of running from it, that we can find love in the darkest and smallest of places. It is then that we will see our infinite nature and transcend the bounds of this singular life and come home to our true nature. It is then that we can embrace both our humanity and divinity in one breath.

The crone understands that no matter what we do time will continue to pass. It matters not what we do, nothing will change the flow of it. You cannot stop time any more than you can stop a river with your hands. If you allow yourself to be taken with the current, you will stop struggling and be able to enjoy the ride.

Life itself is a challenge for many. In embracing this transitory nature of things, we find that everything passes. Bad times, darkness, it all passes. The night always gives way to the dawn. Remember that our lives and our worlds are like individual planets and no two planets experience life the same way. Venus takes 243 days to rotate once on its axis meaning that its night lasts a little over 120 Earth days. That doesn't mean the sun will never rise on Venus again, it simply means, compared to Earth, it's going to take much longer. Whatever planet you're on, however long it takes, know that daylight is coming and this too shall pass.

As with everything, the crone embraces the duality. She knows that as day comes, so does night. Nothing stays still. The crone's power comes in embracing the transition, facing her uncomfortable fears and knowing that this feeling is not forever. Life is not forever.

Her lesson in love is to teach us to be able to accept this movement and duality and love the whole experience regardless. To take great joy in the happy moments and to feel sorrow deep within her bones in the sad ones. To send all of the moments of her life swathes of love for all of them have brought her here to this moment. There is no need for regret because without life, she wouldn't be who she is today.

She extends love to the people that society makes them think they deserve it the least. She holds out her hand to fear and pulls it into a loving embrace to thank it for its presence. *Thank you fear for the growth.* She evolves deeper and deeper into a being of love. She sends love to those who wished her dead, who burnt her at the stake and called her names. She knows they acted out of fear and her power is to respond not with fear but with love.

Love is not a condition of humanity, it is where we infuse and transmute our humanity into love.

The Greek word meraki is often described as untranslatable. The idea of it is that you do something and pour your heart and soul into it. To make something with meraki is not to make it intellectually; it is to make it with love. Meraki originates from the Turkish word 'Merak' meaning labour of love or to do something with pleasure.

The word originally was used within cooking and baking. You would describe your yiayia (Greek for grandmother) as having baked the cookies with meraki. She poured everything into those cookies and they tasted like magic.

And one day when she finally gives you the recipe, you go home and try baking those cookies just like grandma made them. Only they never taste quite right. Your cookies don't taste as good as grandma's did because what you tasted in her cookies was meraki. It was *her* love and her devotion that made those cookies special. You know that now. The extra special ingredient was… *her*. This approach of doing everything with meraki is how the crone approaches life.

My maternal nan was one of the happiest people I have ever known. She spent most of her time smiling, laughing and telling outrageous stories of growing up with eight sisters. She had been humming the same piece of song for so long that no one was sure what the original song was anymore. When she hugged you, she hugged you so tight that you thought your head might pop off.

Her special talent was cooking. Her food was legendary. I'll never forget one Shrove Tuesday when she was making us pancakes. My grandad and I, sitting on opposite ends of the table, were having a competition of who could eat the most pancakes. I was *not* winning. There was no way I was going to manage to catch up to Grandad who had already eaten ten thick dinner plate-sized pancakes.

What I remember most from that night, aside from the scent of sugar and lemons mixed with the coal burning in the fire and the humidity hitting you like a wall when you entered the kitchen, was my nan. She kept popping her head out of the kitchen to where we sat at the table saying 'Who wants another one?' in her sing-song voice. She'd slide it onto a plate and then proudly say, 'Guess how many eggs I've put in there?' I can't remember the number but it was a ridiculous amount that on any normal day, and cooked by any other person, would have created a batch of the most rubbery, awful, inedible pancakes the world had ever seen.

That night, however, they were the most delicious pancakes in the entire world and I've never had pancakes like them since. Because it wasn't about the recipe at all, it was about *her*. She was in her element. Full of light, bouncing around the kitchen. A real feeder, she was more than happy to enable our eating competition because it was how she showed us, and how we showed her, love.

I can see now that food was her love language. I was too young to know what I'd seen at the time. When I think of my nan now, I know that night of ten pancakes was her greatest demonstration of love for us. They may have been made with fifteen eggs and not much else, but they were made with meraki and that is the greatest lesson we can learn from her.

Food is a way the crone demonstrates unconditional love to us in childhood. As we become the maiden, food is turned into a vehicle of control. The association of food and love is inverted to food and hate. We hate food, we hate our bodies. Our relationship with both can become disordered in a bid to control us and keep us small. In there being less of us, our power is diminished. It is in the reclaiming of the association of food and love that we can embrace the crone's wisdom of unconditional love and reject the fear narrative that society has conditioned us to believe in.

It doesn't matter what recipe you use, whether you stick to it or whether it goes horribly wrong and makes a mess. When it comes from a place of love, intention always carries you where you want to go. You will never go awry; you will never lose your sense of self or where you belong when you act from the wisdom inside your heart.

And that's the thing about love, it happens in a moment. It can be so fleeting that at the time we don't even notice it until much later. When you finally see it, you see that it was always there if only you'd opened your eyes to it.

Choose love, it is our greatest teacher and our greatest healer.

A LESSON IN JOY

From love comes joy. Infuse everything with it and drink it like tea. If love is the energy that sustains and centres you, joy is what elevates you. It is the icing on the cake with the cherry on top.

Society has ingrained in us this idea that fear, pain and suffering are our default positions. In the movie *The Matrix*, Agent Smith explains how the matrix originally failed because it was programmed to be too perfect and humans didn't believe it was real. Instead, they programmed a more 'realistic' version of the matrix by which suffering defined us and humanity broadly accepted it, because that's what we've been told is the definition of humanity.

The Bible taught us that we were sinful and we've tortured ourselves ever since. This is how we've been kept under control because we didn't need to be *actively* controlled. We didn't need a demonstration of dictatorship or martial law to keep us in check. We have regulated ourselves within our suffering. No further action is needed. We've perpetuated the pain for ourselves, free of charge because that's what we've been taught that we deserve. The patriarchy has become more passive than it has been in previous generations because we now self-regulate and control ourselves. They've taught us the rules and roles we're meant to play in society and we keep ourselves and our sisters largely in check without much further input from the patriarchy.

The crone knows this isn't true; it's what makes her dangerous. She knows how to enjoy both the simple pleasures and great things in life. She knows her own heart; she knows where the joy dwells. She's carved out a pocket for her joy within her heartspace that cannot be taken away and it is this that the world hates.

When we come back to love and when we remember that we are joyful... we are meant to sing songs to commemorate the passing of seasons and dance around the campfire. When we remember we're meant to sit in circles and laugh as we hold hands and share stories. When we remember those things we step out of the matrix and cannot be controlled or kept quiet.

Our joy is magnanimous and contagious. It radiates off your energy like the sun. A woman who has embraced her joy steps out of the confines and rules of normal society and creates her own extraordinary life. There is no judgement in joy. It is as individually felt as any of our emotions. Let joy permeate your world, bringing life and colour back into it.

The crone is beyond the duties that this world has asked of her. Her time is free, her time is her own to do as she pleases and she revels in this. The crone who has taken joy into her heartspace and invited it to saturate her life, creates lightness and breathes new life into a world that she was told can only be shades of beige.

These joyful women are the ones who dare to go skydiving in their seventies. The ones who become fashion icons in their eighties. The ones who learn hip-hop dancing in their nineties. These are the women who say, *I'm not dead yet* and embrace living. These are the women who know you are never too old to do the things you want to do or try something new.

When I was at college I took up Spanish. Our teacher was in her maga phase of life and was truly embracing it. One day while we were having practice conversations in class, someone asked the person next to them what they had done at the weekend. They thought for a moment and responded, in Spanish, that they'd wanted to go to the cinema but had no one to go with, so had gone to the park with friends instead.

Our teacher stopped everyone at this. She told us how there was nothing wrong with going to the cinema alone and that she did it all the time. She told us how she loved movies and watched as many as she could, especially foreign ones with subtitles.

Everyone scoffed saying it was sad to go on your own. What I saw was a woman who was unafraid to be alone. A woman who knew herself and knew what she wanted and didn't care if anyone came along for the ride or not. A woman who was comfortable in her skin didn't need anyone else's validation and was happy with her choice. I saw someone who wouldn't let the world tell her what to do. She was a woman who wanted to go to the cinema to see a film and she was damn well going to go see it regardless. She didn't need anyone to hold her popcorn, she had it covered.

This moment came back to me years later when I had a similar choice to make.

I have always loved *The Snowman* by Raymond Briggs. It's been a tradition for as long as I can remember that my mum and I watch the TV animation together. We always find time to watch it. Even during the lockdown due to COVID-19, I found out when it was showing on Channel 4, I rang her to tell her it was on and we still watched it together over the phone. It simply isn't Christmas until we've seen it.

Then a few years back I found out they'd turned it into a stage show and it was on in London. I couldn't wait to tell my mum about it. As soon as I said it, she asked if I wanted to go and without skipping a beat I said YES. It was one of those full-body yes moments. The kind where you're too excited to think about all the reasons why you shouldn't but you just go for it. We bought tickets, booked a train and counted down the days.

We arrived in London late morning and had lunch before navigating our way through the underground to the theatre. We were full of smiles and so excited. We didn't notice anything was different until we walked into the theatre itself to find our seats. My mum whispered to me, 'There's hardly any adults'. I looked around. She was right.

Every single adult in the room seemed to have at least one child with them.

Oh.

Oh.

Oh dear.

This is for *kids*.

There had been no indication anywhere that this was aimed at children. I suppose it being the stage show of *The Snowman* should have been giveaway enough. We'd been blinded in our excitement. I scanned the room again. Nope. There was no one I could see that looked like they were solo adults or groups of adults with no children.

My heart sank a little, I felt foolish and out of place.

My mum suddenly broke into a smile. 'That's alright!' she said linking arms with me, 'you're my little big girl!' Instantly we broke into fits of laughter. It was fine. Who cared? We found our seats amongst the children dressed as snowmen and reindeer and all kinds of Christmas-y creatures and had a wonderful time watching the show. It was magical.

In that moment of realising we were out of place, we could have let shame and fear take over and high-tailed it out of there. Thanks to my mum's excitement to be there and determination to see the show that we'd paid for and were absolutely going to love, we stayed and thoroughly enjoyed it.

We kept joy in our hearts at that moment. My inner child was enraptured with the show. I know it was because my whole chest felt warm aglow for the rest of the day. Not only was it a wonderful, joyful show that brought out my Christmas cheer, but I was proud of myself too. Proud of myself for not chickening out and hiding away. Proud of myself for allowing my heart and my joy to be the guide.

My mum continues to call me her 'little big girl' to this day on occasion and every time she does, I smile to myself and remember the day it ensured we got to see *The Snowman* live on stage.

Remembering that sense of joy and silliness and not caring what anyone thinks has opened up my life in so many ways since that day. Most of all it brought me home to myself.

It is in shedding all the weight of other people's judgements and letting go of the need to be validated by society that we find our true north. We realise that our love, our joy and our heart is the only compass we need in life. That the way to build the life we desire is not intellectually, but emotionally. Joy is where the magic happens when you give it space in your life to exist.

The lesson is simple. Follow your joy. No matter how crazy it looks on the outside. If it lights you up, follow it to the ends of the earth. That joyful state of being is our true default positioning. It's okay that you've forgotten it, truthfully we all have. What matters is that you remember it and cultivate it. Allow it to permeate every inch of your being. To live in love and joy is the freedom we seek.

Joy teaches us what it feels like to be in flow and to feel aligned. In asking yourself what feels like a YES, or as I asked myself with the sheltie annual, 'Where is the joy for me today?' We tune into our desires and align ourselves with the frequency of abundance and with greater clarity each time. Joy is the driver for an abundant, flowing and aligned life.

A LESSON IN POWER

We make everything mean far too much. We have been taught to become so wrapped up in our egos that we are blind to everything else. We're obsessed with ourselves and with power and what it means for how we operate in the world. Even women, who've been made to believe they're worth *less* in society, still obsess over power. We clutch at the illusion that we have it, that we somehow have control when in reality, we handed the reins over long ago without really noticing. It's just the way the world is, or so we've been told.

The crone dissolves her egoic self. She is so centred and grounded in her soul self and her truth that nothing causes her to waver. This is when her power and influence become unshakable, because she generates it from within herself, from her soul self and from her heartspace rather than from outside of herself. When we move from this soul self space, we step outside of society and cannot be controlled or told what to do. We return our power to ourselves and operate on our own terms, with our own rules.

We become dangerous. The liability that society has taught us to be afraid of. Loose cannons. Wild, untamed women. Heretics. Hysterical. Insane. Mad. All words intended to induce fear and subdue us, diminish and reduce us to the quiet little good girls that do as we are told. We're safer that way, not for ourselves but for society. When we're good and quiet and controlled, we don't ask the hard questions. We don't make people uncomfortable. We don't make them question their truths and see the bigger picture.

We've become wrapped up in our egos. Seduced by the need to be youthful, beautiful and superficial. You can't cause trouble when you're shallow.

The world has chosen our fates for us and put us in a state of constant adrenalisation. We cling to the illusion that we have a modicum of control – that our ability to be sexy, seduce men and get them to do our bidding is to be in control. It is false control, tiny movements within a patriarchal world that we pretend is freedom. We have been in cages all along.

To go deep into your heartspace is to sit with the uncomfortable truths. To see that in sanctioning society's rules and playing the game, we perpetuate the narrative. We will never escape while we listen to someone outside of ourselves.

The deepest truth you could ever know, the one that will truly create peace in your heart, is the truth that comes from within. It's not the surface answer, the things you think you *should* think, feel, do, say, be. It's not the things society has told you to want. It's the quiet space underneath that whispers your soul's truth if you are willing to face it.

In facing it, you then come up against the fear of going against what you've been conditioned to believe and do. Your soul self operates outside of society's rules and won't fit into the neat boxes that you've been told to squeeze yourself into. Your soul self doesn't know labels, it doesn't understand time or distance. Your soul only knows the here and now and all of time. Your soul only knows what feels good and what doesn't. Your soul only knows what is true for you and what is not. Your soul only knows what brings peace to yourself in the present moment.

To follow this truth is to break out of everything you've been told you can be and everything you've been told is acceptable. It will bring up fear of persecution, fear of being seen, fear of abandonment and that's just scratching the surface. In aligning with your soul truths, you will face everything you've ever feared. In doing so and coming out the other side, there is peace. There is a sense of contentment and wholeness that comes when you live your truth which means you can't go back. You can't go back to fitting in, being told what to do by anyone else. The answers, forevermore, will come from within you; you know that now.

And while initially it may seem like a path you walk alone, it isn't. Every path is carved individually, yes. What you find as you cut your way through the dense forest, away from civilization and away from everything you thought you knew, is that you find there are more souls to your left and right also carving their own paths. You carve separately yet simultaneously, walking towards each soul truth as a united front.

You need to choose to take your power for yourself. To walk the path, you need to remember that your power is yours and you gave it away in what you sanctioned. You continue to give it away in what you sanction from this moment onwards. In not trusting yourself, you allow others to choose for you. In sanctioning other people's opinions and authority over us, you abdicate your power and ability to choose for yourself. This creates a cycle of feeling guilty when we follow our desires, or guilt for even having our own desires outside the narrative other people have decided for us.

In becoming more aligned with yourself and your intuition, it's important to check in with yourself. Are you sanctioning someone's opinion or society's default narrative and allowing it to have a hold over you, your choices and the actions you take? If you are, you can take steps to do whatever you need to consciously and subconsciously release your sanction of their authority over you, leaving you once again, free to choose for yourself going forward.

When I was fifteen and studying for my GCSE's we would periodically do mock exams which are used to predict our final grades. During this time we had a parent's evening where parents were invited to meet with teachers to discuss both performance in class and predicted grades. My mum asked me to go with her. I refused, saying I felt the teachers would be more truthful if I wasn't present, so she went alone.

I was doing a Double Award Science, meaning I had two science teachers and double the science lessons. One of the teachers was brilliant and levelled with the class, making science easy and fun. The second teacher was more dictatorial and made us feel like we were idiots who were beneath her despite being in the top class.

The second teacher had already made up her mind about me when my mum came to sit with her that night for feedback. 'We all know Camilla is not going to ever be a scientist. She will be lucky if she gets a D or ungraded in Science.' My mum was upset and told my other science teacher, who said that I was actually on track to get A's.

When my mum relayed this story to me later, I was indignant. I was angry. This teacher knew nothing about me and didn't like me as I wasn't an active participant in class. This was the teacher who had branded me a mouse, not a human being. In that moment she'd decided my fate and I was fuming. I engaged even less in the class and did the bare minimum to scrape by, becoming all but invisible. My grades in that class slipped to C's and D's and maybe even an E in a module or two. I felt myself finally take a breath when it was announced that the teacher was leaving at the end of the year.

In Year 11, I resat most of the modules from the previous year. I sat in with new teachers during breaks and lunchtimes having crash course refreshers on the previous year's work before going straight into the exams. The second time around, I passed all the modules and my grades significantly improved. I didn't feel so stupid or incapable.

And yet, I didn't feel like I could be a scientist either. Despite my fascination with space and physics, it still didn't feel like an available route. Even when I held my final results in my hands, even seeing I'd got double A's for Science, it still didn't feel like an option for me.

I'd accepted this teacher's judgement of me and closed myself off to the possibility. I'd let someone else decide my fate for me. I'd given my power away to her and it hadn't been ceremonious. It had been quiet. One of those tiny moments that passes by. I'd heard the comment relayed through my mum, I knew my grades and that I was struggling to get a grip on the subject. She must be right. She's the teacher, she knows more than me, how can she be wrong? When an opinion or judgement about us comes from someone else, it has more potency for our subconscious to accept it as truth.

It doesn't matter whether the opinion is good or bad, if we receive it via third parties, it subconsciously carries more weight for us.

What I'd failed to hear in my mum relaying the story of that parent's evening feedback was how vehemently my other science teacher had disagreed, and that I was actually on track for far better grades. That another teacher hadn't written me off and could see my potential.

I also wasn't able to acknowledge how my grades improved the next year once I had teachers who took the time to explain in a way I could understand. In that final year of high school, I had teachers who hadn't decided my fate for me; they just saw someone who needed a different way to understand. They were trying to hand me back my choice and power, however, I couldn't see it, let alone take hold of it.

I continued to live the narrative that I wasn't ever going to be a scientist. Whether I wanted to be one or not wasn't even relevant, all I knew was I couldn't even look at the question.

To know myself is to know that no one else can define me. No one can decide for me or tell me what to do. The most resonant truth that will spur me into action will always be the truth I generate from within myself. It will always be the truth I access within myself.

Having gone through clearing layers upon layers of healing, deconditioning and reclaiming my power, I had no idea a tiny pocket of pain from this memory still existed until I wrote this book. I had been writing at breakneck speed, glancing at the scars of landmarks I've passed multiple times in my exhumation and healing, and then I pulled up short.

The night before writing this chapter, my chest felt tight, and I felt stressed and anxious. No amount of going within showed me what was hanging in the space. The memory had been activated yet couldn't surface. The next morning, I still felt something gripping my chest and for the first morning in nearly five weeks, the words simply wouldn't flow.

I rang Emily and we talked through what had been occurring. I knew there was a message in this chapter that I didn't want or didn't feel ready to hear. We scratched around the idea and whilst out walking my dogs I suddenly found myself with tears flooding down my face as I remembered how I felt the first time I heard what the science teacher had predicted for my life. Indignant. Angry. Shaken. Resentful. Offended. She had chosen a future for me in one offhand remark and I'd accepted it.

I asked my fifteen year old self what she needed. *A hug.* I wrapped my arms around myself as I cried and let the dogs amuse themselves sniffing around. What else did she need? *To tell the story.* Not to be vindicated or to show off what grades I did get. It was a need to share, to show you that this is how easy it can be to hand over your power without even realising it. It happens in the smallest moments as much as the big moments and is pervasive regardless.

What else did my fifteen year old self need to heal this? She needed to hear from me in the present time that I didn't let the story write my entire life. That two and a half years ago, I started choosing for myself for the first time. It doesn't matter that it took fifteen more years to start choosing, what matters is that I *chose*.

It matters that I took my fate, my destiny into my own hands. It matters that I stopped being a background character in my life, took up the pen, became the main character and continue to do so. Not from a space of ego but from a space of following my truth. It matters that I took back control and that I didn't let this define me forever.

I may not be a scientist in this life. Now it's because **I'm** choosing what I become. I'm not creating a self-fulfilling prophecy based on a teacher's comment who had decided she didn't like me. In reminding myself of these things, my fifteen year old self could release the wound and I was once again, able to write.

Consent is the most powerful currency you own. How you choose to spend it is what creates the story of your life. Spend it on what serves your soul, what lights you up, what feels like the truth for you. In sanctioning other people's narratives and judgements of us, we hand them our power. So it's time for a chargeback.

Power is an empty word until we give it meaning. We've collectively understood it to mean that power is something we don't have access to within ourselves. Here's the crone's wisdom, you have everything you need within you. You can find it, as long as you can bear to look.

A LESSON IN TIME

The one thing that the crone innately knows is time will continue to pass regardless. Good times, bad times, in between times, everything passes. Her power is in how she chooses to embrace those times and the lessons they offer. In choosing to revel in the joy and happiness. In not trying to diminish her pain and sadness and to sit with it, listen to it, detach from it and let it pass.

Life is transitory and our lives are a fleeting moment in a grand tapestry spanning millennia. She embraces how tiny and insignificant she sometimes feels herself to be in the grand scheme of things. She embraces how she and the ones she loves are her entire world and how expansive it can be. She embraces every moment for what it is, not what it might be or could have been.

Her strength is in her ability to be in the present moment. She does not hold promise to the next breath for she knows it may not come. She does not hold obligation to the last breath for it has come and gone. All she knows is here in this moment. This is her wisdom. Having gone all the way around the world and back again, she does not flow with the tides any longer. She has become the tide. Unwaveringly consistent, she is unshakable in herself and holds the room with her mere presence, regardless of whether she chooses to speak or observe.

We obsess over time. Whether we have enough of it, hacking to claw back more of it or obsessing over how long we have left.

In the new age spiritual realms, there's talk of how to quantum leap, shift timelines and somehow get ahead, getting a jump on everyone else. On social media, there's constant chatter about how to go from zero to hundreds of thousands in cash within a month. On TV and in magazines we're bombarded with ads that tell us we're running out of time. Hurry and fulfil your destiny now; have children before you get too old! Keep yourself young with these anti-ageing serums.

We're shown highlight reel after highlight reel on social media and made to feel bad about our 'ordinary', 'normal', and 'boring' lives that don't glitter as much as the influencers we follow. How to remedy it? Buy more stuff, of course. Buy their course, buy their products and get the answers you seek.

Everything is handed in a cookie-cutter approach. Strategy has become a buzzword. Everyone is trying to hand you their secret formula because we have all forgotten how to find the answers within ourselves that are uniquely ours.

The truth is you can follow everything the gurus say to set yourself up for a quantum leap. Do the meditations; follow their steps to the letter. Surrender, surrender again, surrender one more time.

However, springing forward isn't done intentionally. You don't wake up one morning and decide that by the end of play, you'll have a quarter of a million in the bank and it's done. You quantum leap in hindsight.

In becoming present and aligned with yourself, in being able to listen to yourself and know your own heart so intimately, you lose track of things like time. It ceases to be something you need to chase or somehow gain more of because you step outside of time. You trust in something much bigger than a clock or calendar on the wall telling you that you're running behind again. That you've somehow missed the boat and can't call it back.

The crone doesn't need to rush because she is always exactly where she is meant to be, *when* she is meant to be. Time is something she has an abundance of, despite society trying to convince us that for her, time is running out.

For her to give you her time is the greatest gift she can offer in our busy modern world. She has unravelled herself from the constraints of the routine. She is no longer a clock watcher. She has nowhere she desperately needs to be other than at home within herself.

It is when we stop chasing time and start revelling in our being, that we find time has leapt. We spend so long trying to find solutions, wondering if we can be or do the things we desire. We agonise over what everyone else might say or think and get stuck in paralysis.

The crone has already gone and left you. She is out there doing what she wants. She cares not what anyone thinks, it's too late to worry. Her time is too precious to waste on anyone who does not know her or has her best interests at heart.

While she's out there doing what she wants to do, time is lost to her. Because she brings her whole self to whatever she chooses to do. When she does finally choose to look at the clock, the time has flown in an instant. She's had the time of her life and travelled the universe while you were sitting on the fence thinking about joining in.

Immerse yourself in life, in love, in joy. Immerse yourself in following your heart and your truth. Time is an illusion meant to distract us from ourselves. Get lost in time. Wrap yourself up in what you love so much that you lose sight of all the other lanes. When you look back, you'll see how far you leapt.

When we say we want more time, this is what we're truly searching for. What we want is to lose ourselves so deeply, to feel so alive in the world that time is lost to us. Time ceases to exist and all that matters is us and the universe. This is the moment we're searching for when we wish we could have more time. To feel the most alive, the most whole, the most human, the most divine and transcend time in a single breath.

EMBRACING THE VOID

The crone is long past serving her expected 'function' in society. Unlike some of the other feminine phases, there is no real rite of passage for the crone in a bodily sense. At best we could consider retirement to be her rite of passage as menopause is long finished for the crone. While maga deals with the turbulence of menopause and still experiences bleeding however sporadic, the crone is complete.

Menstruation provides a regular opportunity for ceremonial letting go and releasing from the body. This doesn't happen for the crone. She has released what doesn't serve and now chooses to retain her wisdom. She has entered the winter period of her life. When I think of this life stage, I think of the fertile void which I realise sounds contradictory on the surface.

The fertile void is a term used in Gestalt theory and is a phase where nothing stands out or appears to be happening. Coined by Fritz Perls, it was described as when 'meaning-making ceases and being begins.'

To me this speaks of the crone, she has lived life and experienced everything. She has found and lost meaning and gained her pearls of wisdom. She is content to simply 'be'. This represents our inner winter. It doesn't look like much is happening on the outside for the crone as she has embraced a slower, more intentional pace of living. She can command a room with her mere presence, without the need to utter a word. This is the culmination of her life experience, wisdom and power – she knows there is nothing more to 'do' or 'have' and only 'being' remains.

In a world that's so busy, it can feel impossible to stop and embrace 'being', however, this is where the truth of our hearts can be heard more clearly. Being busy and rushing is our avoidance tactic. If we distract ourselves with our never-ending 'to-do list', we never need to face the things that test us, the things we truly fear or the things that cause us the most pain. In not having to face them, we don't need to try to move through it.

We've been taught that there is no end to the suffering. That to wallow in the pain is where you will stay and there's nothing; no peace, no happiness on the other side of it. Rather than set ourselves up to fail, we don't even try to address our emotional baggage, or try to heal, transform and let it all go. However, in the wisdom of her experience and life, the crone has seen what is most precious, honest and true and leaves it all behind to revel in the fertile void.

Although on the outside it looks like nothing grows, there is richness in the soil and movement beneath the ground. There is freedom and movement in her soul and she will share it gladly with you if you can make the time. Regardless, she worries not whether she is physically alone because her soul is never lonely.

As the veil thins for her and her connection to the spirit world grows, the crone can find great comfort because she knows there is nothing to fear. Death is a transition, another phase or state of being that we enter into. She looks death in the face and laughs, knowing she has plenty of time and life left to live. Responsibilities dwindled; the crone does what most of us cannot; grabs life with both hands and dances like it's the only moment in the world that matters. She has the joy and relaxed demeanour of someone on the first few days of their holiday as a permanent state of being.

Siga siga means *slowly slowly* in Greek. If you've ever been anywhere Greek, you'll know that siga siga is embedded into their psyche. It's their way of life.

At home in daily life, we walk along the pavement and are frustrated with the people who amble along, take up the entire pavement or worse; stop dead in front of us without warning. That sense of urgency is ingrained into so many of us that we can't stand the people who meander along, taking up our precious time.

And yet, when I visit Cyprus to see my father, I can feel this mentality unravel itself as soon as I step off the plane. I feel it in the humid air with the scent of olive trees, washing over me as if to say, *siga siga Camilla, you're here now, you're home.*

By the time I've reached the queue for passport control, it barely matters to me how long it takes the family in front to fumble for all their passports, or that my suitcase is always the last one to come out on the conveyor. The weight of the world has lifted and life has lost its urgency.

When I think of the crone and how best I want to embody her, this is what I remind myself. *Slowly slowly*. Siga siga.

I always find it funny when people say life is short. Truthfully, it's the longest thing you will ever do; live. Nothing for us as humans can be longer than our life. What people *really* mean when they say life is short is that they spend too much of their lives wrapped up in meaningless things. They spend too much time doing things they don't care about, and not enough time spent on the things they truly want to be doing. When people say life is too short, they mean the amount of time they spend *actually living* is too short, not the length of life itself.

When we do the work to heal and free ourselves from the unnecessary responsibilities that we've taken on over time, we start to live life for ourselves once again. When we call back our power from all the places and spaces in time that we've given it away, we start to return to ourselves. When we start to embrace more of our living and make it have meaning for us, we start to feel less exhausted, spent and resentful about how 'short' life is. This is how we can truly start to accept and implement the wisdom of the crone.

For the crone has experienced the fullness of life. She understands its flow, its transitional states and she understands the fleeting wonder it is to live. She embraces life for everything it is and isn't. She can welcome death with a sense of completion having done everything she wanted to do. She doesn't reach those twilight years with bitterness or regret when she has healed herself. She is content to just be.

The crone invites you to not fear the void, the emptiness, the loneliness, silence or 'finality' of death or any of the little deaths that come from being aligned with your soul. The crone fears none of these deaths despite having looked them all square in the eye. She's here to tell you that there is nothing so scary, nothing so insurmountable that you cannot survive it. That you'll only prolong your suffering in desperate attempts to avoid it.

The embodied crone has gained her inner peace. She's healed, shed her skin and cleared her karmic debt by this point.

She is free to do as she pleases. At peace with the world and thoroughly spent. She shares her time, love, joy and wisdom freely, never fearing lack. She is abundant in all things, having released the turmoil and having borne witness to and lived through the trials and tribulations of life. She fears nothing and embraces everything. Each breath to the crone is new, an opportunity to live life again in a single moment. She knows fully and is content within the now, knowing nothing is promised or owed. She has nothing left to outrun.

There is an acceptance that comes when you are not trying to outrun life or the things that you fear. There's a stillness, a peace when you realise you don't have to keep trying, avoiding or hiding and accept what comes to you, whenever it comes, as you would stand on the shore and let the waves wash over your feet.

It is in accepting that those waves sometimes may catch your toes and sometimes not. Sometimes those waves may come up to your knees and dampen the edges of your shorts, and sometimes not. Sometimes those waves may become large and crash over your entire being, and sometimes not. Sometimes those waves may knock you off your feet or try to take you out to sea, and sometimes not. And that the next wave that comes, may gently tickle your toes once more, or maybe not.

It has taken me days to complete this chapter, much longer than any chapter previously. To help keep it moving, I spoke to a friend about our encounters with death and dying. I remembered conversations I'd had with loved ones. I thought of the story of *The Appointment In Samarra*. My friend talked of *The Tale Of The Three Brothers* from *Harry Potter And The Deathly*

Hallows. I came up with many reasons why I had not continued writing this chapter to excuse myself.

Ultimately, I was avoiding writing it. There's a finality we've been taught to fear for the end. We've been taught by society that we measure success by it being forever, in never-ending, we win. Despite the human nature to seek answers and completion in everything, death is something we cannot answer and it has become taboo. Unspeakable. As I sat in my discomfort, I realised this chapter had become the metaphor for my fears. In not writing, I wouldn't have to face my *own* truths.

This is the ultimate lesson for us from the crone. She has transcended it. She has gone beyond the fear of it and embraces the unknown, the letting go, the transitions of life and death. In *Women Who Run With The Wolves*, Clarissa Pinkola Estés illustrates the embracing of life and death in the story of the skeleton woman and the life, death, life cycle. It is the idea of life and death being cyclical and infinite. This is something the crone has embraced and no longer fears. She knows that she has all the wisdom within her. She knows that the only thing she has control of is herself. She knows the only moment she has is here, now. And that's enough. It's more than enough.

We spend so much time searching outside of ourselves for something more when in fact, this has always been enough and it can be that simple. To embrace this being the answer, we are asked to look at ourselves. To look deeply and go within. To face all the things we've done, who we've been and all we've feared and to love it all. To go beyond it all and to find within the deepest parts of our being; love. Embodying this wisdom, while it can feel very insular, can also be difficult to integrate into your being. Because although the crone is the one that historically, we all look to as she holds the answers, we have forgotten how to truly embody her in the modern age. Reaching for her is a reminder that she is not too proud to ask for and accept help in embodying her truths. The crone is aware of and in full acknowledgement of her limitations whether they are physical or otherwise. She gladly and gracefully accepts the capabilities of others around her to support her through life. Allow yourself to be helped and engage with practitioners to help you embrace and embody the crone's wisdom – it's what she would tell you to do, after all.

The world has taught us that love is conditional and has no real place in our society as a form of control. To go deeply into love is to break out of society's logic and trust yourself above all reason. To trust the answers that come from your very soul. To know that there is nothing outside of you that could bring you closer to yourself. Nothing will be able to bring you home except you.

For the crone, she is there. She has found home in her heartspace and cannot be shaken from that place. No matter the cost, no matter how the world rages around her, she remains in her pocket of inner peace and love and shares it with whoever will take the time to sit beside her. For everything we ever need to know is deep beyond our fears and the answer is always as simple as love.

WHATEVER WE DO, WE'RE FUCKED (AND NOT IN A GOOD WAY)

Women have been set up to fail. Society has engineered this prison for us which means whatever we choose to do or not do, we cannot win. We're asked to play a game with illusive, ever-changing, seemingly non-existent rules. We're expected to play like we think we have a chance of winning. To act like we're winning regardless of the score and to do all of it with the prettiest of smiles on our faces. We are women after all, that's what we're here for, right?

We're not here to play a serious game, we're here to look pretty, keep quiet and attend to our men. That's what we're conditioned to do. That is the 'acceptable' behaviour and relative trajectory of our lives. Be sweet, get a job, marry a man, have babies, quit your job, raise the babies, silently let go of your dreams, don't cause hassle, don't question anything, certainly don't question your man. Keep going quietly until you become irrelevant or invisible if you're lucky, be on tap childcare for your grandchildren, grow old quietly, retire and then die. That's it, that's your lot in life.

Even if you don't follow this path to the letter, you're caught in a state of stress. We can't win whatever we do, don't do or try to do and don't succeed.

Back in the chapter, *The Ways We Destroy Ourselves*, I gave the example of being worth *less* in motherhood as a state of being, not being and being not.

That we are worth *less* if we are to be a mother. That is, to be *only* a mother, a stay at home mum or a working mum.

That we are worth *less* if we are to not be a mother. That is, to actively choose not to have children.

That we are worth *less* if we are to be not a mother. That is, to want to be a mother but not be able to become a mother because we cannot conceive.

All of these options cause us to be in a state of stress. It doesn't matter which you choose, you're damned if you do, damned if you don't. Damned if you're somewhere in the middle. Women are the damned and it hurts us more than anyone else.

However, there's more to it than these three states of being, not being and being not. Each of these states will cause a series of psychological consequences which result in; yep you guessed it, more states of being, not being and being not. Strap in because this is going to be a multidimensional mindfuck. It's taken me a good couple of years to get my head around this concept of being, not being and being not; the psychological consequences, stress and paralysis it can cause, as I found out after Emily introduced it to me in one of our sessions.

Let me break it down for you with another example; the successful woman.

Being a successful woman is a state of stress because you've been told that to become her; it must be at the cost of something else in your life. You can be successful in your work but as a result, you're probably alone so you can't fulfil the only truly valued part of being a woman in society (i.e. being a mother). Stressed much?

Not being a successful woman is stressful because you're now a failure, a deadbeat. You've transcended the socially acceptable version of a successful woman and are actively working to *not* be that. You're trying to be happy, not have big dreams and poodle along in life. You're now the lowest common denominator with nothing of value; you'll never find a partner, get married, have kids or be 'traditionally successful' even though you didn't want it in the first place. Now the world hates you and makes you feel rejected, diminished and invalidated at every turn. Stressed much?

Being not a successful woman is also a state of stress. You desperately want to be a successful woman and you are striving, working hard, doing all the right things and you're still not 'making it'. Now you're a failure who is never going to amount to anything. Once again rejected by society because you also have nothing of value seeing as you can't seem to get your shit together. And yet, because you still desperately want to be successful, you end up stuck in a loop of being exhausted, burnt out with zero boundaries. Constantly reaching for the unattainable carrot that's dangled before you on the promise that you are *so* close, just keep going a little longer. Stressed much?

The fun doesn't stop there. Let's dig into the psychological consequences of these states.

Let's say you do it. Success is yours. You are being a successful woman. Now you'll have the fear of being persecuted. It'll activate your witch wound meaning that now you are *seen* as a successful woman, you'll be hated, vilified and probably burnt at the metaphorical stake.

Or, you don't do it. You chose not to be a successful woman. The consequence of this is your disappointment. You are now not seen. You get to stay alive un-persecuted except now you're invisible, never reaching your true potential and you know it.

Alternatively, you don't become a successful woman despite the fact you're striving for it; however, success seems to elude you. You decide to give up on the idea of being a successful woman. Once again, you are not seen. You disconnect from your genius and stop shining your light. Unseen and un-persecuted by the world means that yes, you get to live but the cost is that you've disconnected and trapped yourself. You've put yourself back in the box and this is how far you'll go forevermore.

To choose success means that we risk death, however metaphorical it may be in this life. Either way, it means we cannot afford to be a success. Yet equally, we cannot afford to not be or be not a success, because these are equally stressful emotional cul-de-sacs that can keep on expanding endlessly until we're in a state of paralysis. We're fucked whatever we do.

Even the state of being not, which is quite a passive state, doesn't give you peace of mind. You're stuck in an endless loop. If you don't want option A, try option B. If that doesn't work, try option C. Whichever one you choose, you'll end up feeling stressed and paralysed because we can't win this game. Success for women is the ultimate impasse when it comes to states of being, not being and being not.

For men, the equivalent is emotional vulnerability. However, to be emotionally vulnerable is not what 'real men' do. To be emotionally vulnerable, to express his feelings and to become a healthy, emotionally balanced human being is seen as a weakness. By this point in the book, it isn't a surprise when I say... patriarchal society cannot afford to have men looking weak, so being emotionally vulnerable is a stressful state for men.

Instead, to not be emotionally vulnerable for men is to be void of emotions, emotionally unavailable, only able to feel anger and have little control over the anger. This state of not being emotionally vulnerable is apparently ideal because it's the vision of the 'real' man by society's standards. It's the one that keeps men in control of their world because it means they don't need to look at their pain or fears.

Finally, to be not emotionally vulnerable for a man is when he feels disconnected and is convinced he's broken and can't be fixed. He so desperately wants to be emotionally vulnerable and feel connected with the world, his partner, family and friends. However, he cannot let himself feel because he is so full of pain and it goes against what a 'real man' would do anyway which is, to be angry or void of emotions. He has failed at being a man by society's standards and is therefore screwed.

All of these states create a state of stress for men and ultimately, they're screwed any which way.

Here's the interesting thing. When you put emotionally vulnerable through the filter of women though, it looks different.

A woman who is being emotionally vulnerable would be seen as weak or someone to be preyed upon, someone to be taken advantage of. While a woman not being emotionally vulnerable is simply a cold-hearted bitch. And finally, a woman being not emotionally vulnerable is not a 'real' woman because she's not emotionally vulnerable enough. Instead, she's aloof and frigid. Not much of a choice, is there?

And these stressful states of being occur all over for women. It's a game that's been rigged against us and we're set to lose whatever we choose. What is the answer?

The answer is what so much of this book has already been about; coming back to yourself. Coming into alignment and listening to your own heart. When we move from and are guided by the wisdom of our hearts and are self-governed in our actions and choices, we stop playing the game. We cannot be controlled by anyone else outside of ourselves.

What you also find is there is no stress from this space because you've chosen it entirely for yourself. Choices that arise from this aligned heartspace don't cause stress because instead of seeing all the opposing states, we only see the one that is aligned for us. We're entirely in the present, not thinking of the past or fearing the implications of the future. The action is smaller, doable, self-generated and therefore, in alignment with yourself.

Take for example the idea of writing a book. So many people wish they could write but rarely get started. Or if they manage to start, they abandon the book pretty quickly. Why? Because they're not only thinking about what they're writing, right now.

Instead when they sit to write at their desk, they're writing with the knowledge of the outward manifestation of the book in the back of their mind. They're thinking about what happens when they finish writing. How do they find an agent, what are the steps to self-publish? How do they sell the book or do book tours? They're thinking about being seen and that'll activate the persecution complex and witch wounding. All of this happens unconsciously the moment they sit down to write the book so if they never start, they don't have to face any of that.

For me, writing this book has been an entirely different process. I felt the energy of the book arrive and I let it sit in the space as I thought it wasn't for me to write. When I realised it *was* for me to write, I thought about whether I really wanted to write it and why I even wanted to write it. The book came from an aligned space. I entrusted the universe to carry me and my intentions for the book and didn't plan too far ahead. I followed my feelings entirely, honouring the days when I felt scared, the days I felt overwhelmed or tired and not making any of it mean anything about the book itself.

There was no stress for me in the actual writing because the moment I sat down to write I let the words flow through me. I didn't question what came through – I could worry about that later in the editing. I simply allowed myself to be the vessel for the words and trusted it would come out as it meant to in as many or as few words as it needed each time. I didn't berate myself when I only wrote a sentence. Neil Gaiman has stated that he wrote *Coraline* at a rate of fifty words a day. Does that detract from the finished work at all? Not in the slightest. Allowing it to flow without trying to force or change myself to make the book happen, made all the difference. This is where it feels aligned.

To step out of these stressful states of being, not being and being not is to realise that we have nothing to solve. The only answer that's right for you is the one that comes entirely from your own heart, not from anyone else's. It's the answer that comes from within you, that isn't shaped or coloured by fear of judgement or desire to be validated. It's the action that you've chosen entirely for yourself and comes with no psychological consequences to cause stress or paralysis because you aren't thinking that far ahead. Only what feels right and good to you in that moment.

That's the only way we can transcend the stress that is to be a woman in a patriarchal society. Instead of fighting for approval, it is to stop listening and looking outside of ourselves for the approval we seek. To know that the way to make ourselves truly happy is to listen to what we actually want. Not what has been decided for us without us ever being called to the meeting to discuss. To turn inwards to ourselves and know that we as individuals have all the answers we'll ever need. This is how we break out of the struggle, and the stress and stop playing the loser's game.

EMBODIED FOUR PHASE FEMININE HEALING

All of the wisdom from the four feminine stages of life forms part of the healing process. It doesn't matter whether you've physically reached those stages yet or not, or if you've long past some of those stages. Each phase holds valuable lessons that we can learn from and embody to truly come home to ourselves. It doesn't matter how you explore and consolidate the lessons within your experience. No two journeys are the same. It is uniquely yours and perfect as it is.

You will find that as your exhumation and healing unravel themselves, it will happen in perfect order. Like a beautifully orchestrated symphony from the universe, you'll be guided to new knowledge and learnings without realising that's where you are heading. Like a jigsaw puzzle, it all fits perfectly. Exhumation and healing are like making a jigsaw without the picture on the lid – you have a pile of pieces and at first, don't know how any of them fit together. In working through it and dealing with each jigsaw piece as you pick it up, you find where it fits. Eventually, you can look back and see the whole picture start to reveal itself. This only comes in time.

The healing process isn't linear and doesn't complete itself tied in a neat little bow. There will be things that you can heal and release with ease in one go. And then there'll be the wounds that reopen in another layer unexpectedly and bring you once again to your knees.

There will be the wounds that bleed, stitches that reopen and you'll wonder how you ended up back here again. With each new layer comes a new level of understanding. Some things do take time to heal.

Some wounds never truly heal in this lifetime, however, they do stop bleeding. The sting goes from them and you learn to live with them, but you're always aware that the scar remains. That at any given moment something could unexpectedly tear it open once more and cut you to the core. Know that no matter how devastating those days are, they happen less and less. The good days far outweigh the bad.

You'll walk on feeling lighter because you won't be dragging aeons of emotional baggage with you. It won't feel like you're trying to hold back the tide.

One day you will realise that you put down the teaspoon, tablespoon and bucket long ago. You find yourself in your boat with the holes plugged, standing with a mop to soak up the last remnants of water. Your boat which felt like it was always on the verge of sinking is now empty and when you look up you can see the harbour coming closer, as if reaching its hand towards you in a warm embrace.

And then you can moor your boat up and hop onto the dock and feel the world steady beneath your feet for the first time in forever or perhaps… ever. You can take a breath on dry land. You can rest and resupply.

It is then that you realise you can choose what happens next and where your story goes. You can jump into your boat and cast off anytime, in any direction. When you set off you know that next time you're armed with extra clothes, teaspoons, tablespoons, buckets, a map and a friend or practitioner. That even if a wave should come and crash over you and swamp your boat, you'll be able to laugh with your company, put on some dry clothes and bail yourself out with the buckets in record time.

You know this and are unafraid. That is the best moment of the journey. When you can sail into a cave with a smile and a look between friends knowing that whatever sea creatures you encounter within, you can handle it. When you know that nothing will stop you on your quest for adventure because you've chosen it and can cope with whatever comes towards you.

This is to know you are truly healed because you realise it's not about erasing the wounds and not having any scars. It's not about having no bones that ache or a heart that never breaks again over memories or experiences new and old. It's about having the courage and heartspace to go forward regardless with an open, loving heart. It's about being able to continue to face the world without shutting yourself down because you know that to be hurt, to feel *anything* is to be human, it's part of living.

It's about knowing that whatever comes your way, you can face it because now you know that it's only the creature in that moment you face. That monster doesn't bring with it the spectre of thousands of unconscious lifetimes of unhealed trauma and wounding, leaving you fighting on fronts you didn't know existed. It's a clean, fair battle and you're armed this time. *You've got this.*

From this point on, we're not healing as much as we are reclaiming ourselves. Because we're not fire fighting, we can look at building the life and world we want to live in. We have the energy and headspace to tackle bigger issues and affect more change.

Exhumation was the process of digging up the old bones that were weighing us down. Healing was the process of cleaning those bones so that they weren't like a ball and chain around our necks. Reclamation is where we go forward waving the bones like they're flags of hope for the future we're writing.

Reclamation is where we choose YES and we choose ourselves. It's where we choose love over fear, loss and regret. It's where we take hope and use it as the foundation for trust, joy and love. We choose what bones of our lives we want to keep. We've whittled them down, chipping away everything that doesn't serve us. Now we're left with a few bones to take forward, ready to build something new. It is with these bones that we play the new song of our lives and write ourselves fully back into existence and history. It is with these bones that we change our worlds both individually and as a collective.

Breathe deep, my friend. By this point in the journey, you'll have faced the darkest nights and scariest monsters. **You are still here.** You are still here and will not have to face those things in the same way again. This is where our heroine's journey moves into the third act; the return. Having battled the demons and won, it's now time to return 'home'.

Only home isn't the place it once was and you can't unknow what you know now. You can't unsee what you've seen or stop being the person you've become as a result of the journey. You can't return to life as you once knew it either, instead, this is the opportunity to carve out something entirely new where you are with the wisdom you've gained. This is your freedom to live life on your terms. This is your reclamation.

Reclamation

EMERGENCE

Breathing into stillness,
soul echoes in silence.
Shedding the skin;
weights of lifetimes.

Having died a thousand deaths
until there is no more left to kill.

There is no great fanfare,
cacophony or symphony of angels
announcing your arrival
on the other side of pain.

It is marked by the first deep breath
and feather light steps.

Every inch feels as new
as the smell of the earth after rain
or dawn breaking on the horizon.
You have come home.

She stands before you once again
placing her hand on your heart.

Closing your eyes, you know her truth,
there is nowhere else to go,

nothing left to fix or do,
only to go deeper within;

The elemental pilgrimage,
a ministry of your heart and soul.

WHAT WE BUILD IN
THE ASHES AND BONES

Healing doesn't ever truly end. However, there comes a point when you've healed enough. That you've healed enough to be able to cope with any wounds that reopen in another outfit, on another layer.

To be healed doesn't mean you've evolved past the point of being triggered or activated, feeling angry or forgetting who you are. It means that you can come back to centre much quicker. It means that the things that used to knock you off balance, don't affect you as they used to. It is not the hill you are going to die on. Not this time.

The things that come up to be healed once you've made it past this major clean up will be new things, as they arise. Not the deep-seated trauma you've been dragging around like a ball and chain since the beginning of time. And the times when something happens that *does* trigger some of that old trauma, well, you'll be dealing with the new manifestation of it, not the years of unaddressed wounding. You will move through that quicker too.

On the other side of this darkest night, when you find that nothing remains insurmountable, is the moment that you know the war is won. On the journey home you might find some stragglers, some wayward bandits and rogues to fend off but the biggest battle is done. The war is over.

In the heroine's journey, this is the third act. We've passed the climax, the culmination, the turning point in your story.

Now it's time to pick yourself up and reclaim what is left of your life. It's time to decide what you're going to build now in the ashes and bones.

The exhumation and healing will have brought everything to the surface. You will have examined every piece of your life under a microscope. What doesn't serve you has been released. New battle lines were drawn and redrawn, fortifying your world. Healing makes you protective of yourself, not in a closed off sense but as an act of loving service to yourself. To be firm in your boundaries is to deliberately keep water in your cup and not pour it out to everyone who asks leaving yourself short.

So then the question comes as to what's next?

This is where you choose what you reclaim. You are no longer at the mercy of karma, trauma or time. The pen is in your hands, what will you write for yourself with it?

This question can be answered at every level. There are the day to day considerations of what you wish your life to look like. This is often where we start when we rewrite our lives. As you shed the skin of who you thought you were and start to feel into who you are becoming, nothing fits anymore. The clothes you wear, how you style your hair or do your makeup. How you treat your body, the way you've decorated your house, with whom you spend your time, how you spend your time, everything comes up for assessment.

There were so many times in my healing journey that I'd wake up and put on five different outfits in the morning, just trying to find what I had in my wardrobe that was nearest to the person I felt myself to be upon waking. It wasn't feasible to throw out my entire wardrobe and buy new clothes – not only because I was still in the process of becoming. In my dismantling of everything that didn't serve, I had dismantled my business too, meaning I didn't have buckets of cash to spend on an entire new wardrobe. While I was frustrated that nothing felt like me and I had little means to align my outsides to match my new insides, this was actually a saving grace.

Being still in the process of figuring out who I was meant I was more deliberate in my actions. I didn't go out on a shopping spree and buy half the shop. Instead, I curated new pieces on wish lists, feeling into them before making a purchase. When I did buy something it was a 'one in, one out' policy, letting go of the old skins with love. This more intentional rebuilding of my world around me was a much more solid foundation to frame things upon.

The aesthetics and how we show ourselves to the outside world are usually the first place we start to reframe and rebuild. Subtle shifts into alignment that will show people who we are. From that come the deeper shifts. Some people look at how they take care of what they put into and on their bodies from food to cosmetics, lotions and potions. There's an appreciation and reverence for your body that builds in this process as we remember this is the only vessel, we've got for this particular conscious human experience; it's important to take care of it.

From taking care of the body is taking care of the heart and mind. How do we spend our time? Are we spending it doing what lights us up and fills us with joy? Or are we going through the motions? The people around us affect our energy, so cultivating friendships and relationships that uplift us and nurturing the joyful hobbies and interests that fill up our cups are the things that make this life worthwhile. This is where chasing your own joy becomes the name of the game.

It isn't selfish to turn your focus entirely inward at this point. In fact, it's necessary, particularly after so long of focusing on everyone else's needs at the detriment of your own. To see yourself as a priority once again is the greatest gift to come out of the healing process. It makes the rest easier because everything comes from a space of love and joy rather than resentment and suffering.

As you start to align yourself and your immediate world with who you've become, the question starts to get bigger again. Usually somewhere in the process of figuring out what lights you up, what you do for work will probably enter the frame. And much as it's a cliché to say 'do what you love and you'll never work a day in your life', there is a truth to this. When we come from a space of joy in everything we do, nothing feels like a chore or work.

This part of the process isn't always the easiest to navigate, particularly when you have responsibilities that need you to bring in money. The idea of ditching your job to retrain or to build your own business can feel both terrifying and not even vaguely feasible. It's a choiceless choice when it comes to keeping a roof over your head and feeding your family versus the 'pie in the sky' idea of chasing your joy.

The truth is, these shifts don't happen overnight. It's the small steps into alignment that help you make this move in a more solid, safe way.

Perhaps you've realised you hate your job but you don't know what you want to do instead. That doesn't mean you should quit your job tomorrow and sit meditating for a year while you figure out the answer. It's more about how can you make work a little more palatable in the short term while allowing yourself to feel into what you could do instead.

And how do you figure out what you want to do instead? Daydream! Give yourself permission to dream again and dream big. Imagine yourself in whatever scenario you can think of, how does it make you feel? What are the things that really light you up, that you could do all day and time flies by – is there a way to get paid to do that? What did you love doing as a child but maybe had cut off as a possibility, could there still be joy in there somewhere now it's healed?

You don't need to immediately jump into a side hustle that stretches you so much that you risk burnout again. Instead, could you maybe do a volunteer day somewhere (and perhaps make it a family activity to give you some moral support and eliminate trying to organise childcare)?

There's an alpaca farm in the next village to me that offers a 'keeper for the morning' experience. You can spend a morning learning the basics of alpaca farming and keeping. It's a short, one-off time commitment that would give someone, like my mum who has a growing obsession with alpacas, the opportunity to try it and see if it feels good to her. If not, no problem, it was only a morning of her time rather than her having spent hundreds and thousands setting up as an alpaca farmer only to find out it wasn't truly for her.

This is your opportunity to get creative, to try the thing, try *all* the things and see if you're hooked. Give yourself the gift of playing with ideas. You don't need to have it all figured out by Sunday. This gets to be fun; it gets to be a process. You get to choose what you do and at a pace that suits you.

Some people go through this process and start to feel the call to be in service of others. To share the wisdom and support others in their transformation is what they are drawn to do. Not everyone feels like that. It is all okay and valid.

If you look at Mother Nature you'll see a world of perfect balance. Without human interference, it is an ecosystem of harmony and equilibrium. I believe as humans we are capable of the same. We are not all built to be carbon copies; one size does not fit all. What I love doing, isn't for someone else and that's as it should be.

What is meant for you is meant for you and it won't pass you by. Doing this healing work is an invitation for each of us to reach our potential and become the best version of ourselves. In becoming the greatest version of yourself, you have no idea of the ripples, impact and legacy you will create for the lives that you touch and for future generations. The whole point of healing and listening to the truth of your heart is entirely that, to listen to the truth of **your** heart and what it speaks to you. Don't allow yourself to be swept up in the excitement of fulfilling a higher calling if it doesn't feel right for you. We're allowed to embody divinity at every level.

For some people that is to go out there on the biggest stage and speak to thousands, sharing their wisdom. For some, it's to coach and support others through personal transformations. For some, it's to bring light into the world through their paintings or candlemaking. For some, it's to work in a library and help people find joy in fantastical, magical stories or to help them learn. For some it's to inspire the next generation of humanity to be kind and loving, working in childcare and teaching. All of it matters. All of it is valid.

When you find the thing that makes you happy, that's the real service to humanity. The uplift and light in the world that only you bring when you are radiating happiness and love in your corner of the world, however big or small you choose to make it.

At university, while discussing with a tutor about our upcoming career paths, I remember being told the story of a student he had once taught. This student had been incredibly smart with a 'bright future'. They got high grades and excelled in everything.

Some years later, my tutor was in a supermarket and bumped into this former student who was working there stacking shelves. The tutor was surprised given that this student had been expected to go on to have a glittering career. He asked how life had been; expecting to hear a sob story of how things had fallen apart and they were working through some stuff. Instead, the ex student explained how they'd resented the pressure and been unhappy in the career they had followed after university. They had packed it all in and got a job stacking shelves in a supermarket a year or so before and this was the happiest they had ever been.

Not everyone is meant to do the big things on world stages. We all have a place where we fit and feel good; it's up to us to allow ourselves to be honest. To listen to the truth of our hearts and to follow it.

Some people will read this book and in the process, be activated and called towards a spiritual path of sharing wisdom and facilitating more transformation across the globe. Others will read this, work through the wounding and come out of the other side realising that they don't have such dreams. Instead, success and happiness to you look like a part-time job in a café where you go home to your cat in a little house by the sea. It **all** counts.

What matters the most is that *you decide* what you will build out of the ashes and bones, not what you actually build. Give yourself permission to tell yourself what you really want and go out there and do it.

KUAN YIN

Hope in the darkness,
mercy for the suffering,
love reaches beyond.

THE HILL THAT HATE DIES ON IS SURROUNDED WITH PINK LIGHT AND ROSE PETALS

The first time I encountered Kuan Yin was when I was the most scared I have ever been in my entire life. What I learnt from her that day was a lesson I had trouble accepting at the time. Now looking back having done much to heal, I can see exactly where she was trying to lead me.

We started having issues with our neighbours back in 2019. I'm not entirely sure what triggered the harassment in this life. Since then though, I have spotted these neighbours within past lives where I was persecuted as a witch. My assumption is something happened in this life to activate an unwitting karmic replay of this behaviour for us all. The important thing to note is that this time the story played out very differently for me and I didn't die as a witch. Instead, I had the opportunity to heal and change the narrative.

At first, though, the whole situation was simply terrifying. All of us, my husband, dogs and I, felt like prisoners in our own home. The harassment escalated and continued daily. We lived in a constant state of panic and all of us ended up on medication for anxiety. We felt increasingly isolated and abandoned by the authorities who were pushing us from pillar to post in our attempts to get the harassment stopped.

The anxiety medication made me feel violently sick so I spoke to a nurse about alternate medication. She asked if I'd be willing to try alternative methods first and if they didn't work, to go back and they would look at the medicated route. She suggested I download the Headspace app and try meditation. I was sceptical of it making a difference but equally willing to try anything.

I spent a few weeks following the basics of meditation on the app. It rapidly became the best part of my day, to have those few flickering glimpses of internal peace and calm. I began exploring other meditation apps and practising active imagination as a way to help me process my feelings.

We'd had a rough week with the neighbours harassing us. I felt so trapped and unsafe. No one seemed able to help us and I felt completely powerless. I silently called upon every angelic being, deity and spiritual being I could think of to help us as I was on the brink of despair. I had no idea how they might be able to help, yet felt it was worth an ask.

Then without further thought, I sat down to do my daily meditation. As I felt myself drifting down the brainwave patterns, I suddenly felt this incredible energy around me. It was hues of iridescent pinks and whites with this gentle warmth and feeling of safety. I don't know how I knew but I instantly recognised the goddess Kuan Yin.

In my mind's eye, I saw the living room where I was sitting and as I watched, I saw Kuan Yin fill the entire room up with pink light and rose petals. I'd experienced the scent of rose petals before, the day I played the Christmas music with my grandad and had attributed it to a general angelic presence. This time, however, it was much clearer to me that it was in fact, Kuan Yin.

I felt the light and rose scent wash over me. All I felt was love. I felt safer than I had done in months. I watched as the pink light and rose petals filled the living room to the ceiling and then spilt out. In my mind's eye, I followed them, watching every single inch of my house fill up with this radiant pink light and rose petals before it sealed around the house like a force field.

The light started to spill out of the windows, and front and back door. It burst through the walls into the front and back garden. I watched it flow down the path towards the garage and carport and then it pulsed like another force field being sealed again. I saw our dogs and my husband wrapped in these beams of pink light and knew we were safe.

I thought it would stop there but it didn't. The pink light started to extend outwards into the neighbour's garden. I saw rose petals climbing up the outside wall, flowing in and around until *their* entire house was also encompassed in this pink light and a thousand rose petals.

I felt confused and my heart tightened.

How could I send love to the people who had struck so much fear into me and my family?

The whole image seemed to pause as if waiting for me to do something. I knew what she was asking of me but I simply couldn't do it. It hurt too much; I had too much fear and anxiety to bring love into the situation.

When I opened my eyes, I could still feel Kuan Yin's energy around me. The whole house felt lighter. I felt calmer and safer. I felt disappointed in myself that I had been unable to take her message to heart. I set about trying to see the situation from different perspectives. We felt frightened and targeted yes, but why had they even started harassing us in the first place? The more I felt into it, the more I could see their own hate, unhappiness and fear. I saw their dissatisfaction with their own lives which had been exacerbated by the arrival of a young, happy couple who radiated a bond that went beyond normal comprehension. As I started doing work on healing my past life wounds with Emily, I even saw them as part of the mob of witch hunters persecuting me.

Eventually, we got the help we needed. The harassment dwindled as authorities got involved, then stopped. We started trying to rebuild our lives.

It was only then, once the active trauma had finished that I was able to go back to that day with Kuan Yin's pink light and rose petals and truly take the message to heart. The day I watched the neighbour move out, instead of thinking to myself, 'Good riddance', I mentally sent well wishes on their journey. I hoped that they'd find the peace and happiness they were looking for, that they'd seen in us and sought to destroy. I mentally thanked them for the lessons and growth I'd received from the arduous journey, spanning years by that point. I sent them away with love in my heart, regardless of the glare that was returned to me as they left.

It was at that moment that I realised it had never really been about our family. It had been an expression of their own pain and fear whether it was from this life or the past life. Harassing us had simply been the outward manifestation. While we couldn't get those years back that we'd lost to hate, we could reclaim what was left of our lives and give them over to joy, happiness and love.

To extend love to the ones who would hurt us is Kuan Yin's ultimate lesson in compassion, unconditional love and mercy.

It does not condone the choices people make or their actions. Instead, it is to say; *the fear stops here with me. I will not reflect your pain and fear back to you. I will not perpetuate this cycle. This is the hill that fear dies on and it is mine. I choose to send back love and compassion because that is the most powerful choice I can make.*

We cannot control what other people do. What we can control is our own actions and how we respond to fear, hate and anger. To return them with more of the same is to fight fire with fire; it will only intensify and continue to rage on. It is by changing our approach and dousing the flames with water that we put the fire out. Sending the same emotions right back doesn't break the cycle, it only maintains it. To break the chain, we invite love to shine a light on the deepest, darkest, most hateful of places. To send love where it's never been before.

This is Kuan Yin's wisdom and mercy to us all. Because it is here in loving that we find our true selves, our most whole selves. This is the place where we encompass humanity and divinity in a single breath. Unconditional love is the well from which all things spring. From here you will find flow and abundance.

The Buddhist icon Kuan Yin is the embodiment of compassion and mercy. Her name means 'She Who Hears The Cries Of The World'. Her legend is vast yet the essence is one of love, kindness and a vow to end suffering in the world. She has been depicted with a thousand arms to reach out to those in need and eleven heads to comprehend the cries of the suffering.

As a Bodhisattva, one of Kuan Yin's stories is that of her incarnation as the mortal princess Miao Shan which is my favourite story of Kuan Yin. In the story, she is to be married to a wealthy man to which she agrees as long as the marriage eases three misfortunes. These misfortunes were the suffering people endure with age, the suffering of falling ill and the suffering caused by death. Miao Shan said that a doctor could ease all of these; however, her father wanted the princess to marry a man of power and wealth.

She refused to marry, so her father punished her. She was forced into hard labour and starved. She didn't complain yet still would not accept the marriage. In his anger, her father ordered the temple she was working in to be burned down. In response, Miao Shan put the fire out with her bare hands. Seeing she did not get burned, her father ordered her to be put to death due to his fear.

There are different versions of what happens at the execution. One story says a supernatural tiger took her down to hell where music and flowers bloomed in her presence. Another tale states that the executioner's axe shattered into thousands of pieces. He tried other weapons and still failed to kill her. Eventually, she absolved him of his guilt and he succeeded in her execution. Kuan Yin with the executioner's guilt went to hell.

There her compassion shone through and she was able to release the suffering souls from their torment – so many that hell started to empty and be seen as a paradise, a chance of redemption and a road to salvation. This displeased the king of hell who sent her back to earth.

Back on earth, she continued her compassionate ways. The story culminates in her father becoming ill with no one able to cure him. The only way he would live, he is told, is to make a cure out of the arms and eyes of someone who does not hold anger. Her father hears a rumour about a compassionate person who lives on a mountain and the request is sent. Kuan Yin immediately, willingly offers her arms and eyes to help. When the king finds out it is his daughter, he seeks forgiveness and sees her true compassionate ways.

Miao Shan is then transformed into the thousand armed Kuan Yin. As she makes her journey to heaven, she hears the cries of the world below and cannot bear to leave. She returns, vowing to remain on earth until all suffering has ended where she remains to this day in her temple on the mountain.

As a deity, Kuan Yin has won hearts and minds with her pure, selfless heart. She inspires us to reach deep within and find goodness in a dark, suffering world. She is the embodiment of hope.

Her story of transforming from Miao Shan shows the abundance that is returned to her tenfold through her selflessness. It's not something she chases or even thinks of being rewarded for her actions, for her the reward is in the giving. It's knowing that she led from her heart and did what she could to help someone in need.

The lesson she shows us is to know that we can give without fear. To know it doesn't cost us anything when it comes from a place of unconditional love. It's the understanding that energy is always flowing and when we circulate it by giving — our time, energy, support, help — it creates space for us to receive.

For me Kuan Yin's story isn't so much about what or how much she gave, but rather the grace with which she accepted and received the abundance that was reflected to her. It's not something we've been taught to do; it isn't particularly socially acceptable to allow ourselves to receive kindness or abundance in any form. We've been conditioned to be independent and do everything alone. That to accept help is a weakness while accepting a compliment is arrogance.

Kuan Yin receives with humility and reverence because she is solid in herself. She knows her beliefs, and her truths and doesn't waver. She is self-assured in her worthiness, not in an arrogant manner but in unconditional love for herself and the world.

She has no need or desire to compete with anyone. There is no jealousy, envy or insecurity. She sees the beauty of the individuality that each person brings and the intricate harmony and balance within the ecosystem of humanity. This is what she celebrates and honours without judgment or trying to change things.

These are things that we have been taught to reject. That it's not the way the world works which is why Kuan Yin is such a beloved icon, a revered symbol of hope in an otherwise dark, hopeless world.

What I found coming out the other side of the healing process was that coming to a space of unconditional love wasn't instant. I didn't suddenly feel unconditional love toward everyone who had ever wronged me or toward myself. It started with acceptance of the things I couldn't change and letting go of the past, knowing I'd done enough to heal it. I kept letting go and letting go; the things I couldn't let go of, I healed more.

I kept doing this until I felt a sense of peace and stillness. Loving neutrality. Lao Tzu once said, 'If you are depressed you are living in the past. If you are anxious you are living in the future.

If you are at peace you are living in the present.' This is what I found to be true. I wasn't dwelling or wallowing in the past, nor was I worrying or mentally projecting myself into the future.

The peace came when I was able to meet myself exactly where I was at that very moment without judgment. I kept meeting myself there in peace until it felt more solid. Until I felt I could try to meet myself exactly where I was, regardless of everything happening around me, and extend love to myself. Although it was for the briefest moment, that was where it started. To meet and see myself with love and nothing else.

All the things society tells us we are meant to do; fear and be suspicious of each other, compete with and be jealous of others, all of those things faded away. Nothing else really mattered other than me and what I chose to do at any given moment. It cut through all the noise of the world. It allowed me to get into my own lane and crack on instead of worrying or wondering what people might think or say. Nothing that anyone outside of myself said or thought mattered. The only one I answered to was my own heart and as long as I could meet my soul in love then that's the only answer I needed. It's self-acceptance, forgiveness and unconditional love of the highest order.

When it feels comfortable, you can practise meeting others exactly where they are and seeing them *in* love, *from* love, *with* love. This is where we truly change the narrative of our lives to one no longer of pain and lack but one of love and abundance. When we can embody that love, all things flow.

However, unconditional love is not an excuse to do whatever you like. There's a lot written about unconditional love in the spiritual space – that it's all about love and light, letting bygones be bygones and allowing everyone to have their truth no matter what it looks like. Yes and no.

Everything that anyone does is a mirror. What they do is a reflection of you. Perhaps an unconscious part of yourself that you don't want to see. If something someone says or does gets your back up and makes you feel triggered, the real question to ask is why it makes you feel like that, not why are they doing what they are doing.

Equally though, it doesn't mean that unconditional love is carte blanche to abdicate responsibility or become pushovers. To meet everything with unconditional love doesn't mean you set your boundaries on fire and give yourself away again until there's nothing left.

Unconditional love isn't an excuse to accept everyone into your field, it's also about discernment. It's about holding **yourself** in the highest unconditional love and then filtering your field through that lens. It's not about allowing people to treat you however they like and it being 'okay' because we are practising *unconditional love*.

In the story, Miao Shan was severely mistreated and didn't complain. The end of the story shows how she willingly gave up her arms and eyes to cure her father, although at the time she didn't know it was him and thought it was a stranger she was helping. She was rewarded for her sacrifice with a thousand arms. A message that teaches us that in giving away everything we have, good karma will reward us with abundance. Taken literally it's a dangerous message because what has been glossed over is that these things happened to Miao Shan because she stood by her principles.

Her terms for getting married were that the marriage would cure three misfortunes. When this was denied, she refused to marry and was subsequently mistreated. Her desire to marry for what she saw as a higher good was the line she drew, the boundary she placed. It was her condition of play. Her father reacted out of anger and would not accept this. She didn't judge his inability to accept her boundaries and crucially, neither did she change her terms to accommodate him. She held her line from a space of unconditional love for herself and her intentions.

We can't abandon ourselves, our principles or our boundaries in the name of unconditional love. Unconditional love is the ability to accept that everyone has their own path, purpose and truth without taking on their responsibility yet not abdicating one's responsibility. It's to hold the duality of the world in love and come home to one's truth to see that when we know better, we can do better. First, however, we know it for ourselves.

To use unconditional love as an excuse or spiritual bypass is to diminish the evolution of what it means to live in a space of unconditional love in the duality of the modern world. We've been taught that love is conditional and therefore, no boundaries need to be placed on unconditional love. This is at the cost to ourselves, our alignment and inner peace. It once again places us conveniently within society's narrative of selling ourselves short, relinquishing our control and silencing our voice and autonomy. The only way to achieve nirvana and be in a state of unconditional love is to betray ourselves in the name of the greater good.

This isn't the message that I believe Kuan Yin offers us. I believe her message is that it's not either or. That unconditional love towards others is not to the detriment of oneself and vice versa. In holding our boundaries, we can extend unconditional love to those who both can and cannot accept our terms and conditions while holding ourselves in love most of all.

The world has taught us to betray and hate ourselves. That our only value is seen through the eyes of others. The purest form of love is that which springs from our hearts and extends outwards, not the other way around.

It is when we reverse this and generate unconditional love from within ourselves that we experience the self-assurance and confidence we have been seeking outside of ourselves. It is then that we open ourselves up to receive, knowing we are worthy. It is then that we experience creative flow, inspiration and abundance when we allow ourselves to be the loving vessel and recipient of the divine. It is then that we can co-create hand in hand with the universe rather than desperately trying to control and create from a place of scarcity, fear and lack. It is then that we manifest our heart's true desires because we've allowed ourselves to truly hear them. It is then that we can be open hearted because we love ourselves and know ourselves to *be* love first and foremost.

THE PESTILENCE OF SUFFERING

Kuan Yin vowed to stay on earth until all suffering was eradicated – it's no surprise her energy is still here. The world has degenerated and twisted the concept of suffering, selling the belief that it is our default state of being. Suffering has become a sport or convoluted art form in which everyone is trying to outdo another in their martyrdom. As if *She Who Suffers The Most* is a desirable title to hold, a prize to be won.

And then we wonder why everyone feels so lost and confused, why there is such a thing as a 'midlife crisis' and why people are so deeply unhappy and dissatisfied with their lives. Have we not learnt by now? Our unhappiness serves the patriarchal, matrix 'suffering' society. It keeps you in a state of insatiable hunger – not for food but for yourself. For love, for happiness, for abundance, for peace, for trust, for a million things we cannot name.

Society has been built on selling a solution for everything so we end up thinking that *surely there must be something wrong with us* because we're buying all this stuff and we're **still** not happy. People buy more and they want it faster and bigger and shinier and better than yours and then wonder why they're *still* not happy. They buy programmes and quick fixes and one-dose solutions promising to solve all their problems. And they're *still* not happy.

We've been convinced that *of course it is we who* are the problem. We just haven't tried or bought everything yet. We're descended from that original sin, so of course we, humanity, are the problem, the blight on existence. It couldn't possibly be anything other than us.

The world has taught us to be isolated, arrogant and narcissistic. We've been taught that we are our egos, not our souls. Egos are the natural self-absorbed, self-centred parts of us so when someone tells us that our unhappiness is our own fault; of course we're going to agree. Everything is about us after all.

We cannot see that society has been engineered to encourage us to disconnect, disassociate and betray ourselves. Instant gratification and mass consumerism have been created as distractions – empty promises of salvation and an oasis that we hang our hopes on like our lives depend on. We're too deeply entrenched in these beliefs and societal conditioning to entertain the idea that it might not all be us. That the world might have been engineered in such a way. Designed to set us up to fail. No, the world is perfect and we are the blight, we are the problem, we are the cancer.

In my own life, I've been taught to believe that I am the blight, the problem, the cancer. Everything happens because of me; therefore I caused my own downfall. I am the architect of my suffering and thoroughly deserve it. If I want redemption or even a brief moment of relief, I could find it by buying these diet pills that say they'll work in just three days! Then I'll be happy, and then all my problems will be solved.

I imagine that as Kuan Yin listens to all the cries of the suffering in the world who think like this, she weeps for what we've become.

The truth is, that suffering doesn't vanish overnight in a puff of smoke. We won't wake up one morning and everything will be solved. Even after exhumation and healing, you don't wake up to a perfect life. There is no fairy waving a magic wand.

Because, despite the lessons you've learned in the healing and the person you've become in your unravelling, we still live in a world that has been built on the foundations of suffering. It simply doesn't evaporate overnight and turn into paradise.

After the systematic dismantling of ourselves, comes the challenge of navigating the pestilence of suffering in society. To walk with this duality of knowing that this is the programmed state of being we've all been taught and yet, understanding it is not the person you are now. You know different. You are different. You have rewritten your coding from the ground up. You know love. You know joy. You know abundance. You know the world doesn't have to be this way.

It starts with you.

As you walk amongst the suffering society, you will be triggered. You will be frustrated by the unawakened and the ones who revel in their martyrdom. You will be angry at the lack of change and how twisted the world has become when you know it to be so beautiful. You will be heartbroken by the rejection and despair at the lack of hope. You will doubt yourself and wonder if you made it up and whether it was all a crazy dream. This is where you will meet doubt once again as you did right at the beginning of the exhumation process.

The difference now is that *you are different*. You have evidence that it doesn't have to be that way and the evidence is yourself. You have broken out of your programming and discarded the limiting beliefs and societal conditioning. You have faced fear, hate, anger and despair head on and came out the other side.

You have seen the likes of forgiveness, unconditional love, joy and abundance. They may have only been fleeting in terms of minutes passed yet were still life changing all the same. They are emotions you can come back to and build upon into something more solid. You know you saw them. You can't unsee it. You can't unknow it.

The choice isn't whether you revert and go back to what you were – to truly transform means you can't go back even if you wanted to, that version of you simply doesn't exist anymore. Going backwards becomes impossible. Sometimes when you feel the weight of the world, going forward also feels impossible.

So shrug, Mother Atlas. This is not your fight. It is not down to you and only you, to save the world. Kuan Yin's vow to remain here while suffering is present on earth is admirable, yet perhaps the biggest wisdom in this healing journey is to realise that she does not save everyone. Instead, she teaches through her actions. In honour of her, we can do the same.

You are one person. When you drop a pebble in the ocean, it causes a ripple. Be the ripple effect. When the world questions you and all that you've become, it's up to you to honour yourself and what you know and hold the line. When you feel rejected and that it would be far easier to fall back into line, remember what it felt like to be in the line in the first place.

We cannot control the actions of others; however, we can take responsibility for our actions. We can commit to never betraying ourselves again. Honour your boundaries. Protect your time and energy. Soften your edges when the world tries to harden your heart. Offer compassion to the ignorant and unkind. Extend love to the hateful.

Show others your authenticity and remain true to it. Walk your true north regardless of whether you walk alone or not. The people in our orbit can choose to both learn from us and respect us or not. When they choose not to, let them leave with love and allow someone else who will honour and love you into the space. Allow your soul to call forth the soul family meant for you and you will find that your one small pebble in the ocean becomes a handful. Mighty oaks from little acorns grow.

It takes courage to walk through this life having healed and keep your heart open. To be healed doesn't mean you will never bleed again. It means that you are not afraid to show the world that you bleed and that you won't let it stop you. Fear and hate will not overcome you for you know a different way and that way is peaceful and loving. It's where we turn this suffering society into one of abundance and bliss.

It does start with just you at the beginning though. You choose how you lead from there. If all you have is this one moment; not the despair of the past or the fear of the future, only this one moment – how do you choose to live it?

A LINE MEANT

We're always searching for answers outside of ourselves. Like alchemists, we try to figure out the secret formulas of life, success and abundance. We're so busy focusing on trying to crack the codes and fast track our route to the top that we don't realise that we're overthinking it and in the process have missed the point entirely.

Life doesn't need to be 'hard'. Once you step outside of the framework of suffering and decide to create your own narrative, you get to choose what life is like for you. What so many people don't realise though is you can choose for it to be **easy**. It seems so obvious, why wouldn't we choose for it to be *easy*? Well, usually it's the last piece that hangs on from the suffering framework. To let go of it completely would mean you cut yourself adrift and step entirely outside of the framework that society has been built on and you don't quite know how to navigate society on your own. Once again, we come down to choice.

You can choose for everything to be easy from here on out, even outside of societal norms, you can choose for it to be easy for you. That doesn't mean millions of pounds will land in your bank account out of thin air or you'll be handed the keys to your dream home and your divine partner will arrive overnight. It doesn't mean that society will suddenly do a 180 and everything will be perfect sunshine and rainbows.

What it *does* mean is that no matter what comes up, you move through it all effortlessly. The things you desire are drawn to you, with ease. Going against the grain of society doesn't mean that you end up destitute and in the gutter, it means that you've simply gone beyond what you've been told and have taken back your control and choice of your destiny. .

On the other side of healing, unconditional love and your ability to choose are your most powerful tools. Everything comes from these two things and both are uniquely yours.

I've found in the spiritual new age world, there's a lot of talk about alignment. Once you're aligned, you become a magnet and attract everything you desire. Alignment is the secret sauce for the law of attraction and there are tons of coaches, practitioners, courses and other help out there trying to help you reach it.

We gobble it all up until we're saturated in other people's words and then wonder why we feel overwhelmed and not aligned. We can't understand why things aren't happening as we think they should be. Where is the overnight success and the £10k a month? Not at the bottom of someone else's strategy. It may work for a short while but one of two things will happen. Either, the bubble will eventually burst and the strategies you've been following to the letter will stop working, or you will begin to feel unsatisfied. You will want more and more and you'll put it down to expansion and evolution, when really what you're truly hungry for is your soul self that you have drowned out in someone else's route to success.

The real secret is that there is no secret formula.

You cannot force yourself into someone else's alignment. Like a stack of cards, eventually, it will fall because you built it on someone else's back. If you want to know the real secret to getting aligned, the truth is there is no secret. The only way you do it is for and by yourself (I don't mean do it alone). I mean that you come into alignment in your own way. No one can teach you, force you or convince you.

When you stop being afraid of hearing yourself and stand still long enough to listen, you'll hear the alignment meant entirely for you. Are you willing to listen?

Alignment isn't about chasing success, it's about standing still long enough to go beyond your discomfort and really hear yourself. What is your truth? What do you *truly* want? What is your version of success? What does life look like when it gets to be *easy*?

There's no formula for alignment because it's fluid. It's a series of constant shifts on a macro and microscale. Alignment never ends, it's your constant companion from here on out. What feels aligned in this very moment may not be the answer tomorrow or in an hour. When you can trust yourself and your intuition, you can trust in the motion of alignment knowing that it will forever shift, coming and going in waves.

When you first get on a boat or a pair of roller skates, the motion feels odd. You feel unbalanced and unstable and long for solid ground. Over time you adjust to the movement and you find that eventually, when you get off the boat or take off your skates, walking feels *really* weird. You somehow can still feel the wobble of that motion as you go to place your feet. You start to miss the feeling of rolling along.

To start to practise bringing yourself into alignment is somewhat like that – at first it does feel wobbly. You don't know how to stand up, let alone stand *still*. You forget how to move one foot in front of the other while everything around you is moving, and it can feel like you're out of control. If it feels too much, you've probably made it too big.

Alignment is **this breath**. It's only ever this one breath that you're in, *right now*. Breathe in with me. And now breathe out. Breathe in again and ask yourself how you feel *right now*. And breathe out. Breathe in again and ask yourself what you need *right now*. And breathe out.

There are a few things I've found that help with the art of alignment. To know and trust yourself innately means that when you ask yourself what feels like an aligned move for you, you trust yourself to know you've heard it correctly. In the moment it doesn't always make sense, however, in learning to trust yourself and your intuition, you can take the action regardless of how much sense it makes.

To be in tune with your body helps you start to understand the nuances of what feels aligned. First, you start to learn what a full-body NO and a full body YES feel like. As time goes on, you can start to tune into your nuances. When it feels like a yes with a lowercase y, when it feels like half a yes, a tentative yes because you're afraid when it feels like you need more time to decide or you haven't seen the bigger picture. Your body is always trying to tell you things; *slow down, take a breath, look after me better, listen to me*. It is subtle at first. If you ignore the subtleties, they get louder until you can't ignore them. Learn the full spectrum of the nuanced messages your body, mind and soul send you.

The biggest thing that factors into alignment is presence. Whether you practise mindfulness or have simply found that the healing process has cut down on your internal mind chatter, being present is the name of the game. When you can set down your worries and simply be without trying to push or judge yourself, you can hear your true self, your soul self and what it's trying to tell you without trying to shape it through what you think you should be doing, or what you might want to hear.

There's an honesty and ability to bear witness to your whole truth that only comes through the healing process. Facing the demons of the past and winning against them is your evidence that you can overcome anything, so nothing feels as scary or like something to be avoided – in that moment you are truly able to face all of yourself.

Here's the thing, while you can face yourself, it's only yourself in this moment. Aligned actions are smaller and more immediate because they're focused on what you can do at this moment. Instead of wanting to write a book and becoming paralysed because your monkey mind has raced ahead to the end where you have to publish it and you suddenly feel intimidated. The aligned action is that you want to write a book, okay, today let's tackle the outline. Today let's write a chapter or even a paragraph. By an inch, it's a cinch, remember? That is what it looks like to be aligned.

There are no worries about the future or wallowing in the past in an aligned state, simply here and now and whatever feels good to you to do at any given moment. No one can prescribe those answers for you, they come from within. It's up to you to trust yourself enough to listen.

Alignment is like a continuous stream of answers to a question that hasn't been asked. It shifts and changes and yet it all comes back to you feeling at home within your body and listening to yourself as you follow the path that you choose. And because it is continuous, you can align with yourself without end. Where in the exhumation process you were unravelling yourself, your life, your programming and your beliefs and it was all splayed metaphorically over the carpet, aligning to yourself is clean. It's another form of unravelling and it is entirely inwards. As you unravel, you simply go within, deeper each time.

To align with yourself is to continually bring your human self closer to your divine self at any given moment. That's not to say we're trying to ascend or transcend the human experience, but to become as whole as we can within the limitations of the human experience. To come home to our hearts and souls within this human body and live a life where anything is possible, where we can manifest and create whatever experiences we desire with ease.

And this is the crucial thing about alignment; it's uniquely yours. Alignment and embodiment go hand in hand. To try and embody or emulate someone else's energy or way of being is to once again, search outside of yourself. The embodiment comes from being comfortable and at home in your own skin. To know you are worthy and valid, to be self-assured and to hold total belief and trust in the probability of the life you desire being available to you right now.

I've always thought the answer to the meaning of life was the meaning we find for ourselves. As part of an infinite consciousness, we relish the idea of experiencing the limitations of humanity, considering how powerful we are in non-corporeal form. To align closer to your soul gives you access once again to that incredible power and then, well, life is yours for the choosing. What experiences are you going to create for yourself out of it? This is when life starts to happen *for* you, not *to* you. You are no longer a victim of circumstances, but instead a co-creator of experiences. The ultimate vicarious storyteller.

It seems to me that alignment is something a lot of people chase and they're going about it upside down and back to front. There is no chasing involved in real alignment. Instead, there's peace. There's love and openness in your heart. There's stillness, there's joy, excitement and passion.

The one thing that people miss about the concept of alignment though is the intention. It's not something that happens to you by accident. It is intentional and deliberate. Not chased and not something you try to grasp with both hands.

For me when I think of alignment, I see the word as; *a line meant*. A line that we mean to draw for ourselves going forward. We can choose whatever direction we want to draw in, we can change direction or speed at will. It's the line, the path, the road forward that we draw for ourselves and then walk ourselves home with it. Like a tightrope, staying on that line we draw for ourselves can feel precarious at times. Things can knock you off unexpectedly or you may step off the line and suddenly feel the loss of the gentle motion beneath your feet. The beauty of it is you can step back on your line, into *a line meant* or alignment, anytime you choose.

Alignment is only ever the next breath away. It's no more or less difficult than that.

MARY MAGDALENE

She sits in stillness
and unconditional love.
Her heart cast wide open
like a rose unfurls its petals.

The bridge between heaven and earth;
she is wholly human
and wholly divine,

A symbol of peace and balance
she holds no fear,
only trust,

as she invites you to spiral inward
and know your own heart

A COSMIC LOVER'S INVITATION TO DIVINE UNION

What society lacks in healthy relationship blueprints, it makes up for in the objectification of women. One of the first models we have access to is God's human creations; Adam and Eve. She is shown to be born from Adam's rib and is subservient to him — not the best starting point for us to model our relationships on, especially after a deep healing journey like this.

We don't have much else to go on for what it *could* look like either, except we *do*. As mentioned earlier in the chapter, *Unspoken Truths We Wish We Knew*, before the Adam and Eve narrative there was Adam and Lilith as God's first human creations. Lilith, Adam's first wife, wanted equality. She was originally intended to demonstrate the sacred union that we all seek. However she was rejected by Adam and subsequently, Lilith left the Garden of Eden. She was vilified at best and at worst, written out of history entirely. She remains, however, the pillar of the woman and the goddess in her own power that we tap into during our exhumation, healing, resurrection and reclamation.

It's natural that at some point in the rebuilding of our lives, we put our relationships and sexual expression under the microscope. Many of us struggle in unhealthy, unbalanced relationships that often have us playing the role of mother or maiden rather than that of equals to our lovers. This is because we don't have access to any reference points for how it could look positively, equally and unconditionally.

Many people don't truly know what's possible, although everyone yearns for more from their romantic love. It's why society has such an obsession with romance stories and fairy tale endings. In a world built on suffering that tells us a happy, loving union isn't possible, our souls quietly niggle at us, desperate to tell and live a different story.

Throughout time, these elusive equal partnerships have had many names such as soulmates, energetic matches, twin souls, mirror souls, sacred union, divine partnership or divine union. The most enduring and polarising name for them is twin flames.

A twin flame is generally accepted as the idea of two people born from the same soul; two halves of a whole and then spending eternity seeking each other to be in union again. When people feel like some part of them is missing, this is often what they feel they're searching for — the other half of their soul.

Depending on the soul missions of the individuals involved, some people may even manifest more than one twin flame in a lifetime.

Not all twin flames are designed to result in union in this life depending on the shared soul mission of the individuals, and sometimes they don't even need to result in romantic relationships. Some twin flames can be entirely platonic friendships, mentorships or other relationship dynamics. The deciding factor is how the shared soul mission of these divine unions is best served.

For twin flames and their journey, the path can be fraught on their way to union. They are usually brought together for a higher purpose; to clear karmic debt, enact their soul purpose and raise the consciousness of the planet. In the online space, it can seem at the moment that everyone and their dog has found their twin flame because there is currently the greatest convergence of twin flames ever. Yet in the grand scheme of the world and its population, only a small number of people will reach union with their twin flame.

Twin flames, their journey, the exhumation, karmic clearing, healing, acceptance and the carrying out of their soul mission that they go through to reach a union built on unconditional love; represent a blueprint for the rest of mankind of what relationships *can* look like. For the majority, they become a template you choose to build your life upon for your own sacred relationship.

When twin flames and divine unions are represented within society, they're generally only ever portrayed up until the destructive separation phase. There's very little in the way of showing us the union, the true 'happy ending' so we don't know what it looks like to even want it. The focus on the painful aspect of the twin flame journey is to prevent us from reaching the union and unconditional love that comes when we have worked through the pain, loss and grief.

Once they reach union, the twin flame dynamic is what the rest of the world models their romantic relationships on because they serve to demonstrate unparalleled love. It's a love that is unconditional and equal in its design. Twin flames are evolutionary and full of growth. They are the catalyst for our growth as they hold up a mirror to us and encourage us to become the best version of ourselves that we can be while holding us in unconditional love regardless. Imagine what would happen to society's current narrative if the whole of humanity decided to live like this. It would crumble instantly.

These are the things we all search for, the place that feels like we've truly come home. The real love that we're hungry to access and once you get a taste for it, nothing comes close to it. This is the sacred union we are seeking, whether you are a twin flame or choosing to live your life on this frequency with another soul.

The following is a poem I wrote to give you a sense of what a twin flame relationship is like and why we hunger for it so much.

What We're Searching For

A twin flame is not a quiet kind of love;
it's passion burning with the fire of a thousand suns,
    kind of love;
planets realigning to orbit around you, kind of love.

Galaxies fanfare into existence, embers of dying stars reignite.
Heart aflutter with butterflies at their voice,
living and dying all at once with their touch.

Eternity in an hour, a languid summer lived in minutes.
It is a peace that could still the world,
and tormented heartbreak that never ends.

Without them,
a wound that never heals. Yet forgiveness exists
in a solitary kiss.

You can't bear to stay and don't want to leave—
it's never enough and always so much.
A magnifying glass to the worst within you.
Statues in honour of the very best of you.

Words are an endless ocean, never to convey the depth.
So speak not—
for their eyes see into your soul.

In a glance; a thousand words, a million lifetimes.
Time and space cease,
for they are the only meaning.

The oasis for which you've long searched,
water to quench the soul. Home in an ever-changing landscape.
The path to salvation, and your own destruction.

A tightrope of adventure into the depths of the ocean,
beyond the known galaxies. By their side
is heaven on earth.

A twin flame is not a quiet kind of love;
it's a soul set on fire, kind of love;
the world pales around them, kind of love.

Once you've found it, come what may—
no matter the trials, tribulations, or treachery of the road—
no other love will do.

———

A NEW RELATIONSHIP BLUEPRINT

The world doesn't have many healthy templates for what these successful sacred unions look like. Many of the current relationship templates are built on objectification, power over and control. Or they are built on the partners being unequal in the relationship, or that one partner needs to save or sacrifice their dreams for the happiness of the other partner.

In our constantly adrenalised state, we've been conditioned to see this as appealing. The unbalanced or addictive, obsessive or controlling behaviours in these relationships give us little hits of dopamine creating this false high and fleeting feeling of pleasure.

We've replaced the love hormone oxytocin which is the hormone that actually *does* create the feelings of intimacy and trust that we're searching for. Instead, we've supplanted it with dopamine and called it love. What we've created is an obsession with unhealthy, damaging relationships that give us intermittent highs and we have convinced ourselves as a society that *this is what love looks like*.

I was a teenager when the *Twilight* books first came out. I remember the rush of reading the first book and being able to put myself in the shoes of Bella. It wasn't that the vampire Edward was in love with her that gripped me and so many other girls around the world; what gripped us was *how much* he was in love with her to the point of creepy obsession. Of course, none of us were able to see it as creepy. What we saw was this handsome immortal vampire head over heels in love with this fairly plain young girl who could have been any of us. It made it feel *possible* like it could happen to us. We could touch that kind of love.

The idea that someone loved us so much, that they would die if anything happened to us made it easy to overlook his less charming behaviours and manipulations. Blinded to the excitement and danger of it all, we were so caught up in the adrenaline rush and dopamine hits that we let the red flags slide without question. Not only is Edward Cullen essentially Bella's Bluebeard, but he's also representative of the slippery slope that is our attitude toward how love is represented in society. At the time of release, he was held up as a pillar of the ultimate man we should aspire to find; strong, handsome, devoted, commanding yet gentle, the 'whole package' and teen girls lapped it up. Yes, even me.

The *Twilight* novels, however, are not the only representation of this controlling narrative; it has been there all along. A few other examples include *Fifty Shades Of Grey*, Netflix's *You*, *Wuthering Heights* and Gaston in *Beauty And The Beast*. The vast majority of the stories and films we consume now are variations of the templates of tales originally written by the Brothers Grimm. Our first stories and fairy tales of happily ever after are tales of the princess needing saving by the prince. This usually occurs after a 'death' of sorts such as in *Snow White* or *Sleeping Beauty*, where we need to remain 'asleep' to our power or let it die to be loved by the prince and live 'happily ever after'.

In my case, I hungrily read the first *Twilight* book and fell in love with the idea – this was around the same time as I met my own Bluebeard. So of course, to begin with, it seemed like there was nothing wrong with this emotionally manipulative and controlling vampire with no boundaries. Their unbalanced and unhealthy relationship seemed... *normal*.

As my own Bluebeard relationship started to unravel, something deep-seated in me knew that something was wrong. I started to look at the stories again through a different lens. The sparkle wore off for me (pun intended). I headed into my next relationship as a broken young adult, crying out desperately for a love that wasn't as conditional as the world would have me believe it was.

Part of our reclamation is to rewrite the relationship paradigm for ourselves no matter how old we are. Whether we have experienced something like the Bluebeard story once in our life or multiple times, or whether we are simply deciding that we crave something more for the remainder of our life doesn't matter. What matters is that we choose something different now, say YES on this crossroad and work towards it.

To re-traumatise yourself in unhealthy, dangerous relationships would be a disservice to yourself and the healing work you've already done. It's a disservice to all the women in divine unions who have gone before us, who have been marginalised and sidelined throughout history to maintain a narrative that keeps us under control.

One of the women who demonstrated the twin flame, the divine union template is Mary Magdalene as the lover of Christ. Labelled as the whore by Christianity, her voice and her story have been systematically hidden from the world. It took until 1955 before her gospel was first published in its most complete form. Even since then it has not been given much airtime or been taken seriously because at the core of it is a message of divine, sacred union with Jesus Christ himself.

The Bible has instead created a more convenient narrative for Jesus Christ to reinforce concepts of celibacy and pious behaviour within Christianity. Mary Magdalene's pivotal role in Jesus' life as his constant, equal companion has been stripped from the story. She has instead been vilified and written with the sin of being a prostitute. This discourages us from connecting with her and her wisdom and obscures the truth of their relationship and what it means as a template of divine union for humanity.

The only evidence that remains in The Bible of her importance to him is that she is mentioned as being present at his crucifixion and she is the first person to see him after his resurrection. Even in this description though, Mary Magdalene is accompanied by two other women; another Mary and a Martha which could have been a convenient literary device to dilute and obscure the significance of her relationship with Jesus. Either way, the truth of their relationship has been hidden and rewritten to peddle a different narrative within the Christian faith.

The Gospel of Philip describes their relationship, stating that Jesus 'loved Mary more than the disciples and he often kissed her on the mouth'. What's interesting is the language used on the original papyrus to describe the status of their relationship. The Greek word koinonós (used in its masculine form) is applied which means companion rather than lover.

They kissed, which as much as it could have been romantic, could be interpreted as an 'exchange of spiritual breath'. In early Christianity, kissing didn't have romantic connotations and was instead used as a form of greeting. It is now known as the kiss of peace. The Gospel of Philip described the kiss of peace as a way of exchanging truths between one another, i.e. the spiritual breath. In that sense instead of it being a romantic exchange, Jesus kissing Mary passes on his truths. It sets her as the Apostle of the Apostles and the new messenger, in place of Jesus after his death. She is his spiritual successor.

Bringing together all these fragments and ideas paints a picture that Jesus and Mary were more than just lovers; she was more than a disciple, a follower and a whore. She was his companion, his spiritual partner. Together they represent the balance, embodiment and union of the divine feminine and the divine masculine. She was not simply his companion or favourite disciple. She was the other half of his soul. Their mission; to raise the consciousness of the world.

In reading Mary Magdalene's gospel, a picture is painted of a very different version of Christianity than the current narrative. Her gospel directs the reader inwards on a pilgrimage of the self through the seven powers which have become the seven deadly sins in modern society – a complete reversal to take us outwards and away from our soul selves.

Rather than encouraging us to seek something outside of ourselves, her gospel shows us that the answers we seek are within. That what we search for is our soul and she provides a blueprint for your own self-discovery to the path of your soul. In coming home continually to yourself, going within, deeper and deeper, this is where you can meet another in a divine union because you've shed the limitations and fears, everything that holds you back from embracing yourself in unconditional love.

For twin flames when they are separated from one another, they often turn outwards in a desperate attempt to reach for each other. The current narrative of twin flames while focusing on separation, emphasises coming into union and aligning with the other person. This means that once again the focus is outside of ourselves rather than turning inward to align with oneself. In turning inwards and continually going deeper, you will heal your wounds that you may have been projecting onto others including a twin flame, or things you were trying to run away from reflected in the other person. By going inwards choosing unconditional love and as a result, exhuming, healing, resurrecting and reclaiming your power, your twin becomes magnetised to union with you.

What a powerful narrative this is that completely changes the face of society and relationship paradigms. This new narrative asks men to let go of their toxic masculinity in such a way that it would crumble the foundations many have built their lives and empires. It invites the men to embrace their divine masculine and to seek union with their divine feminine counterpart, both within themselves and with their twin flame or sacred union partner.

Historically this divine masculine narrative has been so 'dangerous' to society, that it's been buried. Instead, a narrative has sprung up around the concept of twin flames that makes them seem rare, unobtainable and too painful to be desirable. There is a larger amount of these souls finding each other now in our technologically connected world, and at a time when more and more are awakening to raise the consciousness of the planet. They are needed to provide a blueprint for healthy, loving relationship dynamics for the rest of humanity.

At first, it *is* painful. And not because of the other person but because of ourselves. They are the mirror to ourselves; it is *us* we run from, not them. This is why the exhumation and healing are so important. To get to the other side it's not utterly terrifying to face this twin soul and be able to enter a new relationship paradigm built on the foundation of unconditional love.

Mary Magdalene knew this love and relationship paradigm with Jesus as one of the first (and only) documented successfully united mortal pairings, so it's befitting and natural that she appears to guide us on this next stage of the journey.

She shows us her strength, the strength we can all tap into. In Jesus' death, she continued to share the knowledge and work they had begun together. She shows us her softness as she wept for the loss of his physical form and was the only one to stay by his body in devotion in the days after his death. She shows us *his* vulnerability, trust and love for her through her own eyes as it was Mary alone that he resurrected. It was to her he shared special teachings and kisses (and spiritual breath).

She shows us her conviction as she continues to spread their teachings until the end of her life. She shows us the divine feminine goddess, with the grace of divinity in human form. She shows us enduring, unconditional love, trust and an equal partnership despite what the church has tried to convince us.

This is her biggest lesson; to seek no truth outside of yourself. To know your own heart and feel it so deeply that you cannot be swayed or betray yourself. It is through this deep understanding of the self that we attain freedom and the wholeness we are searching for.

We often wonder where our heart is, where is that which would make us feel whole, that other half of our soul. The true mastery is in the realisation that it has always resided in you yet has been hidden in your blind spot.

Finding the other half of your soul, that twin flame or divine union isn't about the parts of you that are missing and another person returns to you. It's about the light they shine upon you, radiating in their unconditional love for you. As you bask in the glow, it illuminates the parts of yourself you couldn't or didn't want to see. They shine a light on the fact that you were whole all along but it took a mirror to help you learn how to love and embrace yourself.

FUCKETY FUCK CAKES

All the changes we seek won't happen overnight. It's a choice we make systematically, moment by moment, minute by minute, breath by breath. How do we choose to respond to this? How do we choose to feel?

The exhumation and healing process affords us the ability to be able to calm and regulate our nervous system to release the long past. When you're not fighting wars on unseen, emotional fronts from all sides, you can deal with the moment in front of you by itself. That's when we're able to make different choices about how we respond to things and make changes.

However, it doesn't stop there. It's not about dealing with life as it comes up or being able to pick yourself up again quicker when you've been knocked down. We owe it to ourselves and our ancestors. To the women and witches who came before us. To the children and daughters who will follow after us. We owe it to us all to go beyond our personal lives and look at what we reclaim and resurrect for our collective psyche and the future of humanity.

It is said that American English is much closer to Old English than modern British English. I love that. I love the fact that while we have a version of English that links us to the past, we are seeing the evolution of English live before our very eyes too. Rooted in its history and origins and yet, simultaneously growing and evolving.

For me, this is how I feel we move forward and shift society. Because although it's important to reclaim the wisdom we have lost and been continuously cut off from accessing, there's no denying that the world has changed. With our technological advances, we can't go back to a world that consists of only the people in our village. It's too late. Pandora's Box is open and there's a whole world out there.

It doesn't mean that the ancient wisdom women hold has no place in society either. It's about how we find its new place in the modern world.

Kintsugi means golden joinery. It's the Japanese art of repairing broken pottery and highlighting those repairs with gold. Rather than try to hide the history of the object, kintsugi seeks to honour it. These items often become highly collectable and the kintsugi is seen as a beautiful addition and development rather than a destruction of the original beauty.

In going first and healing ourselves, we change who we are being in the world. As a result, the old systems will crumble to accommodate the new people we become. It all becomes part of the history and fabric of the world rather than something to be erased from history. If we erase the period of patriarchy and the oppression of women from our history, then we become no better than the men who sought to write us out of history in the first place.

Instead, it becomes facts of life. This is what happened and it hurt like hell and we're not still living there. *This is not the hill we're dying on.* We're healing, we've healed, we're learning, we've learnt, we're changing, we've changed. It would be a disservice to all those who have suffered and fought before us to pretend it didn't happen. We honour them by repairing the cracks in society and painting them with gold. We will never be able to return to the ancient times of the goddess and the wise woman, the world has moved on. That doesn't mean we can't honour the wisdom and the magic and create something new. It is our collective life's work; to contribute to the evolution of the next chapter in society. For those who are building new paradigms in society, it is important there is both an honouring of the old and acknowledging its existence while continuing to move forward to shape the good into something new. To find where the ancient wisdom meets the contemporary knowledge and technology we now have access to and write something new for our future.

And no, it's not the matriarchy. That's just another dictatorship.

It's the *balance*. It's the embodied divine feminine and divine masculine. It's a society built on union, equality, grace and love. Where things like toxic masculinity and oppression of women's rights are footnotes of our history. Reminders of what we've had to overcome to be here, prompting us to remember why it was worth the effort. This is our rebirth.

Rebirth, like any kind of birth, is messy. It's where you leave your dignity and prettiness at the door and embrace your primal instinct. It's where you're guided by your feelings, not your mind. It's where all that matters is this one breath, and then the next one, and the next one.

Rebirth is where women say fuck prettiness. Fuck being perfect. Fuck the glamorous illusions. Fuck being meek and mild. Fuck being *'yes sir, whatever you say sir'* women. Fuck being the trophy wife or the secret bit on the side. Fuck being the demonic home wrecker. Fuck being the obsessive, controlling girlfriend. Fuck being the nagging wife. Fuck being the ball and chain. Fuck being the unholy temptress. Fuck being the one who was asking for it. Fuck being frigid or naive. Fuck being a bitch, a witch or a whore. Fuck it, fuck it, fuck it all.

Go do and be whatever the fuck you want.

Did you find that paragraph a hard read? Did you wince every time I wrote fuck?

Fuck, fuck, fuckety fuck. Fuckety fuck with a cherry on top. Fuckety fucking fuck cakes.

What's the problem? Is it too vulgar? Is it too unladylike? Is it too unholy?

If it makes you uncomfortable, then sit with that feeling and ask yourself why. Is it because it is too vulgar or because you've not allowed yourself to say it? Is it too unladylike or because you've prescribed to someone else's vision of how a 'lady' should behave? Here's a hint; that vision was created by men to keep us pretty, quiet, palatable and safely under control. Is it because it's touching on nerves that makes you question why you ever sanctioned this view of what it means to be a woman?

Is it because you're secretly jealous or perhaps in awe of another being so bold as to type fuck nearly thirty times in as many sentences and to leave it in print forevermore? Bear in mind that as this is published in the UK, I am obligated by law to send a copy of this book to the British Library to be part of the National Archives, so not only will it be in print but it'll be in the British National Archives.

Fuck you patriarchy, how do you like that one? Perhaps if I try hard enough I'll get my book on banned lists across the world for being an affront to men!

And here's the thing, I'm not typing this to make a scene. I'm not even typing this with anger in my heart. If that sounds unbelievable, I invite you to tune into your intuition and heart connection to feel my words and you'll find there is no anger in me as I write this.

I am, however, writing this *with* the anger of a thousand women who have gone before me and couldn't speak their truth. I write this, *with* their anger, on their behalf. I do it for the ones who could not and cannot. I do it to lead from the front. If I can be so bold as to write fuck as many times and humanly possible, while still staying coherent and on point then you can speak the word just once, too.

Reclamation isn't about setting boundaries for yourself after you've healed. It's not even about cutting toxic people out of your life. It's not about self-care that looks like bubble baths and face masks. Taking care of yourself is a basic human right, not a glamorous beauty industry designed to keep you distracted.

Once you've drawn the lines for yourself and your life and decided what you want to create for yourself, reclamation is about clawing things back that you thought weren't meant for you, one at a time. Clawing back the words we've been told are taboo and rewriting our lexicon.

Cunt is widely considered the most vulgar word in the English language. It's also a term used to describe female genitalia since the 13th century, but it wasn't until the 19th century that it began to be considered obscene and vulgar. By this point, I think I'd be in danger of mansplaining to you why not only is it absurd, but also why it's been done in the first place.

However, just in case you missed the memo or perhaps you've skipped ahead to find the chapter where the author writes fuck a whole bunch of times, here's the why.

It disconnects us from our power. In making cunt the dirtiest word in the English language, a word that describes female genitalia, *women* become the dirtiest word, the dirtiest objects in the world. We are the ones with the cunts. We are the original sinners from the Garden of Eden (thanks Eve!) It is us who has caused the downfall of humanity, all because we didn't have a dick. All because we led the men astray. It blatantly has nothing to do with the fact that men are on the whole, too emotionally unavailable and insecure to handle the raw, primal power that women embody so effortlessly. When women come from that space it forces men to look at themselves. Activating and dealing with emotions and feelings they've denied themselves for millennia in the name of being the ones in control and being the ones with the power.

The crucial thing they've missed is that the power comes from embracing and feeling it all. The power comes from not denying ourselves *anything*. In honouring all of it, the good, bad, ugly and fucking disgusting. It's all part of what it means to be human.

We have become so hung up on how we express ourselves through words that we've forgotten it's not the only form of self-expression. That you can express yourself in art, dancing, music, baking, the clothes and make up you wear or how you do your hair. All of it communicates something about yourself whether you are consciously aware of it or not. What is it you really want to say about yourself?

The emphasis has been placed so heavily on words as if they are the only thing that matters. And yet, the language of women has been warped to disconnect us; from ourselves and each other. Words like witch, bitch, slag, slut, healer, priestess, nurse, matron, sister, mother, virgin. They all evoke very specific ideas of who that person is and what they can and cannot do. We decide based on what the world tells us, whether it's okay to be associated with those words or not. We decide whether it's okay based on whether it would get us rejected from the pack and based on hundreds of years' worth of persecution of the female form.

Our bodies have received the same treatment. Cunt is apparently one of the worst words we could ever use. Pussy, aside from the vagina, is often used as a slang term for a weak man. People are afraid to use the word breasts, instead opting for boobs, tits or titties to lighten it. To sexualise them, to make it fun and light. To diminish the importance of our breasts, those which feed our children and are the wings of our hearts. To make them into something to be ashamed of if we use them in any way other than for the pleasure of the male gaze. All of it disconnects us from ourselves and it's time to take our words back. Not in a rebellious or angry way.

Language is live; it's evolving daily due to how we use it. There's a double standard that has been created in the idea of semantic change. While it's okay to create new words or shift meanings of some words, other words like cunt and bitch have this unspoken air around them that gives off this untouchable vibe. If we're afraid to use the words ourselves, no one ever needs to be uncomfortable and no one ever needs to address the change in meaning. By making us afraid of our own language, there's no need to worry about semantic change because it simply doesn't happen. We have self-regulated ourselves in our refusal to use the unpretty, vulgar words that are looked down upon in society.

Once upon a time, to be a witch, to be a healer or spiritual woman, was an incredibly honourable and innate part of being a woman. The crone was to be celebrated, she was trusted and respected. The work of the priestess was holy. Making it safe to reclaim these words, to bring them back into our everyday lexicon and breathe new life into them, to make them mean something positive for ourselves, is reclaiming a tiny piece of ourselves that was once lost. It creates a shift that cannot be ignored.

If we want to rewrite the narrative of women, changing the way we talk about ourselves is part of the shift. As the language of society shifts, it's reflected in our personal usage and in dictionaries where they collate both new words and semantic changes. I believe part of the key to shifting mentalities lies in beginning to make words that have hurt us, *belong* to us. Make them meaningful, **make them ours.** Stop being afraid of speaking out, speaking up and speaking your truth. *Nothing* is too vulgar for you to say unless you believe it is so.

This is how we build something new within society. We take those existing structures, break them apart and examine them. When we put them back together, we paint gold over those cracks to create a new object of beauty. It doesn't all have to be put back together in such a way that everything is new, polished and pristine. We can honour what once was without trying to erase it while still making it work for us in the here and now.

THE HOLY GRAIL WITHIN

From this point onwards, your journey continues deeper inwards. Having unravelled so very outwardly, now you can only unravel deeper layers of authenticity into your own heartspace.

As you get to know the landscape of your own heart so intimately, you start to realise the questions have become bigger once again. The focus no longer lies on what makes you happy or what feels most aligned. These are things you do instinctively in every breath. You have instilled the art of aligning your soul into the fabric of your very being.

The question now becomes, *and what else?*

Because to stay in your own lane, as a little oasis of peace and happiness is a great thing. It is a rejection of everything that society has taught us about ourselves and who we can be.

However, to stay on your island, you will find goes against the grain of who you've become and what you now know. In embracing and unravelling your own loving heart there is also an outwards pull. You no longer want to remain as an island, so you start to build a bridge. At first, it feels like you're building a bridge out into nowhere, into thin air. However, if everyone is also starting to build their bridges instead of burning them, chances seem likely that we'll eventually meet.

And in this beautiful meeting of bridges, we're all building, there is love. Love for the craftswomanship of each bridge. The way they follow and flow with the undulations of the oceans. The knots and notches in the wood. The way it appears like the bridges were grown out of the earth by Gaia herself.

We are not meant to stay as islands lost upon the sea. We are meant to come together, in our network of bridges and build new lands and communities to share with our soul groups.

The ultimate wisdom for women to transcend is that of the togetherness we have lost and been cut off from accessing over the years. Our true strength lies in the power of togetherness. No one was ever meant to do everything or be everything, no one was ever meant to do it all alone.

To know love and to know your own heart and soul is to know this to be true.

Because on the days when the emotional jungle on your island becomes too dense. When you've lost your way inside and don't know if you'll ever see the light of day again. That's when other women; family or the friends you choose as family will come running over those interconnected bridges waving their torches as they rally to come find you in the dark.

On the days where you aren't sure whether to cry in exhaustion or slump in your dinner and all you want to do is wash your hair and eat a chocolate bar in peace. That's when those women you trust and love will arrive on your island, bearing cooked meals, open arms and children, excited and ready to play with yours to give you that five minutes to yourself; because they know, *we know* it takes a village to raise a child and that the load is easier when it's shared.

On those nights when you don't know how to hold it all together and when you feel like your tears will flood your island and swallow it whole. That's when they will take your hand and sit you around the campfire. Where you'll share your burdens and everyone will shed tears. Where you'll laugh until your bellies ache and your eyes leak. Where you'll sing and dance until you morph into primal beasts of passion. Where you'll break bread, eat and toast marshmallows with the sisters you call home. Where you'll fall silent and listen to your heart, honouring those who've come before you.

Healing and reclamation aren't about getting angry at the injustice of the world, it's about learning to sing new songs together. Songs whose melodies will carry themselves over oceans and bridges as clarion calls for more sisters. Siren songs beckoning them to gather and know love in their hearts.

It's about tuning into yourself, trusting what you hear and not being afraid to answer the higher calling. It's when you can feel the pull towards using your ancient wisdom, embracing your spiritual gifts and utilising your magnificent skills, creativity and talents. It's when you surrender entirely to giving them back to the earth and humanity from a space of joy and love.

As you continue to unravel deeper, you'll start to walk through the jungle of your island towards the centre, to know yourself more intimately, to know your own heart and soul. As you walk, you'll see the sisters who've journeyed across oceans and bridges, bearing torches in your name to light your way. As you keep going, entering the temple that is your heart you'll know exactly two things:

One is that you'll never walk alone in this world again, for now, you have the sisters you've embraced.

Two, you already know the secret that resides in the heart of the temple. Instead of being tentative or afraid, you are eager to get there. Gingerly walking ever closer with a grin on your face as you continuously reach the centre of the temple on the island of your heart is where you meet yourself in unconditional love, over and over again.

You are her. She is you. We are she. She is us.

Over and over again. Across all time and space. Across oceans and bridges. From boats and teaspoons, you are always arriving right within the deepest part of your heart.

You can breathe now. You are here.

THIS ISN'T AS FAR AS WE GO

This book is very much alive. It's not something I've forced myself to write – it has flowed out of me and through me and I have been very humbled by the journey of facilitating it. This book has a spirit and a soul of its own. It has always known exactly what it wants to say, in what order and when. It has been a true collaboration between me and the universe to write it and it's been a joy to surrender fully to the process.

Having worked coaching writers for the past three years, I've seen the struggles, the trials and the tribulations. I've heard all of the excuses as to why someone can't write the book they believe they so desperately want to write. Having written this I can honestly say it really does come back to your own soul alignment.

When the idea for this book appeared in the corner of my eye, I genuinely thought it was meant for my practitioner Emily, not me. She was the expert in the divine feminine, not I. Who was I to write such a book when I knew so very little in comparison? As I felt into the energy of the book, it became clear to me that my inexperience and lack of knowledge were *exactly* the reason why I was the person meant to write it. This notion brought up so many fears, yet I couldn't ignore the truth that I felt within my bones.

From the moment I opened myself up to the possibility that it was mine to write, it was like the floodgates opened. The content and structure of the book arrived without me searching for any of it. Although I often had no idea what was going on in a chapter or section, why it had to be in a certain order or how any of it made sense; it flowed.

Nothing stopped me from writing. All of those common excuses; not having enough time or energy, not knowing what to write, lacking confidence or expertise, these excuses were nonexistent. All I knew was that writing this book became a compulsion. I had genuinely itchy fingers when I wasn't writing it. I heard chapters writing themselves in my head while I was in the bath, and I had to rush to get out and type it up on my phone before the words were lost. I nearly burnt the dinner multiple times because I was gripped in writing and the rest of the world had all but fallen away. I never had to think about what was coming next, I simply showed up willing and it wrote itself over forty days.

The number forty is significant in the divine, such as when the earth flooded for forty days and nights while Noah kept the animals on his ark. The Hebrews roamed the desert with Moses for forty years. This was after Moses' original forty years in the desert before he came to free his people from slavery. Moses also spent forty days up Mount Sinai receiving the Ten Commandments. Jesus Christ's ascension into heaven occurred forty days after his resurrection. There are plenty more instances of its significance. Overall, forty days has come to be seen as representing a trial or a test and the ultimate triumph at the end.

This has certainly been my experience of writing this book. It was a test of my trust in the creative process and co-creation with the universe. As I wrote this book, I relived the stages that we wrote about, at speed. While the concepts were certainly channelled from something outside of me, I provided the humanity and context to help them land for you as the reader. To do that to the best of my ability, I needed to be able to feel those emotions once more to write them accurately.

Every stage I've written about in this book, I lived over the last two and a half years as I went on my transformation. In the writing, they've come alive once more, at speed over these forty days. Wounds reopened and I shed tears over things I thought I had moved through when suddenly they once again resurfaced and became live and real.

Emily has also lived this book on my behalf over the forty days of writing. The strength of the relationship we've built on this journey means we have developed a telepathic, energetic connection over the last couple of years. It meant that I was able to pick up on her feelings as I wrote the book. Often at the end of the day, we would talk and I'd describe what I was writing. She would explain what happened to her that day and every time, her experiences and emotions matched what I was writing. As I said, this book is alive and it needed to be lived to be the most accurate representation of the journey to give to you as the reader.

It's a book that has kept on teaching me, not only in the writing but in the editing too, which I love about this journey of personal transformation and co-creation with the universe. We can tap into ancient wisdom and find that the wisdom isn't static; it's still evolving and growing with us. I know that this book isn't where the story ends for all I've learned and everything I'm becoming.

During the editing of this book, I realised that the three main sections of the book that I had laid out; exhumation, healing and reclamation, weren't the whole story either. What I've found is that healing comes in two parts – the healing that comes directly out of exhumation can still be dense and can still send you far back into the depths. Whereas, with time and distance, with more inner work, there's a healing that leads us into reclamation which is lighter, more hopeful and purposeful. This is the kind of healing where we know we're not going back into the depths of pain and exhumation, but we're healing to reclaim the parts of ourselves that we lost so that we can build something into the future. This is when I realised that beyond reclamation, there is creation as a phase to experience.

Once we've chosen what we reclaim in our lives and we've started rebuilding from the ashes, creation is where anything is possible. It's where we can truly start to dream for ourselves and rewrite new paradigms of our existence. As I realised this phase existed in the editing of this book, I considered whether to add it in until I realised that for me it is still too new, I'm still living my own creation phase. To add it to this book would be doing the rest of the story of what comes before and what comes after creation a disservice because I'm still feeling into it. I know this means that eventually there'll be a follow up to Unravelling Inwards and I'm excited by the prospect, without wanting to force it to arrive before it's ready. To this end, I've written the first poem of what will eventually become the creation phase, and I include it for you at the end of this book to give you a taste of what's to come beyond reclamation. I hope you're as excited to find out the rest of what that looks like as I am.

While editing this book, I was also working on my first full length collection of poetry and prose called *Soul Threads*. *Soul*

Threads was a book I had committed to write before *Unravelling Inwards* was even on my periphery and my original intention behind it had been to write about love, sacred unions and twin flames. I had begun mapping it out and then stalled in the process. But as I edited *Unravelling Inwards*, I realised that these two books were meant to live together as companions. *Soul Threads* was in fact, meant to be the Unravelling Inwards journey told through poetry and prose. As I wrote in the introduction to *Soul Threads*;

'[Soul Threads] was meant to be so much more than a story of love through the aeons. Because what I've learnt in navigating this kind of love is that it's a journey of the self. The more I love, the more I'm drawn inwards to myself. The more myself I become, my capacity to love and be loved expands and deepens.'

Immediately I tore up the existing manuscript and began rewriting, rearranging and editing. It was a joy to find that this time; *Soul Threads* flowed and came together with ease and speed as it had been meant to all along.

You can read both books, this one, *Unravelling Inwards* and *Soul Threads* together or independently. They both follow the same journey and as poetry speaks to the soul in a different way to nonfiction writing, it will land differently for you depending on what you read. May you be drawn to whichever combination and order of reading you feel you need to hear it.

That is where I hand this book and soul journey over to you. It's been humbling to write it and yet the work is not done. My word in this book is not a gospel – it is a rough guide. I've written about the common landmarks on the road, given language to the things that you know in your soul and perhaps didn't have the words for or may not know on a conscious level.

It's your turn to take the wisdom from the universe, divine feminine and myself in these pages and use it for your own exhumation and healing. It may not arrive all in the same order, and it may not look the same as my journey. However, it is my wish that on the days when you feel alone on your island, you remember that I've been there and that others have gone before you and struggled in the middle of the journey too. May my words be the first bridge that connects you to something greater than your lonely island.

Although I cannot say I know *exactly* how you feel, I am holding space for you and honouring your journey, however it looks. We all have our paths to carve and choices to make at the crossroads. All I can do with this book is show you that it **is** possible, that you can come out the other side.

My best piece of advice, the one thing I truly hope you take to heart is to not do it alone. Build your soul tribe. Find the friends that you choose as family. The ones who will walk beside you in the torrential rain and pitch darkness. Find the ones who will bring their teaspoon and sit with you in your boat. Find the practitioner who can guide you on the journey as Hecate mentored Persephone in the underworld.

I'm not going to tell you it will be easy. That you won't feel any hurt or pain in the process. I can't promise any of those things. I can tell you that one day, it gets easier. One day, it hurts less. One day the dark night of your soul becomes the brightest day. One day you can look up at the sky and see the light once again. I don't know how long it will take any of us to get there, but I do know that day always comes so long as you're not afraid to face the demons and slay the dragons on the way. Like I said though, please don't do it alone.

Find your Emily who will walk with you on both the brightest and darkest days. Be open to the possibility that she exists out there for you. As you've read in this book, the world has taught us many false truths about women and convinced us to behave in ways that are completely unnatural for us. This healing process is about unlearning those things and tuning into yourself, learning what comes naturally to you.

No one goes through this process and comes out the same. To exhume the dead and bleeding things in your life to heal them means you will never be the same. Change and transformation are not something you need to fear, instead, embrace them. To become the butterfly, a caterpillar dismantles itself entirely into a goo and yet doesn't fear this 'death' for it knows it is simply a part of life.

My wish for you is that you take heart in the journey I've shown you and trust yourself to go through it, knowing you will come out on the other side as your very own magnificent butterfly. In the process of unlearning and rewilding yourself, you reclaim your wings that have been clipped by the world that told you no. In the process, you learn to use your voice to say yes for yourself and others.

Because in going through this process, you find yourself in a position of being called to help others. It doesn't necessarily look like becoming a holistic practitioner; it could be as simple as supporting and holding space for a friend or holding your boundaries to encourage others to look at their own. Everything we do from this space creates a ripple that affects and inspires those around us.

And although once past the healing, the journey becomes a continuous, inward unravelling to the centre of your heart, that doesn't mean that you remain silent and inwardly focused. There is a balance that comes automatically, almost without you even noticing. Where in each breath you know you are turning yourself inwards, aligning closer to your heart. And yet, you cannot look away from the rest of the world and leave it to its fate. In reclaiming your power, there's a desire that grows to help others reclaim their power too. There's a desire to want to shift the world and make it a better place.

That journey and narrative shift for society starts with you. For it is not the wounded and unhealed that can make the change. Coming from a wounded space makes you loud yet also ineffective. There's a wisdom that comes from this journey that makes you quiet, though not silent. It means your actions are much more intentional, deliberate and focused. And you know the power of working together rather than trying to do it alone; this is how we make fundamental, long term shifts.

It's not in the loud acts of rebellion, the bra-burning and the big stunts that go viral on social media. It's not about shouting the loudest for one moment. It's about transforming yourself so fundamentally that you simply cannot operate within society as it currently stands. When you realise you cannot function within those rules or toxicity, you seek to change your corner of the world — when we all start doing that, we become too hard to ignore.

Nothing changes if nothing changes. If we all sit wallowing on our solitary islands, lamenting over the hand we've been dealt in life, the world doesn't change. *It can change.* Don't think for a moment that you are ineffective or insignificant because you are just one person. The impact that you have, the ripple you create on the people and world around you, *is* the change.

It's the moment that you stand up and say; no, I won't be spoken to like that.

No, I don't like your tone.

No, I wasn't asking for it.

No, I won't be treated that way.

No, what you've done is not okay.

No, I don't forgive you.

No, I won't condone this.

No, I won't stay silent.

No, I won't accept what you tell me when it goes against myself.

No, I won't do what I'm told just to make you comfortable.

No, I won't compromise myself for your sake.

No, I won't comply with society just because you tell me I should.

No, I won't betray my sisters anymore.

No, I won't betray myself anymore.

Instead, it's the moment when you decide to start saying yes.

Yes, I trust myself.

Yes, I am connected and in tune with my body.

Yes, I want better for myself.

Yes, I deserve better.

Yes, I know my worth and value.

Yes, I can show you how I want to be treated.

Yes, I can help you as long as it doesn't compromise me.

Yes, I am unafraid to go into the deep.

Yes, I am willing to do whatever it takes to align with my soul.

Yes, I am healing.

Yes, I am freeing myself from my limiting beliefs.

Yes, I trust other women.

Yes, I share my wisdom.

Yes, I follow my heart.

Yes, I am magic.

Yes, I embrace all of myself.

Yes, I love myself.

Yes, I can do this.

Yes, I can make great change.

Yes, I am the change.

Yes, we owe it to the women who went before us, the ones who fought and suffered for our rights to think, speak, vote and open bank accounts.

Yes, we owe it to the ones who will come after us to start making the changes to create a more equal, safe, loving world for them to live in.

Yes, we owe it to them to leave a world behind for them without destroying it.

Most of all, we owe it to *ourselves*. Society has continued its patriarchal narrative for hundreds and thousands of years and has no intention of changing it because it suits them.

It's up to us to stand up and say… that's not okay. To suit you to the detriment of us is no longer acceptable. It needs to work for all of us or it doesn't work at all.

This is the first step. The road may be long. We're going to do it together. We owe it to ourselves to give ourselves the life that we've been taught we don't deserve and yet, our souls have been screaming that we are worthy of it and so much more all along.

Listen to your heart, listen to your soul. You *can* heal. You *are* worthy. None of this is so insurmountable that it cannot be overcome. Just because this is the way it has been for so long, doesn't mean it is written in stone. It can only change if you decide you want to be part of the change and make moves towards it. To sit and complain is just empty words and hot air.

Be the change. Model it for others. It starts on an individual level, with one person. But from tiny acorns, oak trees grow.

The thing about women is we are resilient. Despite how the world has treated us throughout history, we remain. Humanity wouldn't exist without us so it has continued to leave just enough of our souls standing in our bodies to keep running the human race.

You know we are more than the pretty shells they've left us with. Find her within you, embrace her. Let her scream the words of a thousand lives. We've held onto hope, clinging to it like a buoy in the middle of the ocean. And now we grow those seeds of hope, with love, into the thickest, luscious forests that will spread across the earth.

Growing up, my mum always said to me, 'The impossible we do at once, miracles take a little longer'.

And I know this; changing the world isn't impossible when enough of us stand together. It is certainly the most beautiful miracle we can create. In the Cambridge Dictionary, a miracle is described as; 'an unusual and mysterious event that is thought to have been caused by a god because it does not follow the usual laws of nature.'

We are the gods. *We* are the goddesses. *We* are the divine ones in human form.

Let's go out there and create a miracle together.

BEYOND RECLAMATION, THERE'S CREATION...

MOTHER OF ALL CREATION

In the eternal labyrinth of your soul,
the air, sweet and still
beckons deeper.

She meets you there
amongst the flowers and leaves.
Her smile, a silent song calling your soul.

With open hands and loving heart
you receive her wisdom,
as she hands you the seeds of creation.

Ancient chants and primal dance
awaken a fire within,
ready to birth your heart's desires.

Now *anything* is probable –
what will you create?

GLOSSARY

Ancestral Work – clearing and healing ancestral wounds. See *Epigenetics* and *Intergenerational Trauma*.

Ancestral Wounds – see *Intergenerational Trauma*.

Atlas – a Titan in Greek mythology condemned to hold up the heavens for all eternity as a punishment.

Breathwork – breathing practices that help release emotional, physical and mental stress from the body, encouraging relaxation and calm.

Bluebeard – as described by Clarissa Pinkola Estés in *Women Who Run With The Wolves*, Bluebeard is the first man that a woman enters into a relationship with as she is rising into her power. Bluebeard seeks to cut her off from the potential of the maiden.

Bowen Technique – also known as Bowen Therapy, is a gentle, non-invasive complementary therapy using rolling movements to support the body in balancing and repairing itself.

Clairalience – the ability to gain psychic knowledge through a sense of smell.

Crone – the final phase in the four phases of the feminine and the triple goddess (see *Triple Goddess*). The crone represents our final life phase before death with all her wisdom and power. See *Hecate*.

Demeter – Greek goddess of agriculture and grain, mother of Persephone. Representing the mother phase in the four phases of the feminine. See *Four Phases Of The Feminine, Mother, Persephone*.

Divine Feminine – a spiritual construct representing the manifestation of feminine (yin) energy. It is the counterpart to divine masculine energy and part of the constant balancing of energies within ourselves and the universe. See *Divine Masculine*.

Divine Masculine – a spiritual construct representing the manifestation of masculine (yang) energy. It is the counterpart to divine feminine energy and part of the constant balancing of energies within ourselves and the universe. See *Divine Feminine*.

Emotional Freedom Technique (EFT) – a technique that involves tapping on meridian acupressure points in the body to support the release of trauma and emotional, physical and mental stress from the body.

Epigenetics – the study and healing of how decisions and traumatic events affect our DNA, also known as intergenerational trauma. See *Intergenerational Trauma*.

Emotional Stress Release (ESR) – a simple yet powerful Kinesiology technique that calms and alleviates stress by holding fingers lightly on the forehead.

Exhumation – the first stage of the *Unravelling Inwards* emotional healing journey.

Fertile Void – Used in Gestalt theory, meaning nothing stands out or appears to be happening.

Four Phases Of The Feminine – as described by Jane Hardwicke Collings in *The Four Phase Feminine Way*. The four phases of the feminine build upon the concept of the Triple Goddess by introducing another life stage between mother and crone. See *Maiden, Mother, Maga, Crone*.

Gaia – Greek goddess representing the personification of the earth often known as *Mother Earth*.

Hades – God of the dead and king of the Underworld in Greek mythology. He abducts Persephone and tricks her into becoming his wife. See *Persephone*.

Healing – the second stage of the *Unravelling Inwards* emotional healing journey.

Hecate – Greek goddess of the crossroads, the moon and witchcraft. Representing the crone phase in the four phases of the feminine. Hecate also represented the three faces of the Triple

Goddess (maiden, mother and crone). See *Crone, Four Phases Of The Feminine, Triple Goddess.*

Homeopathy – is an alternative medicine based on the idea that the body can cure itself using natural substances to stimulate the healing process.

Hypnosis/Hypnotherapy – a therapeutic tool that brings people into a state of hypnosis or a trance-like state with increased suggestibility and focus to help treat emotional issues and trauma in a safe, relaxed way.

Intergenerational Trauma – trauma that is passed down through generations. See *Epigenetics.*

Journaling – an intentional writing practice to explore your emotional and mental state.

Kali – Hindu goddess of time, ultimate power, transformation and destruction. Kali guides us through the exhumation stage of the Unravelling Inwards journey. See *Exhumation, Unravelling Inwards.*

Kinesiology – an alternative therapeutic tool using the study of human body movement, specifically the response of the muscles to promote health and bring the body, mind, and energy back into balance.

Kintsugi – Japanese art of repairing broken pottery and highlighting breaks with gold.

Kuan Yin – also spelt as Guanyin, is a Buddhist icon and the embodiment of compassion and mercy. Kuan Yin guides us through the reclamation stage of the Unravelling Inwards journey. See *Reclamation, Unravelling Inwards*.

Laying Of Hands – to put your hands on or above the body to send energetic healing to a person.

Lilith – Adam's first wife in the Garden of Eden who refused to be subservient to him. Lilith guides us through the exhumation stage of the Unravelling Inwards journey. See *Exhumation, Unravelling Inwards*.

Love Languages – different ways people can express, and experience romantic love as outlined by Gary Chapman in his book, '*The Five Love Languages: How to Express Heartfelt Commitment to Your Mate*'.

Maga – the third phase in the four phases of the feminine. Maga's rite of passage is the menopause following the end of child birthing and motherhood. See *Tethys*.

Maiden – the first phase in the four phases of the feminine from birth to motherhood. See *Menarche, Persephone*.

Mary Magdalene – travelled with Jesus as his lover, and spiritual successor and is canonically considered one of Jesus' followers within the gospels. She was present at his crucifixion and resurrection. Mary Magdalene guides us through the reclamation stage of the Unravelling Inwards journey. See *Reclamation, Unravelling Inwards*.

Meditation – a practice that uses various techniques such as mindfulness to develop awareness, and attention and achieve a state of mental calm. See *Mindfulness*.

Menarche – first menstruation and physical rite of passage for the maiden. See *Maiden*.

Meraki – Greek term that means 'to do something with love'. Often used for creative pursuits.

Mindfulness – the practice of continually bringing your attention to the present moment. See *Meditation*.

Mother – the second phase in the four phases of the feminine represents the transition into motherhood. See *Demeter*.

Mother Wound – trauma and wounding caused by mothers both in their presence and absence.

Neuro-Linguistic Programming (NLP) – a technique using communication and personal development tools to help change thought and behavioural patterns.

Patriarchy – a social system that places men as the dominant and privileged force in society.

Persecution Complex – Beliefs that someone is going to cause harm or 'persecute' you. Often activated by and connected to the witch wound. See *Witch Wound*.

Persephone – Greek goddess of spring and the Underworld, daughter of Demeter. Representing the maiden phase in the four phases of the feminine. See *Four Phases Of The Feminine, Maiden*.

Reclamation – the third stage of the *Unravelling Inwards* emotional healing journey.

Sacred Union – See *Twin Flame*.

Self-talk – our internal monologue.

Shadow Work – a Jungian psychotherapy focusing on working with the 'shadow self', parts of the psyche that you wish to remain hidden. Shadow work seeks to help individuals reach their potential by healing and aligning the unconscious and subconscious parts of oneself with the conscious psyche.

Siga Siga – Greek phrase meaning 'slowly, slowly.'

Sisterhood Wound – trauma and wounding caused by the sisterhood, i.e. female friends and other women in society.

Tapping – see *Emotional Freedom Technique (EFT)*.

Tethys – Titan goddess of fresh water, daughter of Gaia and married to Oceanus. Representing the maga phase in the four phases of the feminine. See *Four Phases Of The Feminine, Maga*.

Touch For Health – a form of Kinesiology. See *Kinesiology*.

Triple Goddess – Popular in New Age Spirituality, the Triple Goddess represents the three aspects of the feminine; maiden, mother and crone, often depicted by Hecate for all three aspects. See *Hecate, Four Phases Of The Feminine*.

Twin Flame – a term from New Age Spirituality. The concept of two people born from the same soul; two halves of a whole that spend eternity seeking each other to be in union again. Also known as twin souls, mirror souls, sacred unions, divine partnership or divine union.

Unravelling Inwards – the journey and process of emotional healing detailed within this book, spanning the phases of exhumation, healing and reclamation.

Witch Wound – a collective trauma experienced in society by the historical and global persecution of witches, witchcraft, sorcery and magic.

Are you ready to go on
a personal healing journey
and create the life of your dreams?

Kick-start your personal healing journey with our **free**
Unravelling Inwards resources. Join *The Circle*, a private
community run to access free downloads including; book club
questions and discussion topics, summaries, cheat sheets and
action lists, meditations, journal prompts, a first aid box for
emotional stress and more.

Join today to access the free resources at:
https://circle.infiniteunravelling.com/

You've read the book,

now go on the journey with us!

With Camilla and Emily as your coaches, we'll guide you through the journey of your own healing and self-discovery.

Find out how to work with us at
https://infiniteunravelling.com/

ACKNOWLEDGEMENTS

None of this – my personal transformation, this book, this life I'm living, would have happened without my guide, best friend and now business partner, Emily Tuck. She offered me something that I didn't even know was possible and has walked with me every day since. Thank you from the depths of my soul for showing up. How you got my phone number in the first place, I'll never know. Why I answered that call when I never usually answer for strangers I'll never know either, but I'm so grateful that I did. This book is a testament to you and your work; you are the most amazing person I know.

To my husband Aaron; who without question has given me the time and space I needed to work through my emotional baggage and truly heal. Thank you for always seeing my divinity. For a man of not many words, you've always known the right thing to say.

To my dogs; Teddy who made me question my sanity and Mia who got me through the darkest days with her cuddles. Together you showed up in my life to put me back on a spiritual path. Thank you both for being your fluffy barky lovely selves.

To my biggest fans; my parents. Mum, and Dad, thank you for all the encouragement and support as I wrote this and struggled with my fears to put it out into the world. I'm so very grateful for your patience and love on the days when I wasn't sure who I was or where I was going.

Thank you to my Grandad; who has always believed and helped me embrace my magic. You've been more than a grandad to me. There's no one I'd rather talk about ghosts and past lives on the Lusitania with than you.

For my nan who, had she been alive to see this, I *know* would have carried a copy of this book in her bag to show everyone she knew (and I would have pretended to be embarrassed but secretly thrilled). My biggest wish is that she could have been here to see the woman I have become. No one will ever make a pancake quite like you!

To the lovers, family and friends who have shaped me, for both the good and the bad, past, present and future… thank you.

Thank you to those wonderful people who took the time to beta read for me, Katie Gleeson, Linda Docherty, Esther Lemmens, Hannah Parkinson and Julia McFarland. Your thoughtful feedback has meant so much to the girl in me who was told she wasn't good enough once upon a time. You've all helped me make this book even better. THANK YOU!

James Browne, my meticulous editor has helped me make this book shine. You have been so very patient with my dithering. I hope you know how valuable your input is to me. You are brilliant!

Finally, thank YOU dear reader for connecting with my story and words. My biggest wish for you is that you can take this and use it as a guide for transforming your own life. Go out there and find your Emily to walk with you on the darkest of days. It's time to unravel yourself and be amazing!

ABOUT THE AUTHOR

Camilla Fellas Arnold is an executive coach, mentor and creativity facilitator who excels at helping people align to their soul purpose and unlock their creative gifts by combining subconscious tools with the Chinese Five Elements and Interconnectivity Coaching Approach. Camilla believes that creativity is a fundamental component of self-expression. She knows that taking a holistic approach in aligning with our authentic selves, allows us to embrace powerful creative flow, freedom from our limiting beliefs and find our true purpose in life.

Camilla has worked in the creative industries for over a decade across multiple disciplines and is an international bestselling author. Currently, she is training in more subconscious and holistic tools as well as developing programmes to provide better mental and emotional support for creatives and creative coaches to add to their toolkit, to shift the narrative of the suffering/starving artist to creative joy, flow and abundance within the creative industries.

Camilla has been awarded an ILM Level 7 Diploma for Executive and Senior Level Coaches and Mentors and is an EMCC UK Accredited Senior Practitioner. Camilla holds a bachelor's degree in design for publishing and a master's degree in communication design from NUA. She holds membership with the International Society of Typographic Designers and is an RSA Fellow.

When she is not coaching and mentoring, Camilla can be found writing poetry, having afternoon tea or creating fun photo shoots for her Shetland Sheepdogs as part of her passion project, *I Love Shelties,* to create awareness for the breed and raise funds for charity.

Find out more about Camilla, her work and books at
www.camillafellasarnold.com

Sign up to the newsletter for updates on new releases at
www.camillafellasarnold.com/newsletter

OUT 2024

Experience the *Unravelling Inwards* as told through poetry and prose in Camilla's debut full length poetry collection, *Soul Threads*.

Soul Threads is a stunning collection of poetry by Camilla Fellas Arnold that beautifully captures the transformative power of words. Through the author's journey of self-discovery and healing, this collection of poems speaks to the depths of the human experience, offering hope and understanding to readers navigating their paths.

With a focus on the divine feminine and personal transformation, *Soul Threads* is a must-read for those seeking solace, love and understanding. Camilla's words are coded with the rhythms of the soul, reflecting to readers their own stories and truths. Her poetry reminds us that words have the power to cut us to the core as much as they can lift our spirits and that they can heal us in unexpected ways.

With each turn of the page, readers will be transported to a world of raw emotion and profound insight. *Soul Threads* is a heartfelt and deeply personal offering that speaks directly to the soul. It is a book to treasure and revisit, a companion to turn to when the road feels lonely, and a guide to help navigate the twists and turns of life.